HOW NOT TO TEST A Psychic

HOW NOT TO TEST A Psychic

TEN YEARS OF REMARKABLE EXPERIMENTS WITH RENOWNED CLAIRVOYANT

PAVEL STEPANEK

MARTIN GARDNER

Library of Congress Cataloging-in-Publication Data

Gardner, Martin, 1914-
    How not to test a psychic.

    Includes index.
    1. Psychical research—Controversial literature.
2. Stepanek, Pavel. I. Title.
BF1042.G2   1989   133.8′4   89-8403
ISBN 0-87975-512-1

Contents

Introduction

The most famous, most respected living subject of psi investigation is Pavel Stepanek, a lifelong resident of Prague. Again and again, in the literature of parapsychology, Stepanek's achievements are held up as the strongest evidence yet obtained for the reality of that form of ESP traditionally called clairvoyance, or more recently (when the distance between subject and target is large), remote viewing. "His achievement," declared Joseph Gaither Pratt (hereafter JGP), "is one that has rarely, if ever, been equaled in the history of parapsychology."

For a decade PS (as we shall call Stepanek, following the practice of parapsychologists) consistently scored above chance, first in experiments undertaken by Milan Ryzl (MR) in Prague, and later in Prague and the United States in those conducted by JGP and others. PS's overall success rate is usually estimated as 60 percent, though this is hard to pin down in view of hundreds of unpublished tests, most of them made by MR. As everybody knows, psychics who do well on tests usually soon lose their psi abilities. (Parapsychologists find this hard to explain; to skeptics the falling off is attributed to the tightening of controls by later researchers.) PS was an outstanding exception—so much so that his long run of successful scoring earned him an entry (with his photograph) in the 1970 *Guinness Book of World Records* as "the best clairvoyant ever tested."

I first encountered PS in such shoddy, unreliable, sensational potboilers as Sheila Ostrander and Lynn Schroeder's *Psychic Discoveries Behind the Iron Curtain* (wherein two chapters deal with PS and MR) and Jeffrey Mishlove's *The Roots of Consciousness,* that I paid little attention to his career. My curiosity was aroused in 1987 when I was asked to comment on a paper by K. Ramakrishna Rao and John Palmer in which they referred to a 1962 experiment with PS as one of the most definitive ever made. Asked to guess which side of a bicolored card was uppermost in fifty opaque envelopes, PS achieved a perfect score. (We will discuss this experiment in Chapter 4.)

The probability of PS's score being chance, assuming the test was adequately controlled, is clearly 1 over the fiftieth power of 2, or $1/1,125,899,906,842,464$. This is not as low as the $1/5^{25}$ probability that chance accounted for Hubert Pearce's correct calls of 25 ESP cards in a row in an experiment conducted by J. B. Rhine in 1932, but that event is entirely anecdotal. Only Rhine was present, and his several brief, hazy accounts of this miracle leave dozens of crucial questions unanswered. In contrast, PS's almost as miraculous score of $1/2^{50}$ was obtained under what appear to be good controls. By anyone's evaluation this experiment stands out as one of the most sensational in the history of psi research. If ever a psi experiment cried out for replication, this was it. Yet at the time I commented on the paper by Rao and Palmer, I had found no evidence that such a replication had been attempted with PS or anybody else. If this experiment can be trusted, I said to myself, there is little doubt that clairvoyance has been as well established as the constancy of light's relative speed was established by the Michelson-Morley test.

Contrary to what many of my critics suppose, I am completely open to the possibility that ESP is genuine. My skepticism rests almost solely on my inability to find convincing evidence for ESP. I have no a priori grounds for ruling it out, and in some ways would be delighted if I thought it had been established by reliable, replicable experiments. In every case, however, whenever I looked below the surface of the classic demonstrations, I found that Occam's razor provided simpler, more convincing explanations. Would PS's amazing career withstand a similar scrutiny?

I decided to obtain copies of all the papers in English—more than 25—that report on tests made with PS. I also went carefully through four overview reports on work with PS: (1) "A Decade of Research with a Selected ESP Subject: An Overview and Reappraisal of the Work with Pavel Stepanek," by J. G. Pratt, in *Proceedings of the American Society for Psychical Research,* vol. 30, September 1973, 78 pages. The monograph is available from the Society, 5 West 73rd Street, New York, NY 10023. (2) *Hypnosis and ESP,* by Milan Ryzl. Privately published in Switzerland in 1961 and 1976, 112 pages. Available from the author: P.O. Box 9459, San Jose, CA 95157. (3) *Experiments with Pavel Stepanek Performed Between January 1st, 1964, and December 31st, 1964,* by Milan Ryzl. An unpublished, undated typescript of 89 pages. (4) *Monograph About ESP Experiments with PS, Final Version, May 6, 1965,* by Milan Ryzl. An unpublished typescript of about 400 pages, covering all of MR's tests of PS to the end of 1963.

The more carefully I read these monographs, along with the relevant papers, the more I became impressed by the carelessness with which experiments had been planned and executed. At no time did any researcher seek the advice of a magician. At no time was a magician asked to be an observer. On one occasion the noted Dutch magician Fred Kaps was consulted after an experiment had been completed. He is reported to have said that he could think of no way deception could have been involved.

Now to ask a knowledgeable magician to evaluate the controls of a *fait accompli* is in most cases utterly futile. Only in rare instances is it possible to reconstruct possible methods of deception on the basis of accounts by nonmagicians. Nonmagicians simply do not know what to look for, and their memories of what actually occurred can be enormously faulty. I often hear laymen describe tricks by professional magicians who are my friends, and whose methods I fully know. It is not unusual to hear a description that completely excludes the method used. There are, however, some exceptions. To cite only one, two magicians had no difficulty constructing a simple optical device by which Ted Serios could easily have produced all the images on Polaroid film that so excited Jule Eisenbud that he wrote an entire book about them. After David Eisendrath and Charles Reynolds exposed the device in *Popular Photography* (October 1967), Ted's ability vanished. I suspect that by now almost all parapsychologists realize how thoroughly Eisenbud was taken in, and how embarrassing to their profession his book has become.

In most cases, however, asking a magician to explain a psychic miracle is like asking someone to visit the scene of a two-car collision that happened several years ago and tell you which driver was at fault. To give a better analogy, it is like telling a card expert how much cash you lost in a poker game on a cruise taken many years ago, and expecting him to tell you whether anyone at the table cheated and, if so, how. *One has to be there.* If a knowledgeable magician is not allowed to observe a test either openly or through a peephole or one-way mirror, one should at least be consulted in the planning of protocols if there is even a remote possibility that deception could be involved. Note that I say "knowledgeable" magician. Many performers, especially if they specialize in stage illusions using costly equipment designed by others, are not always knowledgeable in what is known in the trade as "close-up magic."

If it is difficult for a magician to contribute anything of value after a test has been completed, then why, you may ask, should I, a lifelong student of magic, think it worthwhile to write this monograph? Let me be clear in replying. There is no possible way I can *know,* at this late date, whether PS did or did not use deception. I grant at once four possible interpretations of his impressive career:

1. PS was, during his golden decade, one of the world's most gifted psychics. At no time did he employ any kind of deception.

2. Although a talented psychic, PS occasionally used deception to boost his scores.

3. PS had no psi abilities. He practiced subtle forms of deception, perfected over his years of testing, that improved his scores whenever protocols permitted the use of his techniques.

4. PS's scores resulted. wholly or in part from an experimenter effect. We can distinguish three varieties: (*a*) In their passionate desire for high scores, experimenters unconsciously exerted their own psi powers in ways that influenced the results. I need not here go into all the curious ways that precognition, psychokinesis, clairvoyance, and telepathy could be involved in raising scores. (*b*) Eager for success, the researchers unconsciously biased their results by shoddy record-keeping and/or biased statistical analysis. (*c*) Experimenters or their assistants deliberately falsified data and/or their accounts of the controls that were imposed.

Needless to say, the history of psi research offers precedent for all three of these versions of the experimenter effect. We know that scientists sometimes cheat. Two outstanding recent instances in psi research are the data-altering of S. G. Soal, England's most famous parapsychologist, and the cheating of Walter J. Levy, J. B. Rhine's associate, friend, and chosen successor. Unconscious experimenter bias is equally well documented—just think of Percival Lowell's detailed drawings of Martian canals, or Prosper Blondlot's observations of the spectra of mythical N-rays. As for the unconscious use of one's own psi powers to bias an experiment, no less a distinguished parapsychologist than Helmut Schmidt is on record as suggesting that his PK may have influenced the behavior of cockroaches in one of his animal-psi experiments.

I do not, cannot, know which of the four possibilities (or some combination) holds with respect to PS's work. I will not deny that I have my own private opinion, but in no way will this monograph settle the matter; nor is it intended to. With only a few exceptions it will deal entirely with the third possibility—that PS had no psi abilities and practiced deception. The reason is simple. It is the only possibility on which I can bring to bear my knowledge and expertise. But I say now, and will repeat it many times: I do not *know* whether PS used deception. Moreover, to argue that he did is not the major thrust of this monograph.

What then *is* the thrust? It is to analyze carefully the published papers about PS and to show how results *could* have been obtained in nonparanormal ways. At no time will I question the integrity of researchers, though in one case I will question the honesty of an assistant. My main purpose is to show that the experimenters, ignorant of deception techniques familiar to card magicians and card hustlers, failed to devise adequate controls. My indictment, let me repeat, is not of PS. It is an indictment of the incompetence of his investigators.

Chapter 1 will cover PS's history and personality insofar as I have been able to extract it from short published accounts. This will be followed by a chapter on each paper that reported tests with PS. In conformity with the bibliography at the close of JGP's monograph, I will take these papers in the chronological order in which tests were made, not in their order of publication.

I am grateful to Chuck Akers, John Beloff, Dick Bierman, Stefan Burr, Persi Diaconis, Nils Jacobson, B. K. Kanthamani, Jan Kappers, Jürgen Keil, Champe Ransom, Milan Ryzl, Lee Sallows, and Ian Stevenson for their willingness to answer questions. I tried to engage PS in correspondence, but (as I will mention later) he ignored my first letter and replied to my second and third by saying he did not wish to answer any questions. I cannot blame him if, after making inquiries, he learned that my book was unlikely to look favorably on investigations of his talents.

K. Ramakrishna Rao, now director of Rhine's Institute of Parapsychology, refused to supply any details about his two unpublished experiments with PS that yielded insignificant results. Many years ago a publisher asked me for a contribution to a book that he said would fairly present arguments both for and against parapsychology. When I learned that the book was to be edited by Rao, and each contribution by a skeptic would be followed by a believer's rebuttal, I declined to contribute and urged several skeptical friends, who also had been approached by the publisher, not to contribute unless given a chance to respond to rebuttals. Evidently this angered Rao enough to give it as his reason for refusing to cooperate with me in any way. Accordingly, my account of his failed experiments (in Chapter 13) is based entirely on brief descriptions in one of Ryzl's unpublished monographs.

JGP died in 1979. His voluminous papers are stored at the University of Virginia, which serves only as custodian. The papers are owned by his widow, Ruth. They are not indexed, and I did not feel it worth my time, assuming Ruth Pratt would give permission, to search them for raw data on JGP's work with PS. It might be fruitful someday for a trained statistician, which I am not, to go over whatever data are available for information that is not provided in Pratt's published papers. Ryzl defected from Communist Czechoslovakia to the United States in 1967. He was unable to take any original records with him. He tells me that those records are permanently lost.

Chapter 1

Pavel Stepanek and Milan Ryzl

Pavel Stepanek (both names are accented on the first syllable) was born in Prague on May 12, 1931, the only child of a father who worked as a streetsweeper. Young Stepanek had no education beyond high school. He has never married, and at the time JGP wrote his monograph, PS was living with his elderly parents in a small two-room apartment in Prague.

In *Hypnosis and ESP*, MR writes that PS had no knowledge of or interest in parapscyhology when the two first met; nor had PS ever had a spontaneous ESP experience. JGP, however, relates an anecdote that PS had earlier told the authors of *Psychic Discoveries Behind the Iron Curtain*. It seems that at the end of World War II PS had a strong feeling that his family should leave their apartment at once. They refused. While PS was away visiting an aunt, the Allied Forces "made the only air raid of the war on Prague. A bomb struck near the Stepanek home, damaging the building in which they lived."

JGP thinks that PS's fear of car accidents may have precipitated spontaneous ESP on an occasion in 1967 when JGP was driving PS to New York City from Virginia. Here is how JGP describes it:

On the way Pavel sat quite still, apparently very tense with anxiety and with his eyes glued to the road ahead. Yet several times when I turned on the signal to indicate that I intended to shift lanes, Pavel would say: "Car behind me!" This only happened when there was a car about to overtake us from the rear, and I could not detect any sensory basis for Pavel's warnings. I think my hearing is sufficiently good so that I do not believe that Pavel could have heard a car coming up from the rear above the noise of our vehicle and other traffic noises without my also hearing it. The anecdote is recorded here as only that; certainly it is not presented as strong evidence of ESP.

PS's "dread of riding an automobile in heavy traffic," as JGP puts it in his monograph on PS, was accompained by a fear of flying. Although he came by plane on his first visit to the United States, his second and third visits to JGP's laboratory at the University of Virginia were made by ship.

MR tells us in *Hypnosis and ESP* (from which most of the information in this chapter is taken) that PS, having been raised a Roman Catholic, wanted to study theology after he quit high school. Instead he took a job as foreign correspondent—he spoke and wrote English—for a Czech exporting firm. Because of an operation on both hands to remove congenital webbing between fingers, he found it difficult to type, and so left the job to become a hotel janitor. This is seemingly contradicted by JGP, who writes that PS has always been employed as an information clerk at the entrance to various firms. "He started in a bank, moved on to an international hotel . . . , then to the Municipal Library where he remained for more than ten years. In 1972 he returned to working in a bank. . . . Pavel has a slight congenital weakness in his hands which would prevent his doing manual work, but he is reasonably skillful as a typist." MR adds that library work was ideal for PS because it demanded little responsibility and allowed him lots of free time to read and daydream.

MR characterizes PS as "introverted, shy, passive, slow and hesitant in behaviour, careless. . . . There was conflict between his lack of push and a desire for self-assertion, which found its outlet in building castles in the air. . . . " MR quotes from reports of two clinical psychologists, one in Prague, the other the American parapsychologist and psychiatrist Ian Stevenson, of the University of Virginia, who also examined PS. They confirmed the traits just mentioned, adding that PS had low self-esteem, repressed "hostile and aggressive impulses," and had an excellent memory. He was often depressed. One report stated:

> PS has a good mechanical memory, good self-control, and high frustration tolerance. He is depressed, socially restrained or passive, lacking vigor, submissive, vitally and socially discontented, and clearly introverted. He is conservative, with infantile traits, and has definite autistic tendencies. His internal (but externally controlled) tension is a source of unrest, stereotyped behaviour, unenterprisingness and unproductiveness. His low self-confidence correlates with great suggestibility, lack of social contacts and activities, and emotional fixation on parents. These of his personality traits were most conspicuous: High internal tension, introversion, low self-confidence, and high suggestibility.

JGP found PS to be friendly, always courteous, but extremely reticent about his past, insisting it "was uneventful and there was nothing worth telling." He was nonpolitical, "strongly motivated by a passion for privacy," and anxious to avoid any sort of personal involvement that would interfere with the simplicity of his life. He had "higher than average intelligence" and an "excellent memory, especially for events connected with his experiences as an ESP subject. Many times when I have asked him if he recalls some incident connected with one of our meetings of eight or ten years previously he has shown immediate recollection of the specific occurrence in question, including the details of what was said in conversation at the time." The dominant trait of PS's personality, JGP continues, is "his strong and pervading feeling of anxiety. His life is governed more than anything else by his need to avoid social complications and personal dangers. He strives to keep matters so arranged that he can be in control at all times."

JGP describes PS's appearance as nondescript—average in height and weight, with light-brown hair, and blue eyes. He is a fast walker "with a somewhat shuffling, flat-footed gait, a man who is easily overlooked in a crowd."

On a trip to Prague in 1970, JGP took along that year's *Guinness Book of World Records,* which he gave to PS without telling him he was included in it. "Eventually he discovered the picture, and he was surprised and overjoyed." A year later he was delighted to learn he was still listed. In 1988 the entry was still there, though PS is cited as one of two famous psychics, and it is noted that his ESP powers failed him when he was tested by John Beloff, as we shall see in Chapter 13. JGP doubts that PS ever told anyone in Prague about his growing fame except his parents and a woman friend "in whose apartment we always carry out our experiments in Prague."

PS was thirty when, in June 1961, he first agreed to take part in one of MR's experiments in hypnosis, having been recommended to MR by a friend. But before continuing with PS's early history of testing, let me introduce Milan Ryzl.

Ryzl (the name rhymes with "whistle") obtained a doctorate at Charles University of Prague, the city's main university, with a thesis in biochemistry on the metabolism of amino acids. The metabolism of nervous tissue was his special area of interest. Among parapsychologists he is best known as the discoverer of PS and the leading defender of the view that hypnosis can be used to train subjects to improve their ESP abilities. This is a controversial view not shared by the majority of parapsychologists. Although some believe that ESP abilities may be enhanced during a hypnotic trance, attempts to train subjects under hypnosis to improve their ESP abilities have met with a singular lack of success by researchers other than Ryzl. The literature on such failed efforts is now fairly large.* Ryzl has not reported on any success in training subjects by hypnosis since he and his wife defected to the United States in 1967.

After his defection, Ryzl worked for a short time at Rhine's institute in Durham, North Carolina, before settling with his wife in San Jose, California. He now teaches at John F. Kennedy University, in Orinda, California, where the emphasis is on paranormal studies. In recent years he has been publishing and selling his own books, correspondence courses, and audiotapes. The courses have such titles as "How to Develop ESP in Yourself and Others," "Advanced Meditation Tapes," "ESP for Money and Success," and "Using ESP in Business." His books include: *ESP Experiments which Succeed; Hypnosis and ESP; Death . . . and After?* and *Biblical Miracles: Jesus and ESP. Parapsychology: A Scientific Approach* was published by Hawthorn in 1970. This was followed by a privately published two-volume sequel, *ESP in the Modern World.* It includes a transcript of precognitive statements by a Czech psychic, which Ryzl believes helped him defect.

Ryzl is convinced that ESP is a natural talent possessed by everybody and that in a few generations, if his training methods are adopted, the majority of people will take ESP as much for granted as they now do electricity. His books tell how even now persons can develop their ESP powers in ways useful for winning at lotteries and in gambling casinos, making sound business investments and decisions, predicting winners in horse races and other sporting events, searching for water, minerals, hidden treasures, and so on. He foresees vast uses for ESP in medical diagnosis. "The patient would not even have to be present at the examination," he told an interviewer in 1976. (See "Profile: Milan Ryzl, Ph.D.," by Steve and Linda Blumenthal, in *Psychic,* March/April 1976.) Uses for ESP in crime detection and prevention are, he declared, obvious. Here is a passage from his *Death . . . and After?:*

> Once it happens, we can expect a tremendous advancement of the human race from all points of view, both as concerns practical everyday uses, and the accumulation of knowledge as well. The use of ESP will ultimately become a commonplace affair of everyday living. This will also allow most people to get a direct insight into the World Beyond—through everyday observation practice, without the need to rely on speculation, wishful thinking, revealed articles of faith, or religious dogmas.

---

*See "Hypnosis and ESP Performance: A Review of the Experimental Literature," by Charles Honorton and Stanley Krippner, in the *Journal of the American Society for Psychical Research,* 63, 1969, p. 214–252; and "An Attempted Revival of the Ryzl Training Method," by D. P. Fourie in *Research in Parapsychology,* ed. by J. D. Morris, W. G. Roll, and R. L. Morris, Scarecrow Press, 1977.

Getting in touch with the World Beyond is one of Ryzl's favorite themes. He expects enormous changes in religion to occur when ESP becomes commonplace. In his opinion, great religious leaders of the past, such as Moses, Jesus, and Buddha, were powerful psychics who used ESP to obtain insights about the World Beyond and to perform seeming miracles. ESP, he is persuaded, not only can be used for locating documents from the past; it can also be used for direct clairvoyant viewing of persons and events in the distant past. Ryzl's *Biblical Miracles* reports on twenty-five experiments he made with trained clairvoyants in Prague who remote-viewed such great religious leaders as Moses, Elijah, Elisha, John the Baptist, and Jesus. Here is how one psychic described the way Jesus looked just before his execution:

> He is about 35, he is rather small, has a very small beard, long hair. He is quite different from how he is usually painted. He is thinner, has dark hair, though not entirely black, longer face, dark eyes, high forehead.

In later chapters we will meet with Ryzl's "impregnation principle." His work with PS convinced him that PS was able to impregnate cards with psychic traces, or footprints, that remained on the cards for long periods of time. In his books Ryzl suggests that such traces may explain why people continue to see the same ghosts in haunted houses. It is not that real spirits are there, but that the psi powers of persons living in the house have impregnated the walls with psi forces that persist and give rise to similar mental impressions in others.

Back now to PS. His original motive for coming to MR was to supplement his meager income. MR paid all his subjects an hourly wage, which (MR says) "was very good by Czechoslovakian standards," thanks to a grant from Rhine's foundation. As one subject put it: "You go there, sleep an hour or so, and get your pay." PS did not mind the long sessions or the "monotonous card guessing. He was paid an hourly wage and was in no hurry."

The sessions with PS were always informal. He and MR would sit in easy chairs, chat about various topics, tell jokes, and drink coffee while PS smoked cigarettes incessantly. When the experiments became successful and PS saw his name in print, "he began to feel famous. Then he became actively interested in ESP. . . . He felt that through ESP he could become a 'man of success' (without effort, merely by utilizing the existing talent); that is, through ESP he could find his own self-satisfaction with achievement."

As we shall learn later, PS's desire for fame and money eventually led him to believe that MR was not doing enough for him on both counts. He developed a strong hostility toward MR, turning instead to JGP as a respected U.S. parapsychologist who was in a better position to bring him fame and fortune. He stopped working for JGP in 1971 and now lives quietly in Prague. He has not participated in any psi experiments since.

The foregoing information obviously suggests two strong incentives—money and fame—for PS to maintain high scores. Apart from his reputation as a psychic, his life was dull and uneventful. Seeing his name in print, and receiving high praise from psi researchers around the world—he treasured a "memory book" in which foreign visitors would write tributes to him—were enormous boosts to his low self-esteem. It is a familiar story. The history of psi research swarms with the names of successful subjects who accomplished nothing else of interest in their entire lives.

"Hypnosis was absolutely without success," MR writes in describing PS's second visit. "After a while, PS himself broke off, commenting that 'it did not seem to work with him.' He seemed to be absolutely refractory to hypnosis." MR attributes this to PS's fear of hypnosis. "He was so full of fears that he was unable to concentrate." JGP, in his monograph, says that Ryzl "was on the point of telling [PS] that there would be no need to come again," but at the last minute MR decided to try once more and another session was arranged. This time PS went into a superficial hypnotic state. Had he not done so, the sessions would have ceased and PS would have lost a chance to make some easy money that he very much needed. At no later time, MR tells us, did PS ever enter a hypnotic state deep enough to produce amnesia. He always recalled everything that happened while he was in a light trance. Later, MR taught him how to put himself into a light trance and efforts to hypnotize him became unnecessary.

It was during the fourth session (July 7, 1961) that MR began efforts to train PS in ESP. The training procedure could not have been simpler. Ten 3″ x 5″ white index cards, painted black on one side, were placed in opaque cardboard "envelopes" and handed one by one to PS. He was asked, while in his light trance, to imagine that each envelope was transparent, and then to say whether he thought the black or white side was facing him. After each call the card was removed and checked to provide instant feedback. After a run of ten cards, the cards were shuffled, "some of them reversed," and returned to the same envelopes for another run of ten trials.

During the first run PS scored only six hits, but on the second run he scored nine, and on the third he got all ten right. There were nine hits in the fourth and fifth runs, making an overall score of 43 hits out of 50, a success rate of 43/50 or 86 percent. "This," MR writes with whopping understatement, "was a very encouraging result."

The same test was repeated with smaller cards. In 40 trials PS scored 39 hits. In the next 40, with aluminum foil around the envelopes, he scored

100 percent. The probability of this happening by chance is $1/2^{40}$ = $1/1,099,511,627,776$. In the absence of cheating or genuine clairvoyance, this is an event comparable to calling heads, then to tossing 40 coins in the air and having all of them land heads.

More tests, all of them informal, were made at other sessions. The construction of the envelopes is not described in the section in *Hypnosis and ESP* on these preliminary uncontrolled tests, but presumably it was similar to those used in the first formal experiment covered in the next chapter. These were made by folding a strip of opaque cardboard, stapling the sides, leaving the top end open so cards could be easily inserted and removed. (Sealing the tops with staples or tape would have greatly slowed down the testing. Besides, the constant removal and replacement of tape or staples would have damaged the envelopes, requiring new sets for each run.) In most of the tests, PS was allowed to handle the envelopes when he made his calls.

After one failure (22 hits in 50 calls), PS rallied with 19 hits in 20 calls. Some tests were made with the envelopes on a table rather than in PS's hands. At first he scored at chance, but in a series of three such tests, of 100 trials each, his hits were 56, 65, and 75. The total of 196 hits out of 300 brought his score back up to almost 66 percent.

There is no point in proposing ways in which PS may have used deception during these poorly controlled exploratory tests. MR's brief account (in *Hypnosis and ESP*) provides no details about the construction of the envelopes or the procedures followed. For all we can know, when PS held the envelope vertically, the extreme tips of his forefingers may have moved the flap nearest him backward about an inch. To see how this works, the reader is urged to construct an envelope (or one of the covers that were used in later tests as containers for envelopes) and hold it up to a mirror. The envelope (or cover) must be held at the middle of the sides by the extreme tips of all the fingers, with thumbs in back. The fingers must be kept pressed together, the tips of the index fingers just above the top staple on each side. An absolutely indetectable motion of the tips of the index fingers will bend the flap back. This is not visible from the front, but it allows a clear glimpse of the card's top. If the move is made with a cover that contains an envelope, it allows a glimpse of the label at the folded edge of the envelope. In Chapter 3, I will have more to say about peek moves and will describe a slightly different way that the move can be made by a thumb.

It is not necessary for both hands to hold an envelope. It can be held in one hand, and the flick made by the tip of the forefinger, or by catching the edge of the flap under the nail of the finger. The move does, however, require practice in front of a mirror so that it can be made with no visible motion of the finger. It is important that the index finger be kept pressed against the middle finger at all times, with no space between them.

Ryzl does not say whether he randomized and inserted cards outside of PS's view or whether PS watched these insertions. If he watched, it would have been easy to observe slight differences on the outsides of envelopes and to recall which color was uppermost when a card went inside. Any shuffling of envelopes, after cards are inserted, would of course not destroy such correlations. I will call this the "imperfection principle," a term used by some card magicians. After a deck of playing cards has been handled for a short time, little imperfections develop on the backs of cards—a flyspeck here, a faint dirt-smudge there, a nick along an edge, a slightly bent corner, and so on. This is why casino dealers and players in private games so often call repeatedly for a new deck. Moreover, if envelopes are made by taping or stapling cardboard sheets at the edges, it is impossible for the tape and staples to be identically positioned on each cover.

It is worth mentioning that although PS's experimenters were aware that he could memorize envelopes by recalling imperfections, they tended to ignore this on the grounds that during the calling they did not see PS searching for such cues. As MR writes in his unpublished *Monograph About ESP Experiments with PS:* "In no case any intention of the subject was noticed to make use of his normal sense in discerning the colors of the cards, or to look for any sensory cues on the outer surface of the envelopes." The statement is naive. Marked cards routinely used by crooked gamblers are marked with such microscopic subtlety that the marks are difficult to see even when they are pointed out to someone. Yet the gambler can identify the cards by only the most casual glance, and often from a distance of many feet.

In my early correspondence with MR, he allowed me to borrow one of the cardboard envelopes he had used in formal testing of PS. It was certainly opaque, but it could easily be identified from a distance of twenty feet. Figure 1 reproduces a photocopy I made of this envelope. Note the black spots that form a triangle. These are not dirt marks, but dark spots embedded in the cardboard's mottled surface. I hasten to say that MR was from the beginning fully aware of the imperfection principle. Before he began testing PS, he had performed similar experiments with a nineteen-year-old biology student identified only as "Miss L. S." He speaks of randomizing the cards after each run "to eliminate the possibility that the subject would remember some marks on the surface of the envelopes, and associate them with the color inside." In many later tests with PS, MR and other experimenters went to considerable lengths to prevent the imperfection principle from playing any role. However, as we shall see in later chapters, the principle can be combined with peeks and with another simple technique, also familiar to card gamblers and magicians, that could have provided PS with significant cues.

How about PS's successes when he held a sheet of cardboard (MR calls it a "screen") in front of his face while he made his calls? Such a sheet obviously is a poor substitute for a large, fixed screen because it is so easy to sneak peeks beneath it. If you sit opposite a person and hold a sheet of cardboard in front of your face, you will find you can obtain a clear view of a table-top even though the person sitting opposite will swear that the top is obscured by the sheet. In his unpublished *Monograph About . . .*, MR explains how the "screen" was used. PS held the cardboard vertically in front of his face while MR placed the target on the table, on top of a piece of white paper. PS lowered the cardboard until it covered the target, made his call, then lifted the "screen" back to vertical while MR replaced the envelope with another one.

Further speculation about how PS could have obtained information about card colors in these informal tests would be a waste of time, because MR himself realized that such pilot tests were uncontrolled. They were, however, sufficiently impressive to persuade him that "the time had come to invite an assistant experimenter and to perform a carefully planned confirmatory experiment with PS."

The invited assistant was MR's wife Jirina. In the many experiments that followed over the years, conducted by Mr. and Mrs. R, JGP, and others, PS never achieved the amazing scores of those first exploratory tests, except for one experiment in 1962 when he made a perfect score on fifty envelopes. (We will discuss this test in Chapter 4). Aside from this exception, his scores tended to be erratic—sometimes moderately high, sometimes moderately low, with an overall success average of about 60 percent. Later we will consider the most famous and most mystifying aspect of his work, the "impregnation" effect mentioned earlier, which JGP preferred to call the "focusing effect." Instead of hits and misses spread evenly over all the bicolored cards, both hits and misses tended to concentrate more than chance allowed on specific cards. In still later testing, the focusing effect shifted from cards to envelopes inside covers, and finally to covers inside jackets and book bags, but we are getting ahead of our story.

Even harder to explain than "focusing" is the fact that PS was successful at no other ESP task except guessing which side of a card, cover, or other container was uppermost in a larger container. Although trivial details could be varied, whenever there was an alteration of the basic task—such as using pictures or ESP symbols instead of colors, or substituting boxes for cardboard containers, or even precognition testing with bicolored cards—PS's psi powers deserted him. "Any other experimental arrangement," MR writes on page 215 of his *Monograph About . . . ,* "always led to an instantaneous disappearance of the ESP manifestation." Writing on "ESP: Proof from Prague?" (*New Scientist,* 10 October 1968, pp. 76–77), John Beloff said it this way: "[PS] is probably the most limited performer ever to gain prominence in the field." Like Ted Serios, the Chicago bellhop, PS was a one-trick man. Only his staying power, his modest track record over a ten-year period, made him famous.

This curious lack of diversification in PS's psi abilities is not easy for parapsychologists to explain. It has been suggested that having been trained under hypnosis to perform a certain task, he was henceforth unable to learn how to use ESP in any other way. This is not a very plausible explanation, especially in view of MR's conviction (as well as the conviction of many other parapsychologists) that almost anyone can be trained for a wide variety of ESP tasks far more extraordinary than just guessing the color of the top of a card in an envelope.

A word about nomenclature will be useful before going on. As experiments with PS continued, JGP and others found it necessary to make use of larger and larger containers, like a nest of Chinese boxes. Terms vary from paper to paper, but I shall adopt the following uniform terminology, starting with bicolored cards and moving outward:

1. Cards. These are the inner targets. They consist of cards with their two sides distinguished in some way, usually by the colors green and white.

2. Envelopes. These are containers for cards, made of opaque cardboard either stapled or taped along the sides.

3. Covers. These are larger cardboard containers, also made by stapling or taping sides, into which envelopes will fit.

4. Jackets. These are still larger containers made by stapling the sides of sheets cut from manila file folders.

5. Bags. These are bags used for mailing books, large enough for "jackets" to fit inside.

The word "container" will be used at times for any of the last four objects. In chapters near the end of the book the phrase "second-level container" will refer to a container immediately inside an outer container.

The first formal experiment with PS, conducted by MR and his wife, took place in 1961. It is the topic of the next chapter.

Chapter 2

Prague, 1961

DATE: July 24 through September 11, 1961
PLACE: MR's apartment in Prague
PAPER: "A Case of High-Scoring ESP Performance in the Hypnotic State." Milan Ryzl and Jirina Ryzlova, in the *Journal of Parapsychology,* 26 (September 1962), pp. 153–171.

MR's first formal experiment, as well as all his later tests of PS, were conducted in his apartment at Praha 2 Vinohrady, Rybalkova 4, in Prague. I mention this because in some later papers by other parapsychologists the place is sometimes called MR's "home" and sometimes a "hotel." All the time he was in Prague, MR tells me, he lived in a brick multi-storied apartment building owned by his mother.

Each of the two parts of this experiment, conducted by MR with the help of his wife, involved 2,000 trials. In the first series, ten 3″ x 5″ white index cards were used, painted black on one side. The "envelopes," each 8″ x 6½″, were prepared by cutting 16″ x 6½″ strips from cardboard folders of the sort used for filing letters, and folding them in half. The 8-inch sides were stapled together, two staples on each side. The authors make much of the fact that such a cardboard container was completely opaque, and I have no doubt it was.

Care was taken to have the staples on the left face in the opposite direction from those on the right. That was so each envelope would look the same on both sides. This precaution indicates that MR realized that PS could memorize envelopes by the imperfection principle, but at this stage of the game MR apparently did not realize how easily it could be done even if the envelopes had no staples. If you are not convinced of this, I urge you to make a few envelopes in the manner described, then inspect them carefully for distinguishing marks. Unless your eyesight is poor, you will readily find slight differences that make it easy, especially after some practice, to memorize a cover. The identifying mark could be a slightly askew staple, a light crease, a faint smudge, and so on. Occasionally dark spots or faint lines will be permanently embedded in the cardboard.

Each envelope had an open end about 4 inches from the nearest staple. If a card were inserted between the two "flaps" and pushed all the way down, one could see about half an inch of the card by lifting a flap. This made it easy to check the uppermost color without having to remove the card.

Jirina Ryzl (JR), working in another room from where PS sat, randomized the insertion of the ten cards by using a table of random numbers. Even digits stood for one color, odd digits for the other. A paper clip was attached to each side of the open end of each envelope to "seal" the end. Note that no labels of any sort were placed on either cards or envelopes. The envelopes, however, were always handled in such a way that at no time was a stack of them turned over. Apparently the reason envelopes were not labeled was to remove visual cues by which an envelope could be memorized by PS—another indication of how little MR at the time comprehended the power of the imperfection principle.

After preparing the ten envelopes, JR carried the stack to her husband in the adjoining room where he and PS sat facing each other. PS had been "placed in a light hypnotic trance" for the duration of the day's session. Resting on his knees was a piece of cardboard, which served as a "table." A second piece of cardboard, size not given, was held vertically by PS to serve as a "screen." Behind the screen MR manipulated the envelopes. First he cut the pack, using a formula known only to himself, and based (he writes) on "figures giving the time of sunrise and sunset for the day." Such a complicated cutting procedure is typical of psi experimenters with little experience. Extreme precautions are applied to a trivial aspect of a test, at the same time allowing major loopholes.

One at a time MR would place an envelope on the cardboard "table" where it was presumably hidden from PS's gaze by the piece of cardboard he held vertically. After PS made his call of black or white, the envelope was put on a chair next to MR, where it would be clearly visible to PS. Both MR and his wife kept independent records of the calls. After ten calls, the stack was taken from the chair, and the colors checked by removing the paper clips and lifting a flap at the open end. If there was a contradiction in the two records (as there was in two runs out of the 200) the disputed run was canceled, and replaced at once by a new run.

After checking the hits and misses in each run, JR took the envelopes to the adjoining room, where she randomized the cards for the next run, basing the new pattern of colors on a new set of random digits. Two hundred runs of ten calls each were made, or 2,000 calls in all. PS scored 1,144 hits, a deviation of +144 from the 1,000 expected by chance. His success score was 1,144/2,000 or .57+. A check of the way the colors were distributed in the entire series found 998 black targets and 1,002 white. As the authors correctly say, this was "very close to the expected fifty-fifty distribution."

It is indeed close. Most people do not realize that the longer you flip a coin, the larger the expected deviation from an equality of heads and tails, although of course in the long run the deviations become smaller fractions of the total calls. I asked a friend to do some calculating for me, and he tells me that the probability of a deviation of no more than 2 from an even split is about .09. This is not too improbable; nevertheless it does raise a slight suspicion about the randomizing procedure.

We are told that after each run JR removed the cards from the envelopes before preparing the next run. Let us now consider the possibility that after a few runs she found it tiresome and unnecessary to remove *all* the cards. Since PS sat behind a "screen," each envelope presumably invisible to him while he made his calls, what difference would it make if most of the cards remained in the same envelopes? Precautions had been taken to make the envelopes look identical, so even if PS saw them, he seemingly would not be able to distinguish one from another. It would be much faster and far simpler to slide the cards half-way out, then rearrange the envelopes to fit the new pattern of odd and even digits. When necessary, a few cards would have to be reversed to make the colors fit the new pattern. We must remember that not only would it be advantageous to save time in a long-drawn-out experiment, but since PS was being paid well on an hourly basis, any shortening of the randomizing procedure would save money as well as time.

Let's assume, however, that JR did indeed actually remove all the cards each time she prepared a new run. Here is a plausible scenario. She removes a card from the top envelope, places it on a table, then puts the envelope directly below it. The second card goes to the right of the first one, and the second envelope to the right of the first envelope. Proceeding in this way she ends with a row of cards, and directly beneath them a row of envelopes. She consults the first digit of the random sequence. It is a "white" digit. She picks up at random a white card and inserts it into the envelope directly below it. The next digit is, say, "black." She randomly finds a black card and puts it into the envelope below it. She continues in this fashion until near the end, when it is possible that the remaining few digits all require one color and the remaining few cards are of the opposite color. So she reverses these last few cards and puts them in their envelopes. This procedure is of course exactly equivalent to the one previously described, although it would be a trifle slower. JR could truthfully say she had removed all the cards from the envelopes, and the procedure may actually have seemed to her a more thorough randomization of cards than the one described in the previous paragraph.

At this point the reader is asked to make the following experiment. Obtain a table of random digits and mark them into sets of ten each. Circle all the odd digits. Now compare each set of ten with its successor. You'll find that the ratio of odd to even digits seldom varies by a difference of more than three. Differences of four are rare, and larger differences are increasingly rare. (A difference of ten would require that one run consist entirely of even digits, the other entirely of odd ones.) Thus, if JR randomized by either of the procedures described, envelopes would be shifted about in the stack, but the probability is high that more than seven cards would remain in their original envelopes in the same orientation.

Put yourself in the place of PS when confronted with the conditions of this test. Assume he has discovered how easy it is to observe imperfections on an envelope and to link that envelope to a call. It would be the only conceivable way he could hope to boost his scores. He need know nothing whatever about how JR would randomize the cards. He would simply hope that in the process *some* cards would remain in envelopes with the same sides up. His strategy, therefore, would be to memorize as many envelopes as he could, and link them with his calls.

Where was the stack of envelopes *before* PS began his calls? This is an important question that MR does not answer. If it was on the chair, PS would see the top envelope before it was placed on the "table" on his lap. Was the stack held in MR's hands where PS could also see it? We are told that the "screen" in PS's hands prevented him from seeing the envelope while it was "being removed from the top of the pack to be placed in position for being called," but we are not told that PS could not see the envelope *before* it was removed. From MR's point of view, since all envelopes were identical, the only important precaution was to make sure PS could not see or touch an envelope *while making a call.* For all we know, as the test proceeded, PS may even have raised the screen to his face after the envelope had been placed, and lowered it immediately after his call.

There is also the possibility that PS could have obtained glimpses beneath the cardboard screen even while he held it. We know the cardboard piece was not large, because we are told that MR could at all times see parts of PS's body while he held the screen to his face. As I said in the previous chapter, if you sit opposite someone who holds a piece of cardboard in front of his face, it is extremely difficult to be sure his vision below the lower edge is completely blocked off. In view of the crudity of the screening process, it is a plausible conjecture that PS had ample opportunities to observe envelopes before and after his calls.

If PS had been capable of memorizing all ten envelopes, then kept repeating the same calls for each one, and assuming that JR randomized as we have suggested, his score would have been fantastically high. But to achieve a modest score of .57 it is only necessary to be fairly certain of hits on just two envelopes. If hits are assured on just one cover out of ten, then 1 plus an expectation by chance of 4.5 hits on the remaining 9 gives an expectation of 5.5 hits, or a success rate of $5.5/10 = .55$. Knowing the contents of two envelopes raises the score to .60, knowing three raises it to .65, and knowing four raises it to .70.

Here is one possible scenario. After the first run, PS has memorized imperfections on four envelopes and also remembered how he called them. After observing the checking, he adjusts his choice of colors according to whether they were hits or misses. During the next run he watches for the reappearance of the four memorized, either seeing them on the stack before they are placed on his "table," or glimpsing them after they go there. He makes the appropriate four calls, hoping they will be hits. As long as they are—remember that the checking of colors is done in his presence immediately after each run—he will continue with the same calls. If a call is wrong, he shifts it next time (for that envelope) to the other color. Allowing for JR to vary her randomizing procedure, and for PS to make mistakes, following just four envelopes could easily account for his modest success of .57.

I do not know if this scenario, or something close to it, actually occurred. But the fact that it *could* occur points up three glaring defects in the test's design.

1. We are told nothing about the procedure followed by JR in randomizing cards beyond the fact that each pattern of colors was based on a sequence of random digits. Had we been assured that after each run she removed all the cards, shuffled them thoroughly, and randomly reversed half the cards before fitting them to a new pattern, the scenario I have imagined would have been ruled out. No such information is provided.

2. Neither cards nor envelopes were labeled. There is no good reason why the cards should not have been labeled, because PS never saw them. Since the stack was always kept with the same side up, there is also no reason why the undersides of envelopes should not have been labeled. A record could then have been kept of the cards and envelopes on which PS obtained hits. If the scenario I described took place, such a record would of course show strong focusing effects both on specific cards and specific

envelopes, and the scenario would have been strongly confirmed. By not labeling cards and envelopes, enormously valuable information about what occurred was irretrievably lost.

3. Holding a piece of cardboard in front of one's face is about as poor a way to screen vision as can be imagined. With very little effort a large fixed screen could have been prepared behind which PS could sit without being able to see any envelopes during any phase of the experiment. Even at the time, such large screens were commonly used in ESP testing by J. B. Rhine and others.

After this first series was completed, we are told, PS was trained by MR to put himself in a "light hypnotic state." From that time on MR no longer found it necessary to hypnotize PS. As the Ryzls put it: "Prior to his beginning of tests in each session he made himself ready through mental concentration. . . ."

For the experiment's second series of tests, four sets of 25 envelopes were prepared in the same way as those used before, except now they were just large enough to hold the cards. They measured 4″ x 6¾″. Each was made by stapling two cardboard rectangles on three sides. The two sides of the envelope were not alike, so the top face was easily identified. In each of two sets of envelopes JR inserted thirteen black-up cards and twelve white-up. In the other two sets, the colors were reversed. Open ends were sealed with gummed paper tape. In sets 1 and 3 JR added to each card a strip of unexposed photographic film. The envelopes were shuffled, then each was wrapped in two layers of heavy dark-blue paper, folds at the bottom, smooth side on top. The paper was stapled to the envelope. The packets of each set were then numbered from 1 to 25.

Ten slips of blank paper, each numbered 1 through 25, were stapled to the upper left corner of each packet. Each slip also bore the packet's number. Ten similar slips were numbered and stapled to the upper right corner of each parcel. It is important to note that Mrs. R kept no record of the uppermost card colors in any of the hundred packets. At no time during the entire experiment did either MR or JR know the target colors until the end, when the packets were opened and the colors checked against calls recorded on the slips.

Each set of 25 parcels was handled as follows. A packet was handed to PS. He made his call, gave the packet back to MR, who recorded the call on the top slip in the upper left corner. The slip was torn off and placed aside. After making a call for each packet, the packets were shuffled and handed to PS for a second run of calls. Each call was recorded on an upper left slip, and the slip removed. Ten runs were made, producing a pile of 250 slips each bearing the number of the parcel and the way PS called it. MR made a permanent record of the 250 calls.

PS was then given the entire set of 25 packets, with ten slips remaining at the top right of each, to take home. He was told to put himself into a light trance, then repeat the same procedure by making ten runs through the packet, recording his calls on the slips, and making sure to shuffle the packets after each run. "This shuffling between runs was necessary," writes MR in *Hypnosis and ESP,* "to make him handle the parcels in a different order, and, thus, minimize the possible interference of remembering call patterns." It is an incredibly naive statement, because each packet bore a number, and nothing could be easier than remembering to make, say, ten identical calls on packet 19. Indeed, because he was working alone, there was nothing to prevent PS from referring back to the removed slips any time he wished.

After completing ten runs at home, PS brought the 25 packets and the 250 slips back to MR, who again made a permanent record of hits and misses. The same procedure was followed with the remaining three sets of 25 packets: First a session of ten runs in MR's presence, then ten runs alone at home—a total of 500 calls for each set, or 2,000 calls in all. Of the 1,000 calls in MR's presence there were 661 hits—a success rate of 661/ 1,000 or .66+. Of the 1,000 calls made alone, 602 were hits, for a success rate of .60+. Combining the two parts, there were 1,263 hits among 2,000 calls, for an overall score of .63+.

As MR correctly perceived, the calls were far from independent events, because PS could have memorized the parcels by their number (the imperfection principle was here irrelevant) and calls on one run could have been influenced by his memory of calls on previous runs. For this reason MR examined the data to determine which targets were designated by PS by a "majority vote." If the majority of calls for a given packet were correct it was counted a hit. If the majority were wrong it would be called a miss. Evenly split calls were considered ties.

In the calls made in MR's presence there were 66 majority vote hits, 27 misses, and 7 ties. Thus PS identified by majority vote 66 of the 100 parcels for a score of .66. This was slightly better than his .62 majority-vote score when working alone. "ESP is the only available explanation of the results," the authors write, "short of falsification of the results by MR in Series II, or collusion between two or more participants in Series I."

We have seen how PS, without any collusion, could have achieved his score in the first series. How could he have raised his score in the second series?

When I first read that MR had allowed PS to take all the parcels home, I could hardly believe it. One simply does not, in any carefully controlled ESP test, allow a subject to make calls on targets in his possession while he or she is totally unsupervised. Was MR unconsciously allowing another huge loophole through which PS could maneuver? It is not only easy to remove and replace paper tape, but even easier to bend and remove a staple, then later carefully reinsert the ends through the original holes and bend them flat again. PS need only have remembered how he had called a few packets during the test's first phase, opened those packets, adjusted cards to fit calls (preserving of course the 12/13 ratio), then sealed them up again.

The unexposed film presents no problem. The authors say they did not tell PS that such film had been used, but being an intelligent chap, he may have suspected this because it would have been the simplest way to guard against tampering. It would have been easy for PS to open a packet in a darkroom with a small red light that would not expose the film but allow him to distinguish black from white. However, let's assume PS did not suspect the use of unexposed film. As soon as he opened a packet with such film, he would thereafter take darkroom precautions. As for the one exposed film, what would prevent him from buying duplicate film and replacing an unexposed strip? Indeed, what would prevent him from replacing many exposed film strips? We are not told that the strips had any unique identifying marks. If they did, and the experimenters recorded them, it would have been an important aspect of the test to mention in their paper.

The main flaw of the experiment was, of course, allowing PS to repeat the sessions without supervision. It was the first and last time anyone allowed him to do this. We will probably never know whether he tampered with any packets, but that is not the point. The point is that because he *could* have, this second series is rendered worthless. If records had originally been kept on the top colors of the cards in the 100 parcels, any turning over of cards would have been detected and PS would not have been able to boost his scores for the calls made in MR's presence. But no such record was kept. This is the second major flaw in the experimental design.

Again I must remind readers that my chief purpose is to show how poorly the experiment was planned, and how little MR comprehended the need for extraordinary evidence to support extraordinary claims. I have no way of knowing if any of my speculations are correct. The positive scores obtained by PS in both parts of this series—calling in MR's presence and calling alone—may have been due entirely to his clairvoyant powers. What I do claim is that the test was too lacking in even the most elementary controls to be taken as evidence for such powers.

The term "focusing effect" was not in use at the time this experiment was made, but analysis of the published data provides overwhelming evidence for it. On each parcel of cards, ten consecutive calls were made in the presence of MR, followed by ten consecutive calls at home. Thus for each packet there were two sets of ten consecutive calls. Since there were 100 packets, there were 200 sets of consecutive calls altogether. Charts in the paper by MR and his wife, as well as in *Hypnosis and ESP,* show that in 33 of these sets the ten calls were *all* hits, and in seven sets they were *all* misses. In 32 of the sets the split was 9 right and 1 wrong, and in 10 sets the split was the reverse, 9 wrong and 1 right. In 31 sets the split was 8 right, 2 wrong, and in 21 sets it was the reverse, 8 wrong and 2 right. In only 8 sets was the split 6 right and 4 wrong. In only 9 sets was it 6 wrong and 4 right, and in only 9 sets was the split 5-5.

The data clearly shows what MR in *Hypnosis and ESP* calls a strong tendency of PS "to repeat the same statement for each target again and again—often regardless of whether the statement was correct or not." MR asks: "How can we explain this unusual distribution, which suppressed chance scores (5-5) and favored extreme scores (10-0, 2-8, etc.)? How can we explain the subject's tendency to repeat systematically even errors?"

MR and his wife say it this way in their report: "There was a strong tendency for the subject to identify the individual packets consistently; i.e., to call each one predominantly either black or white. But . . . the consistently favored choice was not always the correct one, so the frequency with which the packets were called wrongly 8, 9, or 10 times is greater than would be expected on a random basis."

It is indeed not easy to explain this eccentric distribution of calls, and the corresponding eccentric distribution of hits and misses, on the assumption that only ESP was operating. But if you put yourself again in PS's place, there are two reasons why he would choose to concentrate identical calls on certain packets. He may have mistakenly thought that if he kept repeating calls it would enhance his overall score. Of course it would not, because repeated lucky hits would be balanced by repeated unlucky misses. But given the protocols, what other strategy could he adopt?

There was another and more compelling reason. If PS planned to open some of the packets while at home, and adjust some cards, it would have been to his advantage to make large numbers (10, 9, 8) of identical calls on certain packets. Why? Because when alone it would only be necessary to open and adjust cards (if need be) in just those packets. Although MR must surely have kept a record of exactly how the calls were made on each parcel, this record was not published, and the original records no longer exist. This is unfortunate, because an examination of such records would have been enormously helpful in trying to formulate scenarios of how PS may have gone about boosting his score.

The experimenters do, however, provide a record of the total hits and misses for the four sets of 25 parcels, divided into the hits made in MR's presence, and those PS made at home. During the first session, PS made 250 calls in MR's presence, obtaining 162 hits for a score of 162/250 = .64+. Here is one possible scenario:

PS selected four parcels on which to make ten identical calls, and four others on which to make nine identical calls. Later, at home, he adjusted cards in the eight packets so that all 40 + 36 = 76 calls were hits. (Actually, he need adjust only about half of the eight cards—the ones on which he was unlucky.) Of the remaining 250 – 76 = 174, he could expect about half of them, 87, to be hits. Thus his expectation for the session would be 76 + 87 = 163 hits, for a score of 163/250 = .65+. There is no problem about raising his score a comparable amount in the 250 calls made on the same set of parcels at home because he would know the colors of eight cards.

Similar scenarios are easy to devise for the other three sets of packets that would not only explain the percentage of hits but also account for the ways in which ten consecutive calls were split throughout the experiment. Note that if PS selected four packets in each set of 25 parcels for a 10-0 split of calls, and repeated this split on the same four when he recorded calls at home, it would produce 8 × 10 = 40 cases of 10-0 splits. This is just what we are told actually occurred.

Of course there are dozens of different procedures PS could have followed to generate the results given by the published charts, and there is no way we can ever know precisely what happened. However, two conclusions are obvious. By concentrating large numbers of identical calls on a small number of packets, PS could easily have obtained his recorded scores, and of course the procedure would also account for the fantastically strong focusing effect.

As the testing of PS continued, experimenters slowly became aware of the importance of labeling all parts of the test materials as well as imposing better controls—above all of not allowing PS to make calls when he was unsupervised. In the next chapter we shall see how MR and JGP conducted what they considered a more carefully designed test intended to confirm the results of the badly flawed experiment just described.

Before going on to this, however, it is worth mentioning that in May 1962 PS was tested (I do not know where) by H. N. Banerjee, presumably a parapsychologist from India. My information on this rests entirely on a footnote in MR's 1965 monograph (part 3, p. 18). He says he is not including details in his monograph because Banerjee worked alone with PS. The results, he says, were given in *Five Years Report of Seth Sohan Lal Memorial Institute of Parapsychology,* wherever that is, 1963, page 42. I have not tried to run down this report, and can only repeat MR's assertion that out of 1,000 calls on white/green cards PS made 781 hits.

In light of the constant statements by MR, JGP, and PS himself that his psi powers diminished when working with strangers, this high score of .781 is astonishing. There are three ways to view it:

1. PS's clairvoyance was indeed capable of sensational results when working alone with a total stranger.

2. Banerjee fudged his data.

3. PS found Banerjee's controls so lax that he was able to boost his score by nonparanormal means to an extraordinarily high level.

Chapter 3

Prague, 1962

DATE: June 1962

PLACE: MR's apartment in Prague

PAPER: "Confirmation of ESP Performance in a Hypnotically
Prepared Subject." Milan Ryzl and J. G. Pratt, in the
Journal of Parapsychology, 26 (December 1962), pp.
237-243.

During the nine months between September 1961 and June 1962, when
JGP made his first trip to Prague to conduct a confirmatory experiment
with PS, MR made a large number of tests with PS. These were never
published, although MR summarizes the results in *Hypnosis and ESP* (pp.
66–74). No information is given about the construction of envelopes beyond the fact that the ten envelopes used were similar to those used before and that MR shuffled them "behind a screen" (the nature of which
is not revealed) after each run to ensure their random order. The purpose of the tests was to determine if colors other than black and white
could be used, and how strong the contrast need be between the two sides
of a card.

The color combinations tested were white combined with black, red,
blue, yellow, violet, orange, and green; black with red, blue, yellow, violet,
and green; red with blue, yellow, violet, orange, and green; yellow with
violet, and orange; and violet with orange, and green. (The combinations
of black/orange, green/orange, and yellow/orange apparently were not
tested.) PS was given the stack of ten envelopes, which presumably he
held on his lap. One at a time he would pick up an envelope, make his

call, then hand the envelope to MR. MR sorted the envelopes into two piles, one for each color. The envelopes were opened in PS's presence and the number of hits counted. The cards were then removed from the envelopes and replaced (behind the screen) with cards of a different color combination. The combinations were randomly changed between runs. Neither cards nor envelopes were labeled.

Out of 25,000 trials, PS is reported to have made 16,166 hits—a success rate of .64+. His score was highest (.84) on the white/green combination. MR attributes this to something psychological in PS's background. Whatever the explanation, black/white cards were soon abandoned for green and white cards on almost all subsequent testing.

An additional run of 1,000 calls was made with ten white/yellow cards in total darkness. MR reports that PS obtained 686 hits for a success rate of .68+. "The result of this test," he writes, "indicated that illumination is not essential for the operation of ESP." If this surprises the reader, he has a bigger surprise to come.

The high score obtained on yellow/white cards (both in the light and in total darkness), where the contrast between sides was minimal, suggested a new series of tests that MR calls his "dilution experiment." It is described in *Hypnosis and ESP* (pp. 71-74), and I think it both significant and amusing that nowhere in J. G. Pratt's monograph on PS does he mention these dilution tests. Perhaps JGP considered the results so preposterous that mentioning them would weaken his case for what he later called the focusing effect.

The purpose of the dilution experiment was to determine at what threshold in the weakening of a color PS would start failing to distinguish the two sides of cards. This was done by gradually reducing the shade of the black side of black/white cards. No description of the testing procedure is given except that we are told it was the same as in the color testing. Ten envelopes were used, open at one end, and containing a total of ten cards. Before each run the envelopes were shuffled behind the "screen" and handed to PS one at a time for his calls.

The shades of gray were obtained by a progressive dilution of the India ink used to color one side of each card. Fifty runs were made for each set of ten cards, for a total of 500 calls. Here are the rounded-down scores PS achieved for the 14 stages of the dilution.

1. No dilution of the black: .65
2. Very dark gray: .75
3. Dark gray: .80 and .71 (two tests)
4. Gray: .60 and .63
5. Light gray: .59

6. Whitish gray: .63
7. "Discernible from white only in very bright light": .68
8. "Visually not discernible from white": .52
9. White ("even the solution entirely colorless"): .76
10. Same as above, but stronger dilution: .58 and .60
11. Ditto: .81 and .75
12. Ditto: .72
13. "Cards not painted, only the 'white' side marked with a small number": .56 and .57
14. "Cards painted with pure distilled water": .75

The fact that MR mentions identifying marks only for dilution 13 suggests that he distinguished between the two sides in the other cases where the sides were not "visually distinguishable from white" by a close inspection of the surface in slanted light, though how he detected the sides painted with distilled water remains mysterious. Of the 9,500 calls, PS had 6,372 hits for an overall score of .67+.

MR calls these results a "total surprise." The irregular variations, he points out, show no decline as the dilution increases. "Only later on did we find that these strange observations can be explained in the light of what we found out about 'mental impregnation.' " The term refers to MR's conviction that PS was capable of impregnating a card with some sort of psychic impression or "footprint," the nature of which no one could understand, but which enabled PS to identify that side of the card when it was later presented to him. In other words, PS was not responding to the "actual color" of the cards, but to a psychic impression on the card. Because the cards were not labeled, in none of the color tests or dilution tests could MR keep a record of hits and misses on individual cards. He admits that this would have been of enormous value in analyzing the impregnation effect, and he apologizes for this error by saying that at the time "our experimental design was still somewhat groping."

How can we explain these truly bizarre and sensational results without assuming paranormal forces?

First, an important point. MR tells us that after each run of ten calls the envelopes were placed in two piles, divided by color calls. They were then checked and the number of hits and misses recorded. This checking was always done in PS's presence to provide immediate feedback that would encourage him to proceed. In MR's mind there would have been no reason why PS should not be allowed to observe the checking because after each run all the cards would be removed and replaced (behind a screen) with a different set of cards.

In Chapter 1, I introduced the imperfection principle as essential for understanding PS's work, and also explained a simple way to obtain secret peeks at a card by flicking back a flap. Now I introduce another equally important technique. Although it is familiar to card magicians and gamblers, not a single researcher who worked with PS showed the slightest awareness of what I shall call the "asymmetric tactile mark." It is so simple that anyone could think of it, especially a subject who had made thousands of calls on envelopes containing bicolored cards.

Here is how it works. When handed an envelope that contains a card, one grasps the envelope with both hands, at the side edges slightly above the center. Fingers are on the side facing the observer, thumb on the side facing the subject. A thumb or finger, hidden from the front by the hand, goes between the flaps and puts a slight tactile mark on or near the center of the card's top edge. With practice this can be done in an instant, even when the envelope is held by just one hand. In a moment I will explain the move in more detail, and show how it can be done in such a way that it is invisible even to someone standing behind the subject.

What sort of mark? There are four types, any one of which (or a mixture) can be used:

1. Indentations. The thumbnail or the first finger's nail is pressed forcibly against a card, near its top right corner (if the right hand is making the mark), or the top left corner (if the left hand is making the mark). This produces a slight bump on the other side of the card, so small as to be almost invisible, yet easily detected by sliding the tip of a finger or thumb over the bump. If the card is reversed in its envelope, the bump naturally goes to the other side. This technique is applicable only to cards. On heavy cardboard, such as MR used for envelopes and JGP later used for both covers and envelopes, indent marks will not go through to make bumps on the other side.

2. Nicks. These are tiny nicks made by a finger or thumb nail along the top edge of a card, or a cardboard envelope or cover. Again, it is almost invisible, though easily felt by running the tip of a finger or thumb along the edge. Even if noticed, it seems to be nothing more than the sort of mark that cards or covers acquire after a day or so of handling.

3. Corner crimps. A slight bend (magicians call it a "crimp") is made at the corner of a card, envelope, or cover. It can be made in either direction, and is easily removed at any time by bending the corner straight again. Corner crimping has long been the stock in trade of magicians and card hustlers. Needless to add, a crimped corner is easily felt, and it tells at once which way a target is facing inside a larger container.

4. Beeswax. This is the subtlest form of tactile marking. A block of high-quality colorless beeswax is carried in the pocket. The tip of a finger or thumb is rubbed over it, then a spot of wax is placed on the card.

It can go along the top edge, or on the side near the top of one corner. The spot is invisible, but readily felt as a sticky spot when a finger or thumb slides over it.

Such wax, sold in magic shops under the name of "magician's wax," is used by conjurors for many purposes. The reader is urged to obtain some colorless beeswax, such as sold for fine furniture polishing, and see how easily it can be used for asymmetric tactile marking of cards or cardboard containers. Magicians have all sorts of ways of concealing wax on their person so that a finger can touch it without having to go into a pocket. It can be on the back of a button, on the side of a match folder or pack of cigarettes, on a watchband, on the side of a shoe, or even behind an ear. Gamblers do not use wax, but they often use what is called "daub" for putting light smudge marks on the backs of cards—smudges invisible except to someone who knows where to look. It is the card-hustlers who have invented the wide variety of ways of concealing daub on their person or at the gambling table where they can have ready access to it.

There are other ways of putting tactile marks on cards, but they require special flesh-colored devices attached to a finger or thumb, and it is not likely that PS would have known about them or invented them. Psychics who reinvent forms of deception familiar to magicians and gamblers invariably reinvent only the simplest methods. The simplest of course are nicks and crimps. I consider it unlikely that PS would have used wax, not just because its use is more complicated, or because he could not have thought of it or be capable of using it, but becsuse it would have been dangerous. If detected, wax marks would be hard to explain, whereas corner crimps and tiny nicks can pass as blemishes of the sort normally acquired in the course of handling targets.

Observe that in the dilution tests PS's score fluctuated irregularly around .60, sometimes going as high as .75 and .80. To achieve such scores it is not, of course, necessary to put tactile marks on all ten cards. Here is one of a dozen or more possible scenarios.

Assume that the colors are green and white. During the first run PS puts a slight nick on the top edge near the right corner of five cards. The nicked cards are at random positions among the ten. He calls all of them green, and calls all the unmarked cards white. During the first checking process he notes how hits and misses are distributed on the five marked cards. They cannot be equal. Assume it is a 3/2 split—three hits and two misses. From then on he calls each of the five cards green if the nick is on the right side, and white if it is on the left. This guarantees a hit on at least one card in every run of ten. He can expect 4.5 hits on the other nine, giving him a final score that will fluctuate around .55. If the split was three misses and two hits, he would call the five cards white when the mark was on the right, and green if on the left, for the same expected score.

If the split were 4/1, then the same callng strategy would guarantee three hits per run, for a total score that would fluctuate around $(3 + 3.5)/10 = .65$. Occasionally the split would be a lucky 5/0. This would guarantee five hits for a score that would fluctuate around $(5 + 2.5)/10 = .75$.

Here is another scenario. Assume that instead of marking five cards in the same spot, PS marked two cards at different spots along the top edge, one very near the corner, the other between the corner and the center of the edge. By observing whether his calls on the first run were hits or misses, he would be assured from then on of direct hits on two cards. He would expect four hits on the remaining eight, for a total score that would fluctuate above and below .60. If he marked three cards at three spots along the edge, between corner and middle, he would be assured of three hits per run for an expected score of .65.

Did PS make use of asymmetric tactile markings? That is not the most important point. The point is that such a simple strategem could have produced his scores throughout the color tests and the dilution tests, and that MR never considered this possibility. Nor did JGP or any other researcher who tested PS. Because the possibility of secret tactile markings never entered their minds, there would be no need to keep a sharp observation of PS's hands each time he held an envelope.

The technique of marking and feeling can, with a little practice, be indetectable. As we shall see in Chapter 25, it can also be covered by making the "move" while a target is being picked up and transferred to a position in front of the face.

Figure 2 is a photograph of my hands holding one of the two covers I own that were used in later tests of PS by JGP, and which have the same construction as the cardboard envelopes made by MR. The cover is $5\frac{1}{2}'' \times 9''$. The top staples (hidden in the picture by my thumbs) are $4\frac{1}{2}$ inches from the cover's open edge. In other words, the flaps are half as long as the length of the cover. Inside the cover is an envelope, its top edge $2\frac{1}{2}$ inches below the top of the cover.

Although you cannot tell from the photograph, my left forefinger has gone between the flaps and is feeling the top edge of the envelope. From the subject's side, the forefinger seems to be at the back of the cover. From the other side, the forefinger seems to be on the cover's near side. My right hand is pressing the flaps closed, so to an observer on my right (where JGP habitually sat when PS made his calls), the opening between flaps on the left is completely hidden. Of course if an observer is on the left, the move can be made by the right hand while the left hand keeps the flaps closed.

Note that to an observer it looks as if the cover is held by the edges, well below the top opening. As soon as the move is made, the left hand can withdraw, leaving the cover held only by the right hand as it puts the cover aside or hands it to an experimenter. The handling is slightly different when the flaps are smaller and the inside container comes within half an inch of the top of the outside container. On this see Chapter 25.

If you will take the time to construct a cardboard envelope (or cover) along the lines explained by MR, and stand before a mirror holding it as shown, you will see how indetectably the move can be made. The important thing is to keep the fingers visible in the mirror "frozen"—that is, absolutely immobile while the forefinger (or thumb if no observer is behind you) does the "work." Tiny indentations or nicks are almost invisible and can be removed later by pressure. Corner crimps can be made in either direction for identifying two different cards. Wax marks are not visible, though they are detectable by anyone who thinks of running a fingertip along a card's edge. If MR, while randomizing cards behind his "screen," made a habit of giving cards 180-degree rotations before he put them back in envelopes, it would put tactile marks at the bottom, but it is unlikely he would have any reason to rotate cards. Even if it happened occasionally, PS could mark additional cards, or the same cards at the other end.

As for the earlier color tests, the same marking technique could account for the results, though here I will toss out a suggestion that may or may not have any bearing on those tests. We know that India ink in various strengths was used in the dilution test, but we are not told how cards were painted for the color tests. Many paints produce a surface that has a different feel from unpainted surfaces. It is conceivable that in these tests PS did not need to mark any cards, but simply inserted a finger or thumb to feel the texture on one side of each card. I have explained how easily this could be concealed in full light. Surely it would be indetectable in the test conducted in total darkness.

It is also possible, in these as well as in later tests using cardboard containers with large flaps, that peek moves were made. While an envelope is held vertically for a call, the extreme tips of index fingers, touching each side of a flap just above the top staple, can bend the flap backward enough to provide a quick glimpse of a card's color. (See Chapter 1 for details on how this move is made.) In later experiments, when envelopes were put into covers with similar large flaps, the same move could be used to glimpse the number, which was always put at the top edge of an envelope where it could be easily checked by lifting a flap.

Here again the reader is urged to make an envelope of the type described and hold it in front of a mirror to see how easily a peek move can be made, and how invisible it is from the front. If the envelope is tilted a trifle backward, the spread of the flaps can be much smaller than an inch. As I said in Chapter 1, it is essential to hold the sides by the extreme tips of the fingers and thumb, with the fingers all touching one another and the thumb's tip on the side facing the subject. The motion of the index fingertips as they flick back the flap is indetectable from the other side.

It is extremely difficult to gauge another person's exact angles of vision when that person faces you. This fact is essential for dozens of subtle "peeks" of card indices that have been devised by magicians and card-hustlers. An envelope need be tipped backward only a few degrees while the flap is opened slightly and instantly allowed to close. Done properly, there are no visible movements of any of the fingers holding the envelope.

There are other ways that PS could have obtained a peek that are just as invisible from the front. For example, the right hand holds the envelope (or cover) firmly between fingers and thumb at the lower right corner. The left hand grasps the left side near the middle, its thumb pointing upward and resting along the left edge with the fleshy side of its tip touching the flap just above the staple. A slight motion of the thumb will flick back the flap enough for a quick glimpse of the top of whatever is inside. In future chapters when I speak of a "peek move" it will refer to any handling, similar to the two methods just described, by which a quick peek is obtained of an inside container while the outside container is held vertically. Such a move is not applicable, of course, while a container is held horizontally with its closed end toward the subject.

Because JGP and others often sat on PS's right side during the calling, and in some tests we are told that PS kept a container horizontal while he called, I tend to discount the use of peek moves during later testing. It is worth noting, however, that with practice a peek move can be concealed even from an observer on the right. To accomplish this, the right hand keeps the flaps closed on the right by grasping the top corner of the container. The left forefinger or thumb bends the flap back enough on the left side to obtain a peek of the left top corner of a card. If the hands hold a cover that contains a labeled envelope, a slight backward tilt of the cover permits a glimpse of the number at the center of the envelope's top edge.

In the early experiments with PS, conducted by an inexperienced researcher like Ryzl, and by JGP before he had years to reflect on ways PS may have obtained sensory information, the use of a simple peek should not be ruled out. As all card magicians know, peeks can be made rapidly and subtly, under cover of various kinds of misdirection. In the absence of card magicians as observers, no one can be certain that such peeks did not play a role in the early testing of PS, and perhaps also in some later experiments. These are, of course, only conjectures. They may be totally wrong.

As we shall see later, JGP himself began to take precautions against glimpses, perhaps only because of criticism by colleagues. (Throughout his career JGP seemed incapable of doubting the total honesty of any psychic he tested.) In some tests flaps were closed with paper clips, and in one experiment the sides were stapled all the way to the top, leaving no flaps. In Chapter 23 we shall learn that the sides of flaps were taped all the way to the top to make sure they would not spread apart in handling and allow PS unconscious glimpses inside at parts of targets. In Chapter 25 we shall learn that an observer (Ian Stevenson) was stationed behind PS throughout several tests to make sure he did not tip jackets backward enough to glimpse interior covers. Stevenson did notice occasional tipping, and calls made at those times were ruled out of the published data.

JGP discloses in his monograph on PS that "during this time a variety of efforts were also made [by MR] to get PS to show his ESP ability in other kinds of tests, but none of these was successful." I should add that none of these tests was reported in a journal nor has MR written about them in either published or unpublished monographs. This is unfortunate. Knowing the controls under which PS showed no clairvoyance could provide valuable clues about techniques he might have used on successful tests.

We now turn to the first effort to confirm the results reported in the previous paper by MR and his wife. JGP was at the time a coeditor with Rhine of the *Journal of Parapsychology*. He had read the previous paper and was so impressed that he was eager to witness a performance of PS first hand. His trip to Prague was under a travel grant from the Office of Naval Research, with other expenses paid by Rhine's laboratory. He and MR collaborated on planning and conducting the experiment, though the actual writer of the paper was JGP.

The experiment began with a few off-the-record trials made with ten cards and ten envelopes. The envelopes were shuffled between runs without removing any cards. PS's scores were high, but "since PS observed the checking, it could have been possible for him to learn to identify some of the targets by marks on their covers." This sentence written by JGP shows that, like MR, he was aware of the imperfection principle. It was to guard against it that the following procedure was adopted. After each run of ten calls, JGP took the envelopes into the next room and closed the door. He first "cut the pack at random," then reversed exactly five cards inside their envelopes. He next "thoroughly shuffled" the envelopes, turning some of them over in the process. The ten targets were brought back to the test room, taking care to hold them "by the open end so that there was no chance that any of them would come open and reveal the enclosed targets."

MR held each envelope in front of PS while PS made his call. "The subject remained in the waking state during all the tests covered in this report. By the time this work was done, he no longer required the aid of hypnotic suggestion. . . ." After the run, the hits were checked "and recorded by JGP with the subject watching." It would have been wise of JGP to have done this checking in the other room, but he saw no need for it because he had shuffled the envelopes and turned five cards outside of PS's observation.

On the first day of his visit, JGP conducted three pilot studies: the first with green/white cards, the second with yellow/white, the third with black/white. All we are told about this poorly controlled study is that the scores were .62, .59, and .36. Because of the low negative score, the overall score was .52. On the following day, the first of three series of tests were made under what the experimenter believed were unusually tight controls.

There were forty runs through the ten-card pack (400 trials). After each run JGP went into the next room to randomize the white/yellow targets, then brought the envelopes back. MR held them in front of PS while he made his calls. After each run, the colors were checked by lifting the envelopes' loose ends. No description of the envelopes is given. All we are told is that they were "opaque." Presumably they were the same as those used in the previous experiment conducted by MR and his wife. It is important to remember that checking was always done in PS's presence. In this series PS scored 233 hits out of 400 calls, for a significant score of .58+.

The second series involved alternating bicolored cards with standard ESP cards. The results were within chance, so we need not go into details. As we have seen, MR had earlier discovered the curious fact that PS's ESP operated only on bilabeled cards and nothing else, but this was the first confirmation of that fact by someone else.

The third series repeated the first one. This time PS had 219 hits out of 400 calls, a modest positive score of 219/400= 54+ percent.

On the last day, JGP introduced what he calls a "screened touch matching" procedure; but the results were chance, so he gives no details beyond remarking in a footnote that the "level of safeguarding" was low and therefore he felt it improper to combine those results with the others. Here again we see the deplorable tendency of psi experimenters not to give descriptions of tests that fail.

Although PS's scores were lower than those obtained by MR previously, JGP concludes that the experiment was highly successful because PS had produced ESP on demand, and while working with a new experimenter. Indeed, he waxes eloquent: "This is a demonstration of reliability in performance that is unprecedented in experimental ESP research. . . . It could mean that controlled performance in ESP tests may be much closer than anyone has previously had reason to suppose." MR tells us in *Hypnosis and ESP* (p. 79) that "Dr. Pratt immediately after the experiment hurried to the nearest Post Office to send a cable home to share the good news with his colleagues." We now know that JGP's optimism was premature. More than 25 years have elapsed, and controlled, repeatable ESP performances are as elusive as ever.

There are two glaring defects of this experiment. First, neither cards nor envelopes were numbered, making it impossible to record information that would have been extremely useful in determining exactly what occurred. Second, we are given no precise description of how JGP randomized the cards. He does tell us that his procedure was planned for a "minimum of time and effort." He had a limited time to stay in Prague, and it is understandable that he would randomize in the fastest way possible: cut, reverse five cards in five envelopes, and shuffle. Nothing is said about the use of tables of random numbers or a randomizing device such as a die or spinner. The question that cries out for an answer is: How did JGP select the five cards to be turned over?

We may never know exactly how they were selected unless JGP recorded it somewhere among his voluminous papers stored at the University of Virginia. Let me conjecture on a procedure that seems to me the most likely, but first a word about cutting. Cuts are never random for the simple reason that they tend to be made near the center of a pack. It is reasonable to assume that when JGP cut the stack of ten envelopes he did not cut just one or two from the top, or leave just one or two on the bottom. It is reasonable also to assume that after making the cut to further speed up the process, he would reverse cards in the top five envelopes. Having cut the pack, he would see no need to randomize these reversals; besides, he knew that after turning the five cards he would shuffle the envelopes. Using a randomizer or a table of random digits to select the five cards to be reversed would have been time consuming, and JGP states in his paper, as I mentioned earlier, that he adopted a randomizing procedure that would minimize both time and effort. When I asked MR by letter in 1987 how JGP selected the five cards to be turned, he replied that it was his recollection that JGP always reversed the "top half" of the stack of envelopes.

Now let's see what happens when a ten-card pack is cut at least three cards down and without leaving less than three cards on the table. If you try this with ten playing cards, ace through ten from top down, you will see that there are five different spots where the packet can be cut. Now reverse the top five cards. You will find that in every case, no matter which of the five cuts you make, the eight will be reversed and the three will not be reversed.

If PS was aware of JGP's way of randomizing, or if he guessed it, he would have had a subtler strategy for raising his score. All he needed to do was to memorize the outsides of envelopes three and eight during each run, then observe what colors were on top when the check was made after the run. On the next run he would call the same color for envelope three, and the opposite color for envelope eight. This would almost certainly give him two hits.

He can do even better. Cards seven and nine would be among the five turned with a probability of 4/5, and cards two and four would have the same probability of *not* being reversed. If PS made opposite calls on seven, eight, nine and the same calls on two, three, four, he stands a good chance of getting six hits during each run. If he were to hit on all six, and got two of the remaining four correct by chance, his success score would be 80 percent.

Let's assume that PS knew nothing about JGP's way of turning five cards, and did not even guess the procedure. It is not difficult to memorize ten envelopes by the imperfection principle and to recall (even without a mnemonic system) the calls made on these envelopes. Since PS watched the checking procedure, he would know on just what envelopes he made hits and misses. After a dozen or so runs it would soon become apparent that certain envelopes in each run were getting their cards reversed, and certain other envelopes were not. In my opinion it is stretching it a bit, but I suppose it is possible that PS could have picked up this information without being conscious of it. However, on our assumption (which of course may not be true) that PS discovered clever ways of boosting his scores, the technique I described could easily have raised his score to .58 and .54 on the two successful tests. By following only one envelope he could boost his score to .55, and if he followed two envelopes he could boost it to .60. A plausible scenario is that he followed two envelopes, but that JGP occasionally cut extremely high or extremely low so that PS made occasional wrong calls on those two envelopes.

We see here how extremely informative it would have been if JGP had numbered both cards and envelopes and kept a record of the way those numbers correlated with calls. The raw data could then be investigated for deviations from randomness that would indicate exactly how JGP determined the cards to be turned, and whether PS adopted a calling strategy that took advantage of such deviations to raise his score. Such a guessing strategy obviously would produce strong focusing effects. Later, as we shall see, JGP recognized the importance of labeling both cards and envelopes—not for detecting methods of deception, but for providing more evidence for focusing.

The experiment also shows the importance of using random numbers or some sort of randomizer to determine where to cut a pack, and to determine which envelopes to select for reversing cards. I do not know for sure whether JGP always reversed cards in the top five packets, though it seems extremely likely that he did. I do not know for sure whether PS consciously or unconsciously based a guessing strategy on this. I do insist that because of the glaring flaws in the design of this experiment, it has little evidential value.

Chapter 4

Prague, 1962

DATE: August 1962
PLACE: MR's apartment in Prague
PAPER: "A Model of Parapsychological Communication," by
Milan Ryzl, in the *Journal of Parapsychology,* 30
(March 1966), pp. 18-30. A shorter account of the ex-
periment had earlier appeared in the Czechoslovakian
journal, *Sdelovaci Technika (Communication Technol-
ogy)*, 12, 1964, pp. 299-302.

Although this was the most extraordinary of all experiments made with
PS—indeed, it is one of the most sensational in the entire history of psi
research—there is some doubt as to just when it was made. The date is
not given either in the 1964 paper or in MR's *Hypnosis and ESP*. The
latter reference describes it as occurring before JGP's first visit to Prague
in June 1962, but JGP, in his monograph about PS, says it took place
after his visit, "probably" in August 1962.

The purpose of this unusually complicated test was to determine if
ESP could be the basis for a code that would communicate numbers with
perfect accuracy. MR likens the test to the first crude efforts to transmit
messages by radio waves. He was convinced that in the future, when the
training of subjects would be vastly improved, ESP could be used for sending
coded messages across vast distances. He realized that his experiment was
no more than a clumsy effort to prove such a dream is possible and to
encourage others to work on improving the technique.

The technique, which in more sophisticated form has become

commonplace today as "error-correcting codes," is to make use of redundancy in amplifying a message, or in the familiar phrase of Lewis Carroll's *Hunting of the Snark,* "what I tell you three times is true." The technique is involved of course in the "majority vote" that MR had previously used, but now he adopted an ingenious procedure of steadily amplifying calls until strong enough criteria were met for deciding when the repetitions were sufficient to constitute an unambiguous hit. Here is how it worked.

An assistant, who is not named, arbitrarily assigned to each of five three-digit numbers (chosen, we are told, "by lot") a string of ten binary colors, green (G) and white (W). The only number given in the paper is 242, which was coded by the color sequence $GWWWWGWGGW$. A set of ten envelopes similar to those used in earlier tests were labeled on the back with capital letters A through K (J omitted). Then green/white cards were inserted in the envelopes so their top colors formed the pattern from A to K that coded 242.

To aid the amplification process a second set of ten envelopes were labeled on the back with lower case letters a through k (j omitted). It contained the same string of bicolored cards, though in negative form: Each G in the coded sequence was a card with its *white* side up, and each W was a card with its *green* side up. This ensured an equal distribution of colors in the two sets, and also provided a parallel, independent test of PS's accuracy.

A third set of ten envelopes, called "index covers," numbered 1 through 10 on the back, contained G/W cards in a random but known pattern. This set was used solely to determine if PS's clairvoyant powers were operating. MR had decided in advance that if ESP failed to show on this test, the entire experiment would be canceled.

All thirty envelopes were sealed after the assistant made a record of their color patterns. MR does not tell us how they were sealed, though presumably it was with paper tape, because such tape was used to seal envelopes in both earlier and later tests. The thirty sealed envelopes were then handed one at a time to PS, who held them while he made his calls. After each run of thirty calls, MR shuffled the envelopes. There were 50 runs, making a total of 30 x 50 = 1,500 calls.

Before proceeding with the amplification technique, the third set of ten envelopes, with the random pattern, was opened to see if ESP was operating. Of the 500 calls made on this set, there were 285 hits, for a respectable score of 285/500 or .57 exactly. Convinced that PS was in good form, this set of envelopes was discarded and not used again.

The experiment now continued, based on the following procedure. Calls for the first ten envelopes were checked to identify the envelopes on which PS made forty or more identical correct calls out of fifty. These "outstanding hit" envelopes were now checked to see if they met the following two criteria:

1. On each run of ten consecutive calls for that envelope, there had to be a split of 8-2 or better favoring the color designated by the forty or more calls on the set as a whole.

2. The color designated by the forty or more calls had to be supported by a favorable split of at least 30-20 on the corresponding envelopes of the set in which colors had been reversed.

Envelopes meeting the two criteria were removed. They were replaced with what MR calls "new index covers," containing arbitrarily turned cards. PS then went through the new pack of fifty envelopes to make a new set of fifty calls, after which the original "test covers" (the index covers were disregarded) were again examined to see if they now met the criteria for reliably indicating a color. If so, they were removed, more "index covers" were mixed in, and the procedure was repeated until all ten of the original envelopes had been reliably identified. In the example given, for envelopes that were coded 242, three repetitions of the procedure were required before all ten colors had been designated.

The entire process was then repeated for the other four three-digit numbers. After the five independent series had been completed, the colors that had been amplified to the point of providing what MR considered a reliable indication of all fifty colors, and not until then, were the designated colors checked against the record of the color-patterns kept by the unnamed assistant. One assumes that the test envelopes were also opened at this time to make sure the colors actually matched the assistant's record, although for some reason MR does not say this. We are told only that the five target numbers "were thus identified without a single mistake." Altogether PS made 19,350 calls, of which 11,978 were hits; so his overall score was almost 62 percent. The entire experiment took about fifty hours, not counting the hours spent in analyzing the data.

Pause now to consider the amazing accuracy of this test. PS succeeded, by the amplification procedure, in correctly identifying the top colors of fifty cards in fifty envelopes. This is comparable to calling heads, then tossing fifty coins in the air n times, and deeming a coin "heads" if it fell heads more often than if fell tails. The probability that all fifty coins will be deemed heads is exactly the same as the probability that all fifty will fall heads in one toss. It is $1/2^{50}$ or $1/1,125,899,906,842,624$.

Of all the experiments with PS that have been reported in published papers, this is the most difficult for the skeptic to evaluate, not just because of its complexity, but also because of the vagueness with which it is described. I have already mentioned the uncertainty about the date. There also is uncertainty about who the "assistant" was, although he or she played a crucial, perhaps even the major, role in the experiment. When PS finally answered one of my letters, telling me he did not want to correspond about any of his tests, he said that this experiment had happened so long ago that he could not recall who the assistant was. Ryzl responded to the same question by writing that it was a "friend," but that he used so many friends as "hired help" he could not be sure which one assisted in this particular test. As we shall see, his memory was later refreshed.

I found MR's forgetfulness astonishing. It was almost as if Albert Michelson could not remember who helped him in the famous Michelson-Morley test. MR can counter by saying that, after all, his "hired help" were not trained researchers but only inexperienced persons paid to assist him. But in that case, are we not justified in asking about the person's trustworthiness? Did the pay provide an incentive to get positive results so he or she would be hired again? Could this incentive, perhaps combined with a strong desire to please MR, result in an "experimenter effect" that would play a role when the assistant and MR made their complicated statistical analysis of more than nineteen thousand calls?

In keeping with my plan to focus only on techniques by which PS could have raised his score by nonparanormal means, I will not consider the following three possibilities: (1) Conscious fudging of the data. (2) Unconscious fudging of the data (experimenter effect). (3) Collaboration between PS and the assistant.

Excluding the above (and I do not believe they are relevant), there remain two ways the results can be explained on a nonparanormal basis.

First, it is possible that someone who knew the target patterns was present while PS made his calls and that he picked up unconscious reactions, modifying his calls accordingly. Nowhere in his papers does MR say he was ignorant of the color patterns chosen by the assistant, or that his assistant was never present during PS's calling. However, MR has assured me that he knew none of the patterns until the experiment was over and that his assistant was at no time present during the calling. He also assured me that his wife played no role in the experiment. I accept all of this.

A more plausible conjecture—of course I have no evidence whatever for it—is that over the period of fifty hours, with an assistant so untrained that MR could not remember his name, PS may have been left alone for brief periods with the targets. We know that MR had total trust in PS's honesty. Besides, were not all the covers sealed? There is not a line in MR's paper, or in his description of the test in his unpublished monograph, about taking precautions to guard the targets or, for that matter, to guard the assistant's record of the color patterns. Were there times when MR left the test room to go to the bathroom, to the kitchen for a drink, to answer the telephone, and so on? It would take PS only a few seconds to peel back paper tape, take a quick look at a card, moisten the tape, and reseal the envelope. He made more than nineteen thousand calls, spread over a period of many days, perhaps many weeks. It is not inconceivable that as the experiment progressed he gradually learned the ten colors necessary for a perfect score. Learning the color for one envelope would, of course, automatically tell him the color of the partner envelope of opposite color.

Data is given only for calls on the envelopes that were coded 242. A chart shows that during the first session PS reliably identified only one pair of envelopes (*H* and *h*). On the second run-through he got five more. One more was identified during the third run-through, and the last three envelopes were identified on the third run-through.

MR believed this to be the first experiment to demonstrate that ESP could provide perfect identification of a set of target numbers. He saw it as a monumental breakthrough. In both his paper and in *Hypnosis and ESP* he is eloquent about the possibility that ESP could be used in the future for transmitting coded information swiftly and accurately over vast distances, and without the use of physical mechanisms. Now an experiment of this magnitude, with such incredible success, cries out for careful replication on the familiar grounds that extraordinary claims in science demand extraordinary evidence.

Parapsychologists impressed by this experiment may be surprised to learn that MR himself tried three times to replicate his most famous experiment, failing all three times; but the three failures were never published. In *Hypnosis and ESP* the first two failures are not mentioned, though there is a brief reference to the third failure on page 101. JGP, who must have known of these failed replication efforts, does not mention them in his monograph on PS. I learned of the first two only after I obtained access to MR's two unpublished manuscripts.

The first unsuccessful effort is described in the 1965 monograph, Part 4, pages 76-86. Instead of obtaining a number by lot, then translating it into a predetermined binary code, a sequence of ten colors was directly obtained by "tossing a coin." The colors were represented by white/green cards sealed in ten envelopes by MR's assistant, in this case his wife. A second set of ten sealed envelopes contained the same sequence but with colors reversed. We are told that JR did not keep a record of either sequence. The guessing procedure was the same as before, using the amplification technique previously described. MR reports that eventually six cards were correctly identified, three were not identified, and one card was wrongly guessed. Because the objective was to correctly identify all ten colors, "the observed error doomed the whole experiment to be a *failure*. Therefore, the experiment was discontinued. . . ."

The second attempted replication began in July 1963, but because it was continually interrupted by other tests, it did not terminate until the middle of 1964. It is described in MR's monograph on 1964 testing of PS, pages 13-20. Preoccupied with other things, the work was delegated to an unnamed male assistant.

Only one three-digit number was involved. The assistant obtained it by tossing three differently colored dice, each with ten faces bearing the digits 0 through 9.* A code was used for translating this number to a pattern of ten green/white cards. They were put in ten envelopes, numbered on the back and sealed with paper tape. As in the previous amplification experiment, a parallel set of ten envelopes carried the same color pattern in negative form. This time a record was made of the pattern, and placed aside in a sealed envelope to be checked at the end of the test.

As a further way to amplify the number, it was multiplied by 100, and the product translated into another pattern of G/W cards that went into twenty more sealed and numbered envelopes, one set of ten being the negative of the other. A third set of twenty envelopes contained a pattern that coded the target number multiplied by 200. It was agreed in advance that the experiment would be deemed a success only if at least two of the three patterns were perfectly identified.

The 3 x 20 = 60 envelopes were mixed with sixty other "control targets"— envelopes containing cards of known top colors. There were thus 120 envelopes in all, or double the number used in the successful amplification experiment. All envelopes were labeled on the back with numerals. The set of 120 envelopes was turned over to MR, "who either himself, or in cooperation with other assistants, carried out the repeated calling experiment."

PS made ten runs of twelve calls each, or 120 calls, one for each envelope. These were recorded on one page, alongside the envelope numbers. After the 120 calls, the envelopes were shuffled by tossing them repeatedly about on a table, and another series of 120 calls were made. This continued at various intervals over a period of almost a year, until 50 pages of "minutes" were obtained. They were the records of 50 x 120 = 6,000 calls. The amplification process required three more run-throughs. Thus altogether there were 4 x 6,000 = 24,000 calls on the G/W targets.

The criteria used for evaluating the results were even more complicated than before, and require three pages of typescript to explain. I will not go into them here because the experiment was another failure. PS showed no ESP success on the actual colors. There was some evidence of a focusing effect. The failure of the test was taken by MR to indicate the beginning

---

*Ryzl calls the dice "ten-faced," but does not describe their shape. No Platonic solid has ten faces. Perhaps he used icosahedral dice, each digit appearing twice on the twenty faces.

of a temporary loss of ESP ability on the part of PS, which MR attributed to a variety of psychological factors.

When I first learned about this failed replication, I wrote to MR to ask if he could tell me the name of his assistant and, if not, could he tell me if it was the same assistant who helped in the successful amplification test. MR replied that he did not recall ever attempting a replication, and he wondered where in the world I could have gotten such information. He added that he could not remember even planning such a test or discussing it with anyone. I wrote back to say I had found it described in detail in his own monograph of the 1964 experiments with PS. This immediately produced a postcard on which he congratulated me for knowing more about his experiments than he did!

The postcard was followed by a fascinating letter dated November 27, 1987. MR had read his old monograph, he said, and it had refreshed his memory. He was now able to supply details not in the monograph, although he was not sure his memory was accurate. The assistant in both the original test and the second failed replication was "probably" Ctibor Sorbus, at that time a twenty-year-old student at Prague University. MR described him as the most "enthusiastic" of all his assistants—a man who spent more time helping him than anyone else had. He said he had lost track of Sorbus's whereabouts. He confirmed the fact that original records of all his experiments had been stored with people in Czechoslovakia when he made his escape to the United States. They have since died, he said, so the records must be presumed lost.

As for the results of the second replication effort, and a third one which I will come to shortly, MR said he found them "confusing" and "quite worthless." He repeats what he alludes to in *Hypnosis and ESP,* that early in 1964, after JGP's second visit to Prague, PS decided to break off working with MR and shift to JGP as an experimenter who could bring him more fame and money. With this shift in mind, MR thinks that PS began deliberately to stop producing positive results. He says he placed no value on the two failed replication tests, hoping at the time that he would someday be able to repeat the experiment successfully with another subject. He adds that he never viewed PS as "unique," in the way he has been viewed in the West, but only as one of his good subjects. He says he had every reason to hope that later he could repeat the failed experiments; but because of events beyond his control, the opportunity never materialized.

I turn now to MR's third failure to replicate. It was undertaken during the same time interval as the second attempt, with PS calling as before in MR's apartment. As MR describes it in his monograph on 1964 tests (pp. 21-25), the target was not a number but a phrase of "17 letters." The phrase is not disclosed in MR's typescript, but he now recalls it as either

"Peace and Freedom" or "Freedom and Peace." Each phrase has only fifteen letters. Perhaps a symbol was added for the two spaces between words. In his letter to me Ryzl added that English was chosen because at the time he hoped to cooperate with American parapsychologists and to publish the results (had they been favorable, I assume) in the West.

The phrase was translated by a code into a pattern of bicolored cards, which for some reason were yellow/white instead of green/white. For each of the seventeen symbols, nine envelopes were prepared to hold the cards in the required color pattern. Thus there were 9 x 17 = 153 envelopes altogether. They were sealed and numbered. MR prepared the targets himself, which were then turned over to an unnamed assistant (presumably, Sorbus) who supervised PS's calls in MR's absence. PS made fifty calls on each envelope, or a total of 7,650 calls for the experiment's initial phase. The amplification process required two more run-throughs. Altogether, therefore, PS made 3 x 7,650 = 22,950 calls on the white/yellow cards. The experiment was abandoned when analysis of the data made clear that PS was scoring negatively on the colors. Putting the two failed replication attempts together, they involved 22,950 + 7,650 = 30,600 calls.* It is little wonder that the two experiments extended over a period of almost a year.

I need not go into the confusing criteria used in evaluating the data because it showed no evidence of either ESP or focusing. In fact, PS's score on the colors was negative. As I have said, MR attributes this and the previous failure to a deliberate attempt by PS to block his paranormal powers. Two other possible explanations are obvious:

1. PS found the two experiments so complicated, and extended over such a long period of time, that he abandoned all hope of boosting his scores by nonparanormal methods.

2. The assistant and MR were extremely careful, in both replications, to make sure that at no time was PS allowed unsupervised access to either the target covers or the records of their color patterns.

In his unpublished monograph on 1964 experiments, MR conjectures that the negative score of the second replication effort may have resulted from a "defect in the experimental set-up." Although the assistant assured him that he devoted all possible care to the test procedures, MR "suspected

---

*Different figures are given in the brief account of this experiment in *Hypnosis and ESP*. We are told that the test was started in July 1963. It was discontinued because MR's tests of impregnation (covered here in Chapter 12) were "more challenging." The experiment was resumed "during the first half of 1964," but the results were not evaluated until "late summer of 1964." The first part of the experiment had a total of 12,000 calls of which 6,679 were hits and 5,321 were misses. But the second part, consisting of 34,950 calls, had 18,465 misses and 16,485 hits, a negative score. I do not know how to reconcile these figures with those given in the unpublished typescript.

the assistant to have erroneously presented the subject the reversed sides of the targets for ascertainment instead of those that had been determined for the experimental series in question." Some assistant! What MR is saying is that instead of presenting the envelopes to PS with their numbers on the back, the assistant presented the envelopes with the numbered sides facing PS! It is hard to believe that PS would not also have noticed this abrupt change in procedure. Of course if he called all the colors in reverse, what would have been a positive ESP score naturally would have become a negative one.

Let me sum up. In view of the lack of important information about the original amplification test, on which PS made his perfect score, and in view of PS's failures on three attempts at replication, I think the original experiment should be relegated to that class of psi miracles that happen only once, and about which, after a long lapse of time, nothing new can be learned. I place it in a class with Rhine's constant claim that ESP had been established beyond any doubt by Hubert Pearce when he correctly called twenty-five ESP cards in a row; or the claims by Harold Puthoff and Russell Targ that Uri Geller, when they tested him at SRI International, provided uncontestable evidence of clairvoyant viewing of pictures; or the claims of several witnesses that they had seen D. D. Home, the British medium, float horizontally out of one second-floor window and then float back in at another one.

If five three-digit numbers can be transmitted by ESP without a single error, this is so revolutionary that it would fully justify the claims by parapsychologists that the scientific community is on the verge of a gigantic paradigm shift comparable to the Copernican revolution. Unfortunately, MR himself, using the same subject as before, failed three times to replicate his sensational results. According to his own statements, he considered those failures so unimportant that he even forgot he had made them!

Parapsychologists who persist in holding up the original test as one of the most persuasive ever made should be under a moral obligation to add that three efforts to replicate it failed. I find it shameful that JGP, in his monograph on PS, describes the original test but omits any reference to the failures. MR, living for many years in California, has had more than twenty years to train another subject and try to replicate the experiment. Why has he never done so? Why has no other parapsychologist attempted it? When an experiment this extraordinary sits in the literature for twenty-five years, with three failed replications with the same subject and not a single successful one, it is a good bet that some aspect of the original test was defective, even though we may never know what the defect was.

In their paper on "The Anomaly Called Psi: Recent Research and Criticism" (*Behavioral and Brain Sciences,* 10, December 1987, pp. 539-

551), K. Ramakrishna Rao and John Palmer hold up MR's original experiment as an outstanding example of how the amplification of a weak effect can be intensified by a "majority vote" technique to identify with 100-percent accuracy which color was up on fifty concealed bicolored cards. In my comment on this paper (ibid., pp. 587-588) I mentioned that a "more plausible" way to amplify psi is to let a group of people simultaneously invoke psi. As an example, I cited the notorious failure of psychics to move a tiny arrow suspended frictionless in a magnetic field under a bell jar from which the air has been removed. Palmer and Rao, responding to criticisms by me and others, wrote: "We fail to understand, for ESP at least, why Gardner thinks that amplification is more 'plausible' when based on a small number of guesses from each of a group of subjects than when based on a large number of guesses from one subject."

This gives me a chance to explain. I leave aside the fact that it is much easier and faster to record the simultaneous guesses of, say, ten talented subjects than to record ten guesses by one talented subject who makes them serially over a period that can vary from a few minutes to many days or even longer. Judging from hundreds of published papers, psi powers are extremely sensitive to a psychic's state of mind. If a subject is inhibited by a headache (as we shall see in Chapter 22, two of PS's failures, when he was forced to wear a mitten on his right hand, were blamed on a two-day headache), or any of a dozen other psychological factors, it presumably can cause a loss of psi power. Now, if a subject is inhibited by a psychological factor and asked to guess a target ten times in a row, the inhibiting factor will surely apply to all ten guesses. But if ten psychics simultaneously guess, it is reasonable to suppose that not all of them are psychologically inhibited at the same time. The amplification technique should therefore be more dependable.

This is even more obvious with respect to psychokinesis (PK). In the rotating arrow test, amplification by many psychics seems clearly "preferable" to amplification by repeated efforts of one psychic. If PK can influence falling dice, bend spoons, float objects, and move pill bottles, it should be able to move the arrow. But if one psychic cannot muster up enough PK to rotate the arrow at noon, surely he or she will be just as unable to do so ten minutes later. However, PK should be strongly amplified when coming simultaneously from many psychics standing around the arrow. One person may not be able to lift a heavy table, but ten people may be able to lift it with ease. One psychic, for a variety of psychological reasons, may be unable to "see" the color of a concealed card no matter how often he or she tries. Out of ten gifted subjects, surely two or three will do better than the others, producing a majority vote above chance. I find it puzzling that Rao and Palmer cannot understand such simple reasoning.

Chapter 5

Prague, 1963

DATE: The paper says January 1963, but JGP in his monograph on PS, says February.
PLACE: MR's apartment in Prague
PAPER: "A Further Confirmation of Stabilized ESP Performance in a Selected Subject." Milan Ryzl and J. G. Pratt, in the *Journal of Parapsychology,* 27 (June 1963), pp. 73–83.

As the authors state, this was essentially a repetition of their previous experiment (here reported in Chapter 3) except that twenty cards and envelopes were used instead of ten. One hundred runs were made, for a total of 2,000 calls. The bicolored cards were 3″ × 5″ white index cards, painted green on one side. The envelopes were the same as in the previous test: folded strips of heavy cardboard, stapled on the sides, with flaps left open at the top for easy insertion and removal of cards.

PS sat as usual in an easy chair, engaging in "friendly conversation" between runs and smoking cigarettes. There was no attempt to screen envelopes from his gaze. MR held the stack of twenty envelopes on his right knee while he presented them one at a time in front of PS, who made his calls at a rate of about two seconds per envelope. After each call the envelopes were placed aside on a chair in two stacks, one for green calls, one for white. MR then checked the cards in PS's presence by raising the top flap of each envelope enough to see the card's top color. The two experimenters kept separate tallies of the calls. The total testing time was seven hours. PS made 1,133 hits out of the 2,000 calls for a score of .56+.

"The only interpretation of the data that can be made," the authors write, "is that they are due to ESP."

After each run JGP took the envelopes to the next room to randomize the orientation of the cards. He used the same process as before, except now we are told he "cut the pack a few times" before reversing half the cards (in this case, ten) and reinserting them in the envelopes.

Again, nothing is said about how JGP selected the cards to be reversed. As we saw in Chapter 3, MR's recollection is that to save time JGP simply reversed cards in the top half of the pack. After all, having cut the pack several times he would see no need to randomize this selection. Now, as all card magicians know, and JGP did not, no matter how many times a pack is cut, it is equivalent to a single cut. This is surprising to people who are neither magicians nor card players. Cut a deck a thousand times and the final order of cards is one that a single cut would have produced. Had JGP wished to truly randomize his selection of the ten cards to be turned, he could easily have chosen a single cutting spot by using a spinner with numbers 1 through 20.

"A few" commonly means three. If JGP habitually cut three times, cutting near the middle each time, it would be the same as a single cut near the middle. You might pause at this point to try another simple experiment. Arrange twenty playing cards so that the top ten are, say, the ace through ten of hearts in sequence, and the bottom are, say, the ace through ten of spades. Give the pack three random cuts, then examine the top ten cards. You will find that there is a very high probability (if you repeat this many times) that the five and six of hearts will end up among the bottom ten cards. The probability of the four and seven of hearts also being among the bottom ten is almost as high. Even the three and eight have a better than even chance of being among the bottom ten.

Exactly the same probabilities apply to cards near the center of the pack's bottom half. There is a very high probability that the five and six of spades will end up among the ten cards at the top of the pack, and almost as high a probability that the four and seven of spades will also be in the top half.

What does all this mean? It means that if JGP made three random cuts and then reversed the top ten cards, there is a high probability that cards at positions five and six before cutting would not be reversed and cards at positions fifteen and sixteen from the top would be reversed. We know that PS was allowed to observe the checking for hits after each run. He would know, therefore, after the envelopes had been checked, the orientations of the cards in the envelopes at positions five, six, fifteen, and sixteen. If he also had a way of memorizing the four envelopes at those positions (using the imperfection principle), he need only watch for those envelopes when they turned up at random spots during the next run. He would then repeat his previous calls on the envelopes formerly at positions five and six, and make opposite calls on envelopes formerly at positions fifteen and sixteen. He would have an excellent chance of making hits on all four envelopes, which would elevate his overall score to .60. If he hit on only three, it would boost his score to .57+, and if he hit on just two it would give him an expected score of .55. The actual score was .56+.

Let me anticipate an objection. After JGP cut the pack and turned the ten cards inside the envelopes, he went to considerable lengths to randomize the order and orientations of the envelopes. Here is how he described it:

> To achieve this purpose, JGP threw the 20 covers [envelopes] one at a time onto a large table, separating them into 10 to 15 small stacks and turning approximately half of the covers over in the process. Then the scattered covers were reassembled into a single stack by picking them up in a haphazard order. After the stack was reassembled, JGP further shuffled the order by cutting the stack a few times, inverting one part each time before completing the cut. Only when this randomization was completed did JGP open the door and return with the enclosed randomized targets to the experimental room.

Given this kind of randomizing, and the fact that the outsides of the envelopes were not labeled, PS would have to know the imperfection pattern on both sides of each of the four envelopes if he followed the scenario suggested above. There are several ways he could have known this. Suppose, for example, PS was allowed to examine the envelopes prior to the experiment. Given the informal atmosphere, and the fact that the experimenters would see no reason why he should not be allowed to do this (since he would be seeing the twenty envelopes throughout the testing), this is not an unreasonable assumption. The experimenters would regard it as too irrelevant to mention, but of course it would give PS an opportunity to memorize both sides of each envelope. You might suppose that memorizing twenty pairs of sides would be too difficult a task, but remember that PS, over a period of two years, had made hundreds of thousands of calls. Moreover, he could by this time have developed a mnemonic system that would make the task much easier.

Let's assume, however, that at no time during the seven hours of testing was PS allowed to handle the envelopes. Was it possible for him, during the calling and checking procedure, to observe both sides of the envelopes before they were taken away for randomizing? The answer is yes. The experimenters were careful to handle the envelopes exactly the same way for each run, but the description of the handling does not rule out the possibility that at three points in the procedure PS may have seen the other sides of the envelopes.

We are told that JGP brought the stack of envelopes to MR, who placed it on his right knee. PS sat in a chair with his back to a window. MR sat in a chair on PS's right. When he put the stack on his knee, we are told, he always turned it so that the closed ends of the envelopes pointed toward PS on his left. Thus the envelopes had their open sides pointing to MR's right. Think a moment, and you will see that it would have been natural for MR to pick up the top envelope with his right hand, taking it by its right edge (the edge nearest him), then without turning it over in his hand, present the envelope's underside to PS for a call. Knowing that JGP had turned over envelopes at random during his shuffling process, there would be no reason why MR would need to present PS, at each call, the side of the cover that had been uppermost in the stack on his knee.

If this was MR's procedure, it would of course give PS a chance to see both sides of each envelope before he made his call. This would enormously simplify his strategy. It would only be necessary for him, during each run, to memorize both sides of just four envelopes—the two that would end up at positions five and six in the stack after checking, and the two that would end at positions fifteen and sixteen in the final stack. We are told that after the calls MR placed the envelopes in two piles on a chair, one pile for white calls, one pile for green. At the end of the calling, MR picked up the green pile, turned his back on PS, and placed it on a table behind him, where JGP had been sitting and recording the calls. The white stack was then picked up and placed on the table, and JGP made a record of the targets and hits "beginning at the bottom of the run and working upward." It is not too clear just what this means, nor are we told whether after the recording the white stack went on top of the green or vice versa. However, it is not important to know this. Since the procedure was followed exactly after each run, PS would know precisely which envelopes would end up at positions 5, 6, 15, and 16 from the top of the final stack that JGP would take to the next room. Those would be the four envelopes that he had memorized along with the orientations of their cards. On the next run he would watch for the four envelopes and make the four calls that would almost certainly be hits.

Because the four envelopes would come up in random positions, it would be necessary for PS to memorize a different set of four envelopes for the next run. It is conceivable that after a few hundred calls PS would have memorized both sides of all twenty envelopes. Once this was done, his task on each run would be greatly simplified.

Assume now that, in picking up the envelopes to hold in front of PS, MR always presented the side uppermost on the stack. There is another point in the procedure at which PS could have seen the other side of a memorized envelope. When MR placed a called envelope on the chair, we are not told whether he placed it called-side down or called-side up. All we are told is that the order of envelopes was reversed, and that at the finish MR was careful not to turn the two stacks (the white and the green) over when he placed them on the table in front of JGP. If he placed the envelopes called-side down, of course he would turn the down side toward him when he lifted a flap to check the color that had faced PS when he made his call. Nothing in the paper rules out this procedure, which of course would give PS a chance to see both sides of an envelope *after* making his call.

There is a third point at which PS may have seen the other sides of envelopes. Let's assume that MR always placed the envelopes on the table with called-sides up. We are not told where he sat at the table while he lifted flaps and registered hits and misses. It is possible that MR sat in such a position that, as he checked the card colors, PS would be able to see the opposite sides of each envelope.

In brief, the vague descriptions given of the calling and checking procedures does not rule out three points at which PS may have seen the verso sides of memorized envelopes. Here again we see the importance of providing precise descriptions of procedures. Of course neither experimenter would have seen any need at the time for such detailed accounts. Because JGP was thought to have thoroughly randomized the orientations of cards after each run, such precision would have appeared totally unnecessary.

Suppose that calling and checking were handled in such a way that at no time could PS see the "other" sides of envelopes. Would this rule out all strategies by which he could have boosted his success to .56+? It would not. There are dozens of possible strategies. I will consider only one, selected because it also accounts for two seeming anomalies in the data: PS's marked preference for green calls, and the fact that he scored a higher percentage of hits on white calls than on green.

Assume that when MR checked for hits after each run he sat with his back to PS, allowing PS to see the sides of the envelopes he had seen when making calls. This is plausible, because we are told that MR turned his back to PS when he placed the called envelopes on the table where JGP sat. It is not essential to assume this, because PS could hear the checking process, but it makes things simpler for him.

In making his calls on each run PS would (in our conjectured strategy) first call green on four envelopes picked at random, and then he would call green on six envelopes chosen because their imperfections were easy to memorize. After this, two more randomly selected envelopes would be called green. Thus he would scatter twelve green calls among the twenty, for an overall ratio of 12/20 or 60 percent of the total of 2,000. This would be a total of 1,200 green calls. The actual total was 1,193, a score of 59.7 percent.

We are assuming that after the checking process the stack of green-called envelopes went on top of the white, so that when JGP began his cuts the twelve green-called envelopes would be on top. As mathematicians like to say, we can assume this with no loss of generality, because had the "white" stack always gone on top PS would have reversed colors in his strategy and the colors would have been reversed in the published data.

Among the twelve green envelopes at the top of the stack, the memorized ones would be at positions 3, 4, 5, 6, 7, 8. As we have seen, there is an almost certain probability that those six would go to the bottom after three cuts, and therefore none of the six envelopes would have their cards turned. However, JGP's random shuffling and turning of envelopes would on the average turn over three of the memorized six, so that during the next run PS would see only three of them. Having observed the checking of those three, he would know how to call them so as to make an almost sure hit on each. He could expect, therefore, almost certain hits on three out of the twenty envelopes. Of the remaining seventeen, he would expect to score 8.5 hits, so the expected number of hits would be 11.5/20 or .575. The actual score was .565.

Let's see how these hits break down with reference to colors. PS would expect on each run to make 1.5 hits on green calls for the three memorized envelopes. His expected score on green hits would therefore be 6.75/12 or .562. The actual score was .548. The variation is certainly reasonable in view of the slight uncertainty on the memorized envelopes.

It would be expected that the percentage of white hits would be higher because there were fewer white calls. PS would average 1.5 almost certain hits on white during each run. The number of white calls per run is eight. Therefore the expected score on white calls is 4.75/8 or .593. The actual score was .597.

It is folly, of course, to be more precise in trying to reconstruct calling strategies that would generate the published data. The situation is far from what statisticians would call well defined! (Perhaps someday a computer expert will model various strategies, in light of plausible assumptions, that will shed more light on what may have gone on.) Nevertheless, I think it reasonable to conclude that PS could have taken advantage of the imperfection principle, combined with JGP's poor method of randomizing, to obtain the scores he made on green and white calls. Did he actually do this? I have no way to know. It is possible, as I shall keep repeating, that the published data arose entirely from PS's clairvoyance. What I do maintain is that the conjectures here point up three glaring weaknesses of experimental design:

1. Allowing PS to see envelopes before, during, and after his calls, and throughout the checking process.

2. A flawed method of randomizing the selection of cards to be turned after each run.

3. A failure to label cards and envelopes so data could be recorded and analyzed for calling anomalies.

By the end of this experiment both MR and JGP strongly suspected that the imperfection principle—they refer to it as sensory cueing, which they believed to be completely unconscious on PS's part—was playing a role in focusing effects. As we shall see in the next chapter, this suspicion was the main reason they began putting envelopes inside covers. JGP also soon realized the importance of labeling both cards and envelopes. If this had been done in the experiment just discussed, and PS had followed a strategy similar to those I conjectured, there would have been strong and peculiar focusing.

It is amusing to note that at the beginning of their paper, where the authors summarized the test by MR and his wife that we considered in Chapter 1, they mention that in the second half of this test all the envelopes were sealed. It sounds impressive. They do not tell their readers that on those sealed envelopes PS made all his calls at home, totally unsupervised!

Chapter 6

Prague, 1963

DATE: February 1963
PLACE: MR's apartment in Prague
PAPER: "A Repeated-Calling ESP Test with Sealed Cards."
Milan Ryzl and J. G. Pratt, in the *Journal of Parapsychology,* 27 (September 1963), pp. 161–174.

This experiment, which immediately followed the previous one, marked two turning points in the testing of PS. First, there was an increase in the tightness of certain controls, perhaps as the result of criticisms of earlier testing. Second, in analyzing the data, MR and JGP became much more aware of what JGP called "focusing" and MR preferred to call "impregnation." The effect had been noticed before in a vague way, but (as we have pointed out) a failure to label both cards and covers had made it difficult to pin down. In this experiment the amount of focusing proved to be extraordinary. It was post hoc in the sense that the test was not designed to reveal it, and so surprising that almost all subsequent testing of PS was designed to better comprehend the strange nature of the phenomenon.

The targets for this experiment were twenty white/green cards. It was not necessary to label them because throughout the experiment they remained sealed in what the paper's summary calls "black envelopes." They were made in the usual way, by folding strips of cardboard, presumably black, using "gummed tape" to fasten the two sides. The fourth side was left unsealed.

The randomizing procedure was as follows. First MR took ten cards into a room where he was alone, and closed the door. The cards were randomized both as to order and which side was up, then placed in a row. The remaining ten cards were put in another row in a negative order—that is, each card at position n in the second row was turned so its top color was opposite that of the top color of the nth card in the first row. There was no real need to make one row the negative of the other, because this played no role in the experiment. Perhaps the experimenters were expecting some sort of correlation between the two sets of targets. All twenty cards were inserted in envelopes and the open ends sealed, presumably with gummed tape. They remained sealed throughout the test.

MR now left the room. JGP entered and closed the door. On the table were two rows of envelopes, one with top colors opposite to the top colors of corresponding envelopes in the other row. JGP then randomly exchanged pairs of correlated envelopes, using a die with ten faces bearing the digits 1 through 10.* For example, if the die showed 3, he would exchange the third envelopes in each row, taking care not to turn either of them over. The die was tossed ten times. The designated interchanges were made regardless of whether the number shown had appeared on an earlier throw. The only purpose of this rigmarole, apparently, was to make sure MR had no knowledge of what cards went in what envelopes. Since cards and envelopes were all identical, the ritual seems pointless.

JGP now labeled the envelopes in one row, from left to right, 1a, 2a, 3a, . . . , 10a. The envelopes in the other row were labeled 1x, 2x, 3x, . . . , 10x. The backs of the envelopes in the a series were labeled 1b, 2b, 3b, . . . , 10b, and the backs of the x series were labeled 1y, 2y, 3y, . . . , 10y. Thus envelope 7a would have 7b on its verso, envelope 7x would have 7y on its other side, and so on. The color uppermost on side 7a would be opposite to the top color of 7x, and of course the undersides of the two cards would also be opposite.

JGP then shuffled the envelopes, randomized them as to which side was up, and inserted them into opaque cardboard "covers" of the type previously called "envelopes," perhaps even the same ones. These covers were not labeled, apparently because the experimenters wanted the covers to be as identical as possible—a wholly unnecessary precaution in view of the ease with which covers can be memorized by the imperfection principle. This also was a major defect of the controls. If the covers had been labeled inside their flaps they would have provided valuable information about PS's guessing strategy.

---

*Here again, as in Chapter 4, we are told that a ten-sided die was used. Because no regular solid has ten faces, I assume JGP used an icosahedral die with each number from 1 through 10 appearing on a pair of faces.

The preparation of the covers clearly made it impossible for either experimenter to know the orientations of any of the cards inside their envelopes. Moreover, since the envelopes remained sealed throughout the test, there was also no way PS could know the orientation of any card.

The experiment now proceeded in the same manner as the previous one. MR held the covers one at a time in front of PS for his call of white or green, and then placed the covers on a chair in two piles, one for white calls, one for green. JGP, seated at a table on PS's right, kept a record of the calls. MR then lifted the flap of each cover to allow JGP to see the label on the envelope. We are told that this was done "silently," and in such a way that at no time was PS allowed to see either the exposed envelope or the records. However, PS did see the placing of the covers on the chair, and the manner in which they were stacked before and after the checking process. It is worth mentioning that the care taken to make the checks silently, and without letting PS see the exposed envelope labels, suggests that the experimenters realized they had been careless in this respect in the previous experiment.

After each run of twenty calls, JGP took the covers to the next room and randomized them in the way he had done before, except now the sealed envelopes took the role previously played by the cards. As JGP writes in his monograph on PS: "The *envelopes* were really taken by PS as the ESP targets in this experiment (as well as in others using the same method of doubling-concealing cards and leaving them in the same envelopes throughout a series)." Nothing is said about JGP using his ten-faced die for the process of reversing half the envelopes in their covers, although it would have been wiser to use it here than for the meaningless earlier ritual.

In *Hypnosis and ESP,* MR writes that the randomizing "was done in the usual way, by turning over half of the envelopes in their covers." I mentioned in a previous chapter that MR's recollection was that JGP always turned the contents of the top half of the stack of covers. If he followed his usual practice he would cut the pack "several" times before turning the envelopes. Cutting twice would obviously be absurd, because it would tend to leave the stack unaltered. So it is reasonable to assume that he cut either once or three times. After turning envelopes in the top half of the covers, he would shuffle the covers, turning some of the covers over, and then bring the entire stack back to MR for the next run.

The experiment was concluded after 250 runs, or 5,000 trials, conducted over a period of five days. Because the experimenters had no information on which to pick a "favorable point for ending the test, the optional stopping question, therefore, does not arise." I quote this to show that the experimenters were aware of how optional stopping could bias results. Although optional stopping may have played a role in some earlier tests with PS, as well as in some later ones, I have not and will not consider it for any tests discussed in this book. At any rate, it was not a factor in the present test.

Because PS had no way to learn the top colors of the cards, one would expect that his scoring on the colors would be at chance level. This is very close to the actual results. Of the 5,000 calls, 2,636 were hits—a low success rate of 2,636/5,000 or 52+ percent. However, as the authors point out, green was uppermost more often (2,531 times) than white, which would add slightly to PS's success score because of his strong preference for green calls over white. In the previous test, 60 percent of his calls were green. In this test he called green 2,791 times, or 55.8+ percent of the calls.

One envelope proved to be exceptional, and that was the very first one prepared, 1ab. On this envelope PS made 194 hits out of 250 calls, a success rate of .77+. This was much higher than his next highest score, which was made on envelope 2ab, the second one prepared. On 2ab his score was 165 hits, or .66. These high scores were balanced, however, by scores of .44+ (110 hits) and lower on five cards. Eliminate 1ab from the data, and the overall score drops to 2,442/4,806 = .508+, with the .008 easily accounted for by the excess of green in both calls and uppermost colors. If we eliminate both 1ab and 2ab, the overall score drops to 2,277/4,641 or .49+, which is slightly *below* chance. That the two highest scores would be on the first two envelopes prepared by JGP is, from any point of view, an amazing coincidence. There is no conceivable reason why PS would focus his psi powers on those two envelopes. I will return later to this anomaly.

Although PS's score on the colors was almost at chance level, analysis of the data showed astonishing focusing effects on the envelopes. "Each side of the card behaved as an individual unit," MR writes in *Hypnosis and ESP,* "which seemed to be entirely independent from the other side. . . . Also, there seemed to be no dependence of the phenomenon on the color of the target. Highly overchance results, chance results, and strongly below chance results occurred in white sides as well as in green sides. . . . Extremely positive and extremely negative scores mutually canceled out, and made the total result close to chance."

Here is how JGP, in his monograph on PS, summarized the focusing effects:

> The primary importance of the results obtained in this experiment was the discovery (on a post hoc basis in this series, but confirmed repeatedly in later tests) of what we named the focusing effect: the subject did not show a uniform consistency of response in relation to all twenty of the hidden envelopes containing the sealed cards. Rather, he showed very

striking preferences for calling white or green in relation to particular envelopes while giving only random responses to others. In some instances he showed a strong calling preference for only one side of an envelope while responding with a chance or fifty-fifty distribution of calls to the other side. In other instances the subject's calls were within the chance limits for both sides, while for still other targets he showed the same strong calling preference for both sides, as when he showed a tendency to say green regardless of the side of the envelope presented upward.

The strong focusing effects were confined to six envelopes. The other fourteen were close to chance distributions of calls, and can be ignored. The strongest focusing was on envelopes 1*ab* and 2*ab:*

1*ab*. On side *a,* PS made 143 calls, of which 131 were green (all hits) and only 12 were misses. Thus instead of an equal number of hits and misses on the two sides the hits were almost eleven times the misses. On side *b* the hits and misses were not far from equal, but the focusing on side *a* raised the total hit score to 194, where only 125 would be expected.

2*ab*. Here the focusing was on side *b*. Of 116 calls on this side, 90 were hits on green, 26 were misses. This together with a majority of white hits on side *a* raised the total hit score to 165.

If PS adopted a strategy that would produce strong focusing on envelope sides he seemingly concentrated his attention on six covers. We will probably never know if he followed such a strategy, because the covers were not labeled and so no information was kept about how he distributed his calls on the covers. We can only speculate. I will outline two conjectures.

In the published paper on this test we are told absolutely nothing about how JGP randomized covers after each run, except that his procedure was "closely similar to the one described in the last issue of the journal." (The authors here refer to their paper about the experiment discussed in the previous chapter.) The next sentence reads: "To repeat the full details here would therefore be superfluous. Suffice it to say that JGP randomized the envelopes in the covers before each run. . . ."

The last sentence is curiously ambiguous. The envelopes are in covers, and JGP randomized them. The sentence does not explicitly say that after each run he took half the envelopes out of their covers and turned them over. This is such a crucial aspect of the procedure that one would have expected the authors to have emphasized it. Is it possible that JGP's "closely similar" procedure was simply to shuffle the covers, randomly turn half of them over, and shuffle again, thus leaving the envelopes in their *same* orientations inside the covers?

It is easy to see why JGP might have omitted removing and turning envelopes. Since the cards were sealed inside the envelopes, and their orientations unknown to anybody, reversing envelopes inside unlabeled and identical covers may have seemed to JGP a useless waste of time. If JGP did not reverse ten envelopes after each run, it would make PS's guessing strategy childishly simple. He could select six covers, having memorized their faces and backs, concentrate lots of green calls on certain sides, and lots of white calls on certain other sides. On each cover he would arbitrarily assign green to one side of its envelope, white to the other, then focus his calls any way he liked.

I cannot take this too seriously because I cannot imagine the experimenters being so careless, and also because both of them, in monographs written much later, say that the envelopes *were* turned. However, we have only their memories on which to depend for his. I consider it possible, though highly unlikely, that JGP skipped the turning of envelopes and forgot that he did so when he wrote his monograph ten years later.

My second and more plausible conjecture is best explained by considering the cover holding envelope 1*ab*. As in the previous experiment, we can assume (with no loss of generality), that the green-called pile of covers always ended up on top of the stack that JGP carried to the next room. (If the white-called covers were on top, PS simply reverses the colors in his strategy.) JGP's cutting technique would bring the green stack to the bottom where covers near the middle would almost surely not have their envelopes reversed. It is not even necessary to assume that when JGP carried away the covers, the pile on top was always the same "color." There may have been no uniformity in the way the piles were finally stacked. Since PS could see how the piles were assembled before JGP carried them off, he would always know how to adjust his calls for the next run.

Assuming the green pile is on the bottom when JGP reversed envelopes in the top ten, here is how PS's calling strategy works. PS calls this cover green during the first run, doing his best to make the call as near as possible to the center of his ten or so green calls for that run. He can't always do this, but most of the time he can. He makes three, four, or five green calls, waits until the cover holding 1*ab* shows up (of course PS does not know it contains 1*ab*; we are just assuming that this is the envelope in the cover that JGP has decided to track, possibly because its blemishes are easy to see). After calling this cover green, he makes three, four, or five more green calls. Call the side of the cover that faced him the *M* side, and call the other side *P*. Because that cover goes to the center of the bottom stack, it is extremely unlikely its envelope will be reversed when JGP randomizes.

On the next run, the cover PS is following may come back with either its *M* or its *P* side toward him, owing to JGP's random turning of *covers*. If he sees side *M* he calls it green again. If he sees side *P*, he calls it white, once more doing his best to put the call near the center of about ten calls. The probability is now high that the envelope inside this cover *will* be reversed. Therefore, when PS spots the cover on the next run, he calls it green if *P* is up, and white if *M* is up.

If JGP's cuts were always equivalent to one cut exactly in the center of the stack, PS could end the test with identical color calls on side *M*, and identical opposite-color calls on side *P*. This would give him a perfect focusing pattern, with a fifty-fifty chance of a perfect score of hits on the card's colors. Of course JGP's cuts could not be perfect every time. Nevertheless, it is clear that if PS followed a strategy similar to the one outlined, he could generate strong focusing effects on envelope 1*ab*. More-over, as we shall see, there is a way he could have adjusted his calls to take care of imperfect cutting as well as mistakes on his part.

If PS could do this for one cover, he could do it for more than one. More than two would be hard to keep in mind, but he could easily track two covers for, say, a third of the experiment, then switch to two other covers for the next third, and two others for the final third. This would produce focusing effects on all of the fantastic six. Or he could concentrate on two covers for the first half of the test, then two more for the next quarter, and two others for the last quarter. There is no point in speculating further on this conjecture because the published data is complicated, and the relevant probabilities are ill defined.

We now consider the possibility that during the silent checking after each run by JGP and MR, PS could observe the movements of JGP's pencil or pen. JGP sat at a table to the right of PS's chair while he wrote down both calls and envelope labels. It seems obvious that PS could see the movements of JGP's writing instrument. "Pencil reading" is a familiar art to magicians and fake psychics, though only in recent decades have parapsychologists become aware of it. If Rhine had known about it he would never have written the most embarrassing paper of his career—the youthful report in which he praised the mind-reading prowess of a horse named Lady Wonder. (See my *Fads and Fallacies* for the amusing details.)

If PS engaged in pencil reading during the checking, it would allow him to correct calling errors arising from variations in JGP's cut (the product of three cuts) or his own mistakes. There is no way to know whether PS took advantage of pencil reading, but perhaps it is worth noting that the numeral 1 is the easiest of all numerals to recognize from the movement of a pencil, and 2 is almost as easy. Of course *a, b, x, y, W,* and *G* are also easy to distinguish. It is possible, therefore, that if PS planned on pencil reading, he would have selected six envelopes with easy-to-read numerals (the numerals of the other four were 2, 3, 9, and 10) as the envelopes whose covers he would track. As for the colors on the concealed cards, half would tend to be hits and half tend to be misses. The overall score would be near chance, as it actually was.

I have already called attention to the anomaly that the two highest-scoring envelopes were 1*ab* and 2*ab*, and will return to this in a moment. First let me call attention.to another anomaly. Each target was called 250 times, so by chance there would be an expected 125 hits on each. The actual number of hits, in ascending order, were: 94, 103, 105, 109, 110, 115, 118, 122, 125, 126, 126, 128, 134, 141, 150, 150, 160, 161, 165, 194.

Note that eight of these scores are exact multiples of 5. Since every fifth integer is a multiple of 5, one would expect about four of the twenty scores to end in 0 or 5, but we have twice that number. How probable is this? It is equivalent to the following question. Five cards, four black and one red, are repeatedly shuffled. You randomly draw a card twenty times, each time replacing it. What is the probability that in eight or more of the draws you will select the red card? A friend calculated this as .03+, or roughly once in 31 times. This is a lower probability than for the anomaly cited in Chapter 2, but again, not low enough to prove anything. It is only low enough to arouse some suspicion about the accuracy of the published data.

Now for the coincidence of the two covers on which PS made his highest scores. Although the scores are within the range of chance, given our conjectures about calling strategies, they impressed the experimenters as so amazing that they actually opened those two envelopes first to see if both had focused on hits. I assume those were the two envelopes opened, although the authors never explicitly say so. They tell us they were impressed by the first two "pairs" of envelopes in their chart—presumably they meant 1*ab* and 1*xy*, 2*ab* and 2*xy*, pairs that were correlated by having their green side up in one envelope and white side up in the other. They then say they opened "one envelope of each pair." Because 1*ab* and 2*ab* had the higher focusing, I assume those were the two they opened, although it is puzzling why they did not specify the two.

It turned out that both envelopes focused on color hits. The probability of this clearly is 1/4, so the result may be mere chance, but let me toss out another speculation. We are told that extraordinary precautions were taken to guard the targets during the periods between the days on which the test was carried out. It is conceivable, however, that after the experiment was over, such careful guarding would seem unnecessary. After all, every call had been made and recorded, and the envelopes were still sealed. We are informed that JGP, outside of MR's presence, checked the colors inside ten envelopes by unsealing them and sealing them again because he wanted to use those envelopes on another test and needed to know the orientations of their cards. If he could do that, so could PS. In the relaxed atmosphere following the testing, I can imagine PS being left alone for a few minutes with the targets. He would know that his strongest focusing was on the covers that held 1*ab* and 2*ab*. He could locate those covers, unseal their envelopes, adjust one or both cards (if necessary) to fit his calls, and seal them again. This would ensure his success on the colors of both cards, which, as we have seen, lifted his overall score to the modest level he actually achieved.

It is worth mentioning that if either envelope had shown high focusing on color *misses,* the authors surely would have cited this as evidence of negative ESP on the two cards, as well as a mild negative ESP for the experiment as a whole. As we shall see in Chapter 13, when John Beloff made a test that resulted in a negative overall score JGP considered it not a failure but evidence of negative psi. And in Chapter 18 we will learn that PS, after a test was well under way, asked permission to score negatively. When he did so, JGP hailed it as a huge success.

Once more I add that these are merely hypotheses for which I have no evidence. PS's high scores on the two envelopes and his strong focusing on others could have resulted from psi powers, though why they would have their highest concentration on the two envelopes that were first prepared remains mystifying. As always, my main purpose is to bring out flaws in an experiment's design. In this case the flaws are:

1. A failure to label covers. Here, from his monograph on PS, is JGP's own admission of this flaw:

> Specifically, we did not record the responses in relation to the sides of the outer covers presented upward in each run. Because of this omission we might have overlooked sensory responses occurring on them intermingled with the ESP responses on the concealed targets. Fortunately, the fact that the envelopes were not shifted among the covers but were only randomized as regards their positioning inside them (after which the covers were randomized as to order and sides upward) makes it possible to draw some inferences from the data regarding sensory effects related to the exposed containers . . . .

2. A crude method of randomizing the orientations of envelopes between runs. The test would have been enormously more secure if JGP had removed all twenty envelopes from their covers, shuffled them, randomized their orientations, then reinserted them in covers. This of course would have been time-consuming, and JGP had only a limited time to remain in Prague. As it was, the test extended over a five-day period.

3. Allowing PS to see the covers while he called them. PS had earlier performed well behind a screen. Why was the screen abandoned? A large,

fixed screen, behind which PS would make calls, and behind which experimenters would silently make their records, would have added greatly to the value of the experiment.

4. Allowing PS to observe the checking.

As we shall see as our saga continues, the history of work with PS is peculiar in this sense: Instead of steadily tightening all controls, each succeeding experiment that closed certain loopholes either left others open or introduced new ones. When all controls were tight, allowing for no possible visual or tactile cues, PS's success on colors fell to chance, and even focusing on containers disappeared.

Chapter 7

Prague, 1963

DATE: February 1963
PLACE: MR's apartment in Prague
PAPER: "The Focusing of ESP Upon Particular Targets." Milan
Ryzl and J. G. Pratt, in the *Journal of Parapsychology,*
27 (December 1963), pp. 227-241.

Before JGP left Prague to return to the United States, he and MR conducted two more experiments with PS. After JGP left, MR continued alone for four more tests. As the title of their paper implies, all six were designed to study the focusing effect that had caught them with such surprise in the previous experiment. "The present investigation," they write, "represents the first step in experimentation specifically aimed at further elucidating this phenomena." It is, they say, "only exploratory and preliminary" to investigations they hope will follow.

The authors are rightly puzzled by focusing. Is PS leaving some sort of psychic trace on envelopes that causes him to repeat his calls, regardless of whether they are hits or misses? The results "seem to us to raise anew the question whether the so-called token object, long associated with mediumistic practices, may play more than a purely motivational or suggestive role." The reference here is to mediums who ask for a possession of the deceased—a bracelet, watch, handkerchief, and so on—to assist them in making contact with the departed. Or perhaps, as parapsychologist W. G. Roll had suggested, there are "psi properties" that cling to objects. The authors express their belief that focusing may be a basic aspect of psi performance, overlooked in the past because of insufficient labeling of targets and the absence of recording details.

The first two tests, conducted by both authors, are called Series A and Series B. Only four targets were used. Two of them were envelopes 1*ab* and 2*ab*, containing the same bicolored cards they contained in the previous experiment. The two envelopes were selected because they were the ones on which PS had made his highest hit scores in the previous test. The other two targets were envelopes 5*ab* and 6*ab*. They were chosen because in the previous test PS had made chance scores on both.

On 5*ab* the score had been 125 hits, or exactly half the 250 calls. On one side of this envelope PS had scored more than twice as many hits as misses, but this was canceled by more than twice as many misses as hits on the other side

Envelope 6*ab* was selected because it had shown chance results on both sides: 55 hits against 56 misses on side *a*, and 71 hits against 68 misses on side *b*, for an overall score of 126 hits out of 250 calls.

It is easy to see the amusing plan the experimenters had in mind. If PS had somehow impregnated envelopes 1*ab* and 2*ab* with some sort of psychic property, then maybe the "footprint" would persist over a period of several days and he would produce similar high scores on the same two envelopes. If no footprints had been planted on envelope 6*ab*, perhaps he would again score chance on both sides of the card in that envelope. As for 5*ab*, PS had seemingly impregnated one side with a hit footprint, the other with a miss footprint. Would this, too, persist in the new test?

As before, the four cards remained throughout both tests in their original envelopes, which were presumably sealed, although the authors do not say so. The four envelopes were inserted in four covers as in the previous test. The covers were not labeled—a serious defect of the previous test that went uncorrected. Fifty runs were made through the four covers, or 200 trials in all.

Instead of going to another room to randomize between runs, for reasons difficult to fathom JGP dropped this safeguard altogether. He randomized with PS in the room. However, to conceal the randomizing, it was done behind what the authors call an "opaque screen." That is the screen's total description. Had it been a large stable screen of some sort, surely it would have been described as such. I can only conclude that it was similar to the "opaque screen" used by MR in earlier testing—namely, a piece of cardboard that PS held vertically on his lap. If it was indeed a more adequate screen, it is a grave flaw of this paper that it was not described.*

---

*I asked MR in a letter about the size and nature of this screen. He said his best memory was that, while JGP did the randomizing, he (MR) was engaged in casual small talk with PS, and that JGP may even have done the randomizing in another room. He had no memory of a screen.

No details are given about how JGP randomized beyond a statement that the "basic experimental procedure followed in each of the six series described in this paper was the same as that used in the preceding report." I take this to mean that after each run JGP inverted two envelopes in their covers, then shuffled the covers, randomly turning some of them over in the process. Whether he began with a cut is not known. More than likely he would have considered cutting just four covers unnecessary. How he selected the two envelopes to be reversed in their covers also is not known. It would have been easy to use a randomizer or a table of random numbers for this, but presumably JGP considered that too much of a burden. If the covers had been labeled and adequate records kept we would of course know exactly how he randomized.

After JGP randomized the covers behind the "screen," he handed them to MR, who then held them one at a time in front of PS for his call. (Although the screen was used to hide the randomizing, it was not deemed useful in hiding the covers from PS's gaze.) How were the calls recorded, and how were they checked against the labels? About this we are told absolutely nothing. Was the recording silent as before? If so, it would have been important to say so. That we are not told it was silent strongly suggests it was not. Presumably the experimenters went back to their earlier practice. One recorded the calls, then at the end of a run one would lift flaps and call out the labels. The recording of calls and labels obviously was done in PS's presence. The envelopes, we must assume, remained sealed throughout the test. Whether the envelopes were opened after the test is another lacuna in the paper. If a record had been made in advance of which color faced which side of each envelope, it would not be necessary to open the envelopes. Whether such a record was made before or after the test is not answered in the paper.

To the dismay of the experimenters, there were no signs of focusing, and the number of hits on all four cards were at chance levels. Of the 200 calls, there were 97 hits, a nonsignificant below-average score of .48+. Each of the four covers was called fifty times, producing hits of 30, 28, 21, and 18.

When an experiment with a gifted subject fails, parapsychologists almost always find something consistent with their belief in psi to blame for the failure. In this case, the onus fell on two visitors, Mr. and Mrs. Russell Ogg. They had come to Prague (the authors do not say from where) to interview MR and PS, and to photograph the test. Mrs. Ogg, we are told, took flash pictures throughout the first half of the session. "It appears that the presence of two strangers and the activities of being interviewed and photographed were the factors that caused the decline in success."

If our conjectures are right about ways in which PS could track targets, then of course there is an equally plausible explanation. With outside observers not only watching but taking pictures, the experimenters would take strong precautions to make sure that PS could observe nothing about the randomizing process, and PS himself would be careful to give no indication he was trying to observe. At any rate, because this first part of the experiment was a failure, we need spend no more time on it.

Series B began about fifteen minutes after the end of Series A. The visitors had gone, leaving only MR, JGP, and PS in the room. It was another series of fifty runs (200 calls) on the same four covers and their sealed envelopes. A chart in the paper shows that the cards in the four envelopes had the same orientations in their covers they previously had, so we can assume that the envelopes had remained sealed during the fifteen minutes that elapsed between Series A and Series B. We are told that the procedures were as before. JGP randomized behind the "screen," then handed the covers to MR, who held them one at a time in front of PS for his call.

Once again the overall record of hits was at chance level. Moreover, it was *exactly* at chance level, a fact that arouses some suspicion about the accuracy of the data. Out of 200 calls, PS made exactly 100 hits and 100 misses, for a success rate of precisely 50 percent. On the two envelopes that scored at chance in the experiment described in the previous chapter, the hit scores were again at chance! Incredibly, they were *exactly* at chance! Out of 52 calls, each envelope had 26 hits.

Let me pause a moment to make clear what strange anomalies we have here. Most people naively suppose that if you flip a penny 52 times, an outcome of 26 heads and 26 tails is more probable than a deviation from an even split, but this is not the case. If you flip a penny four times, the probability of an even split of heads and tails is 3/8. The probability of a 3 to 1 split (three heads and one tail or three tails and one head) is 1/2. In a family of four children, the probability that sexes will split three to one is considerably higher than the probability of two boys and two girls. The probability of a 26/26 split in 52 tosses of a coin is about .11. The probability of a 100/100 split in 200 tosses is about .06. If nothing is at work here except PS's psi powers, the three splits—100/100, 26/26, and 26/26—are not easy to account for.

Although the overall hit score was exactly at chance, the test sprang a big focusing surprise. The card in envelope 1*ab*, the highest scoring hit card of the earlier test, scored almost as high this time, with 36 hits, a success rate of 36/50 = .72. However, this was offset by the fact that the number of hits on 2*ab*, the second highest hit envelope in the earlier test, dropped to a mere 12. In other words, the extremely high success score on 1*ab* was balanced by a psi missing score of 38/50 = .76.

It is not hard to guess how the experimenters would explain this curious shift of a high psi-hitting target to a high psi-missing one, and still retain their belief in psychic impregnation. I quote:

> This finding may suggest that the focusing effect for particular targets is a psychological phenomenon which may be described as an unstable condition of equilibrium. After the period of chance scoring during Series A, card 2a/2b came back into focus as an ESP target, but this happened in a reverse, or psi-missing way. This finding may also suggest the presence, in the target, of some peculiar characteristic quality relevant from the point of view of the subject's ESP performance which possibly, during the testing procedure, may be gained, changed, lost, or sometimes even transformed to the opposite.

In other words, somehow the psychic property PS had planted on one side of envelope 2ab had switched to the opposite side. I cannot deny that this is a possible explanation of the change of 2ab from a high-hit envelope to a low-hit envelope, but surely, by applying Occam's razor, there is a simpler explanation. My hypothesis is that PS made no attempt to track the sides of envelopes 5ab and 6ab. On 5ab his split of calls when the white side of the card was uppermost was exactly 13 hits/13 misses (another, albeit smaller, anomaly), and 11 hits/13 misses when green was the top color. On 6ab the split was 12/8 on the white side, and 16/14 on the green side. These scores are all within chance limits.

The question now before us is: How could PS have tracked the sides of envelopes 1ab and 2ab so as to produce high focusing? Of course we will never know exactly what strategy he followed because the covers were not labeled and recorded.

Since only four covers are involved, let's assume that JGP abandoned his procedure of always turning envelopes in the top half of a stack, and simply picked two covers at random. Because we are told nothing about how he randomized behind the "screen," and nothing about the nature of the "screen," let us speculate on a possible scenario.

If the screen was no more than a piece of cardboard that PS held in his lap, as in previous tests, we have no problem. PS could simply have observed below the screen's edge, or by watching JGP's arm movements, which covers he chose each time for envelope inversions. The simplest way for JGP to randomize would be to take the covers, as they had been stacked after the last run, and place them in a row on a table. It is possible he did this not on a table but on his lap. He would then pick two arbitrary covers and reverse their envelopes, after which he would shuffle the four covers in some way, turning some of them over. Of course all PS need observe to track the top sides of envelopes in two covers is which covers had their envelopes inverted. Once he knows this, any later shuffling or turning of covers is irrelevant.

This is not the only strategy by which PS could track envelope sides. As we have noted, the paper says nothing about how the calls and the envelope labels were recorded. We are not told that this checking process was silent, so it is reasonable to assume that PS heard the checking, perhaps also witnessed it. This would not, of course, tell him which two envelopes had been inverted before the run, but it would provide a check on any error he had made by watching JGP's arm movements, or perhaps observing his hands directly by looking below the screen. If, for instance, PS mistakenly thought a certain envelope had been reversed when it hadn't, hearing or watching the recording process would reveal the mistake. More than that, it would tell PS exactly which sides of all four envelopes were uppermost in their covers.

Although PS had a simple way of focusing his calls on specific sides of envelopes, he would not know how the color cards were oriented in their envelopes. It is true that the experimenters did not alter the orientations of the cards from what they were in the experiment discussed in the previous chapter, but PS would not have known that. Indeed, the authors write that in this experiment they did not tell PS the purpose of the test, and that "he was not even told when changes in the target situation were introduced." All he was told was that the envelopes contained green and white cards and that he should try to guess the top colors. We are not told whether the same four covers were used that had contained the four envelopes in the earlier test. If they were, then of course PS could have long before memorized both sides of all four covers. If they were new covers, he would have to memorize both sides of two of them—certainly an easy task.

In focusing his calls on the two covers that contained 1*ab* and 2*ab* (it would be natural for PS to select those two envelopes because he knew they were the high-hit ones of the earlier test) there were four possibilities: he would hit on both covers (call them *x* and *y*), he would miss on both, or he would hit on *x* and miss on *y,* or he would hit on *y* and miss on *x*. Had he hit on both (probability 1/4), the outcome would have been hailed as a great victory for the impregnation theory. Had he missed on both (probability 1/4), it would have been hailed either as an example of strong negative psi or as confirmation of the ease with which footprints get reversed. As it was, he hit on one and missed on the other (probability 1/2), with the result that the high and low scores canceled, producing an overall chance score.

We turn now to Series 1, 2, 3, and 4. JGP had returned to the United

States, leaving MR as the sole experimenter. Eight covers were used in all four tests, each containing a bicolored card inside an envelope. They included the four covers with sealed envelopes and cards that had been used in Series A and B, plus four new covers with unsealed envelopes and cards. The unsealed envelopes were inserted open side down in their covers "to eliminate the possibility that the experimenter or the subject might get a glimpse of the card inside the envelope during the check-up." These new envelopes were labeled *AB* (*A* on one side, *B* on the other), *EF, MN,* and *XY* at their closed ends so the labels could be checked by lifting a flap of the cover. Each of the four tests consisted of 100 runs, or 800 calls in each test.

On colors, the overall hit scores for Series 1, 2, 3, and 4 were, respectively, .71, .71+, .59+, and .55+. These positive scores were, however, eclipsed by sensational focusing effects on certain sides of the envelopes—some hits, some misses. But before speculating on how these results could have been achieved by nonparanormal means, I offer some general comments on the quality of the paper in which they are reported.

As all philosophers of science know, and as parapsychologists are slowly comprehending, not only do extraordinary results require extraordinary evidence, but when they are reported they demand extraordinary attention to details about experimental conditions. In this paper we have extraordinary results presented with an extraordinary lack of details. Indeed, the four pages dealing with Series 1, 2, 3, and 4 are so vaguely written that I suspect the *Journal of Parapsychology* would never have accepted the paper had it not come from one of its editors. (JGP was then sharing the editorship with Louisa E. Rhine, JB's wife.)

First we should recall that JGP was not present when the four tests were made, so the pages describing them are based on data sent to him by MR. The two previous tests, Series A and B, in which JGP participated, were failures. There was therefore a strong incentive for MR to show that PS performed with greater success when he, MR, was in complete control. In brief, it was an ideal situation for generating a strong experimenter effect. Here are some questions that the paper should have answered, but did not.

An "experimental assistant" is mentioned but not named. Who was he or she, and what roles did he or she play? We learn no more than that the assistant, between Series 2 and 3, shifted two pairs of cards in two pairs of envelopes, and presumably was also the person who shifted the outer covers of two pairs of envelopes between Series 1 and 2. Did the assistant also participate in the checking process after each run? We are not told.

What sort of screen was used? We read: "[MR] randomized the targets in back of the screen before each run, either with his eyes closed or his gaze averted, following the usual procedure of turning over half of the envelopes in their covers, after which he further shuffled the pack by inverting some of the covers while changing their order. In other words, MR took care to insure that he would not know any of the targets when the subject was calling them."

Was the "screen," as in earlier tests by MR, a piece of cardboard that PS held vertically on his lap? If not, how large was it and where was PS while MR randomized? Did he sit opposite MR, holding the cardboard in front of his face? Obviously he was somewhere in the room or the screen would not have been necessary.

After each run, how were the records made? Was the procedure silent as before, or did MR call out the envelope labels while the assistant wrote them down? Was the recording made behind the "screen" or did PS observe the checking? Did the assistant verify the checking?

We are told that the four tests were spread over a period of six weeks. This is a long time for just four tests, each involving only 100 runs through eight covers. Was each test done at one sitting, or were the tests broken into parts? If broken into parts, how carefully were the targets guarded? Did MR ever leave the experimental room, say to go to the bathroom, or to the kitchen to prepare coffee for PS, who liked to drink coffee while an experiment was in progress? If MR left the room, did he always take the targets with him?

In view of our hazy knowledge of the experimental conditions, we can make only vague guesses about ways in which PS could have tracked certain envelopes by techniques we have proposed for previous tests. If the covers had been labeled, and a record made of how PS called them, a vast amount of valuable information would have been available about guessing patterns. Nevertheless, the published data about his focusing on certain sides of envelopes lend support to certain hypotheses. Again, I remind the reader that my purpose is to show how nonparanormal methods *could* have been used. For all I know, PS may have in these tests displayed extraordinary clairvoyance. In what follows I shall also assume, as I have throughout this book, that the published data accurately reflect the lost raw data.

SERIES 1

The eight covers consisted of four from the previous experiment. They contained sealed envelopes 1*ab*, 2*ab*, 5*ab*, and 6*ab*. The first two were chosen because they were the two on which PS had made his highest scores in the test covered in the previous chapter. The other two were selected because they had chance scores in the earlier test. The four new covers contained envelopes *AB*, *EF*, *MN*, and *XY*. Their envelopes were not sealed. PS made one-hundred calls on each of the eight covers, so his expected number of hits per cover was 50.

As the paper says, "Among the four old cards, the two 'good' ones remained good and the 'bad' ones bad." On 1*ab*, PS's score was 88 percent. Of forty-four calls when the green side was up, he hit thirty-eight times. Of fifty-six calls when the white side was up, he hit fifty times. On 2*ab* his hit score was 69 percent, less than on 1*ab* but still impressive. His hit score on 5*ab* and 6*ab* remained at chance.

Of the four new cards, PS scored high on *EF* and *XY* and chance on *AB* and *MN*. On *EF*, out of 56 calls on the *E* side, he had 47 hits on green. Out of 44 calls on the *F* side, he had 42 hits on white. Total hit score: 89 percent. On *XY*, out of 57 calls on the *X* side, he had 54 hits with green, and out of 43 calls on the *Y* side he had 42 hits on white, for an overall score on *XY* of a whopping 96 percent—only four short of perfect! The odds against this happening by chance are, of course, astronomical.

In line with our earlier conjectures, PS could have been tracking four covers and ignoring the other four. He would know the orientations of the cards in envelopes 1*ab* and 2*ab* because they remained sealed and unaltered from the previous tests with those same envelopes. As before, PS needed only to recall the markings on their covers and follow MR's arm movements behind the screen (or peek below the screen if it was no more than a hand-held piece of cardboard) to learn whether the envelopes in those two covers were reversed or not. Also as before, he would be able to confirm or disconfirm what he observed when he listened to the checking after each run. (I am assuming it was not a silent checking or MR would have said so.)

How can we explain the extraordinary hit scores on *EF* and *XY*? If PS had no knowledge of the orientations of the cards, he would simply have focused his calls on the two covers, hoping that this would result in hits instead of misses. The chances of hitting on both covers would be $1/4$. My conjecture, and it is no more than that, is that under the informal, spread-out conditions of the testing, PS found an opportunity to look at the cards in unsealed envelopes *EF* and *XY*. It would have required only a few seconds to slide out the envelopes and look into their open ends. It goes without saying that PS would have had no difficulty in applying the imperfection principle to the covers, memorizing both their fronts and backs.

SERIES 2

We are informed that before this series began the outer covers of envelopes 1*ab* and 5*ab* were interchanged, and similar cover exchanges were made for envelopes *MN* and *XY*. No assistant is yet mentioned in the paper, so either MR made this·switch or an assistant had been participating all along, otherwise we would have to assume that MR did the checking alone and unobserved. This would, of course, have introduced the possibility of recording errors in the direction of hoped-for results.

We can summarize the results as follows. Envelope 1*ab,* now in another cover, continued high with 90 hits (49 on one side, 41 on the other). The score on 2*ab* also continued high, with 76 hits. This suggests that PS continued to include 1*ab* and 2*ab* among the envelopes he tracked. Of course he would become aware of the switch of envelopes during the first checking. In *Hypnosis and ESP* (page 84), MR naively concludes that the fact that the shifting of covers had no effect on scores proves that "the outer covers play no role in the 'focusing phenomena.' "

SERIES 3

Before this series began, we are told that an assistant made a more subtle switch—one that PS could not have learned about from the checking. The cards inside envelopes 1*ab* and 5*ab* (one "good" card, one "bad") were switched and the envelopes resealed. Cards inside 6*ab* and *XY* (one a moderately good old card, the other a good new card) were also switched. A look at the published chart shows that in both switches the "up" colors were exchanged. We are told that when the assistant made the switches he or she was careful to see that neither cards nor envelopes were turned over, but because the cards in each pair were oppositely oriented the switches automatically reversed the "up" colors. In other words, each of the four envelopes now contained cards whose colors were oriented opposite to the way they were before.

If PS now continued to track 1*ab,* not knowing its colors had been reversed, his high score would automatically drop to low, and that is exactly what happened. Out of 51 calls on side *a* he had 48 misses, and out of 49 calls on side *b* he had 38 misses. His overall *miss* score was 86 percent. PS, in our scenario, also continued to track 2*ab,* on which he continued high with a hit score of .68.

On 5*ab,* which in our scenario PS had not tracked before, he now scored 80 hits, with high focusing on both sides. This suggests that PS had added 5*ab* to the envelopes he was following. Not knowing its colors, he was either lucky (his chance of hitting being 50 percent), or he had somehow managed to learn the orientation of colors in 5ab.

PS's score on 6ab, not previously tracked in our tentative scenario, was now fantastically high: 93 hits. He also scored 80 hits on AB, 90 hits on EF, and below chance with 39 hits on MN. This suggests that PS continued to track EF, and had added 6ab and AB to his tracking list.

Our scenario is strengthened by the results on XY. XY now held an envelope in which colors had, without PS's knowledge, been reversed. One would expect, therefore, that if PS could track it, his previous high score of 88 hits would shift in the opposite direction. This is what happened. His score on XY dropped to a mere 14 hits, a miss score of .86.

Here is how MR sums all this up in *Hypnosis and ESP* (p. 85): "Both chance cards which were placed into outstanding 'hitting' envelopes, turned into strikingly missing cards. They had outstanding missing scores on both sides. It was evident that the scores were influenced by the envelopes, and that the subject continued to call the color which he was used to name for each particular side of the envelope—regardless of the fact that, for the card it contained by that time, his statement was wrong. . . . This was an important finding which indicated that the property carried by individual sides of envelopes did not consist in stimulating 'hitting calls,' but in stimulating calls 'green' or 'white' regardless of whether they were correct or wrong."

I leave it to the reader to decide on the simplest explanation: whether PS switched his clairvoyant focusing, or whether in his tracking of the two envelopes he was unaware that the top colors of the cards had changed.

SERIES 4

Before this series began, someone (we are not told whom) removed the cards from envelopes 6ab, AB, EF, and MN, turned them over, and reinserted them in their envelopes. Presumably 6ab was resealed, and the other three were pushed open end down into their original covers. No changes were made in envelopes 1ab, 2ab, 5ab, and XY. PS was not told about these reversals.

On the unaltered envelopes 1ab, 2ab, and 5ab, PS scored close to what he did before. Envelope 1ab continued low with 26 hits out of the 100 calls. Envelope 2ab remained moderately high (64 hits), and 5ab continued high (76 hits). Hits on XY rose abruptly from a previous low of 14 to a high of 73. This, you recall, was one of the envelopes whose card was turned over in Series 3, causing PS to drop from a former high of 66 to a low 14. My conjecture is that by now he had learned of the change of colors in XY, so he tracked it with a reversal of calls to change his very low score to a high one.

Turn now to the four envelopes on which, unbeknownst to PS, the colors had just been switched by turning over the cards. On AB his score dropped from the previous high of 80 hits to the chance level of 48. On EF his score fell from the previous high of 90 to the below-chance score of 29. On MN his score rose from the previous low of 39 to a high 73. And on $6ab$ his score dropped from a previous high of 93 to a chance 56.

To the experimenters, these changes proved the instability of focusing. From our perspective they simply reflect PS's continual tracking of certain envelopes. Not knowing when colors had been reversed, his scores went from high to low on one, and from low to high on another. The drop to chance on the other two suggests he had abandoned tracking them.

In his published report of the experiment, and in his monograph on PS, JGP stops after Series 4 and says nothing about more testing by MR. But MR, in *Hypnosis and ESP,* writes about a fifth series, part of the same experiment, in which PS made another run through the same covers. No alterations of cards or envelopes were made, and we are told that PS's scores remained "approximately the same" for all eight covers "with only one exception." Nothing is said about the exception. When I asked MR about it in a letter, he was unable to recall what it was. Why JGP failed to mention Series 5 is puzzling.

MR goes on in his monograph (pp. 86-88) to speak briefly of more tests along the lines of Series 1, 2, 3, 4, and 5. The results suggested that "PS could be using his ESP to recognize the identification marks on the envelopes and associate them in his recollection with specific responses." From our perspective this is precisely what PS was doing, though not by ESP. MR continues: "The theory is inconsistent with the general character of PS's ESP performance (he gave good results with respect to colors, but never with letters, numerals, and other symbols)."

To test the possiblity that PS was focusing ESP on envelope labels, MR secretly interchanged the labels on opposite sides of each envelope. This had no effect on PS's scores. From our view, this is easily explained by the fact that PS never saw the labels during his tracking. We are given no details about this test. MR concludes that the results "confirmed our opinion that the phenomenon under study did not depend on physical identification marks on envelopes."

MR next ran a test—again no details—in which two envelopes on which PS had scored high were opened and their cards removed. PS was not told that these envelopes were now empty. On the empty envelopes he continued to score high, as if the cards were still inside the envelopes in their same orientations. From our perspective, this is no surprise because PS at no time saw the cards. MR concludes that "the empty envelopes really carried some tendency to stimulate certain responses, which remained as a residue of the former tendency of the envelope-card combination."

MR now conducted two more experiments, which he calls Series A and Series B. Series A used four top-hit cards with four new cards, and Series B used four chance cards with four new ones. Runs of 100 calls with targets from A were alternated with similar runs for targets from B. In Series A, PS continued with high scores on the hit cards, and chance scores on the others. According to our conjectures, this indicated a tracking of four high cards. In Series B the former chance cards remained chance, and the new cards became high hits. From our perspective, PS tracked the covers of the four new cards.

There is no point in trying to guess PS's strategies in these tests because MR provides no information on which to base guesses. We don't know whether new covers were introduced, how the checking was done, whether a screen was used, whether an assistant was present, or when and where the tests were made. MR summarizes the results as follows: "Selected outstanding targets remained outstanding . . . and originally near-chance targets remained near chance." The surprising feature was that new cards mixed with outstanding ones gave chance scores, whereas new cards mixed with chance cards gave outstanding scores.

These results tend to confirm our hypotheses. Both JGP and MR, analyzing results from all the tests with eight covers, go to absurd lengths in trying to justify the shifting of focus from target to target on the basis of a mysterious instability of psi imprinting. They may be right. I contend, however, that the changes are more simply explained by assuming that PS tracked certain envelopes by a combination of cover memorizing, the watching of arm movements while MR reversed half the envelopes after each run, and checking the accuracy of his observations by listening to or watching (or both) the procedure by which calls and envelope labels were recorded. On some occasions PS may have had an opportunity to examine unguarded targets.

I should add that PS (as JGP reports in his monograph) always insisted thoughout these tests that he concentrated his psi effort solely on card colors and at no time paid attention to covers.

This brings up again how much more informative the data would be if covers had been labeled. Here is how JGP apologizes in his monograph for this obvious flaw:

> So strongly were the experimenters oriented toward the concealed targets that we assumed without question that nothing of interest could be occurring in the way of nonrandom responses to the exposed covers. Consequently no thought was given to recording the covers. Blom did, it is true, comment

during our main experiment [covered here in Chapter 11] that we might be losing data by not recording the covers, but we took no step to correct this oversight.

It now seems clear, on the basis of evidence presented earlier in this survey, that highly significant responses to the covers were being made all the while. But this bit of insight, which seems so simple and obvious in retrospect, was not easily achieved during the course of the decade. It came about gradually as a result of the fact that the relative strength of the ESP responses to the hidden targets gradually became weaker while the sensory responses to the covers remained strong. In consequence the investigators were forced to recognize that a shift in the response hierarchy had occurred.

Even so, the appreciation of what this change in the subject's responses meant was not achieved immediately in one easy step. The first research calling attention to it interpreted the focusing effects as being connected with the concealed envelopes rather than the outer covers. Only when, at long last, the practice of recording the covers became a regular part of the testing procedure were we able to break out of the earlier erroneous mental set.

Because covers were not labeled, we have no data for deciding between two hypotheses: (1) that PS displayed extraordinary clairvoyance— sometimes focusing on colors, sometimes on sides of envelopes without respect to hits or misses on colors—and (2) that PS used nonparanormal tracking strategies. The main thrust of this chapter is that powerful focusing effects on the tests just described cry out for a better account of controls than the joint paper by JGP and MR provides. For this reason alone I contend that the tests covered in this chapter should not be taken seriously.

Chapter 8

Prague, 1963

DATE: April 1963

PLACE: MR's apartment in Prague

PAPER: "An ESP Experiment in Prague." Milan Ryzl, J. T. Barendregt, P. R. Barkema, and Jan Kappers, in the *Journal of Parapsychology,* 29 (September 1965), pp. 176-184.

MR writes in *Hypnosis and ESP* that when he welcomed three Dutch parapsychologists to Prague he had two objectives in mind: to accustom PS to working with strangers, and to study further "to what degree the selection of outstanding targets [from past experiments] can increase the scores." In other words, he wanted to confirm his hypothesis that psychic imprinting was the basis of PS's extraordinary focusing.

The three visiting researchers, selected by the Amsterdam Foundation for Parapsychological Research, were J. T. Barendregt, P. R. Barkema, and Jan Kappers. They were the authors of the report, although Ryzl's name was added to the byline. Barendregt and Barkema are no longer living. I have had the pleasure of corresponding with Dr. Kappers and will discuss this correspondence in an addendum to this chapter.

Sixteen target cards were prepared, one side of each card white, the other side painted green. The sixteen envelopes were made in the usual way by folding a strip of cardboard, closing two sides with tape, and leaving the fourth side open. They were labeled at the folded ends. The cards went into these envelopes and the envelopes were pushed, open side down, into unlabeled cardboard covers that also were prepared in the standard way.

A drawing shows that each side of a cover was closed with two staples, one near the folded side, the other at the extreme end of the open side. Putting a staple close to the open end was a vast improvement. Eliminating large flaps made it impossible—certainly enormously more difficult—for PS to use a peek move. The tactile move could, however, still be made by the forefinger of a hand holding the top corner of a cover as shown in Figure 6 of Chapter 5. With no one sitting behind him, PS could more easily make the move with a thumb instead of a finger.

At MR's request, the covers were divided into two sets of eight each. One set, its envelopes labeled *AB* and *EF,* contained cards on which PS had scored high in earlier testing. The other set of eight covers, its envelopes coded by 1/2 and 11/12, contained cards not used before. MR's plan was to see if PS would score higher on the first set, but he did not disclose this plan to the Dutch visitors. If PS scored significantly higher on the "good" targets, it would support MR's "footprint" theory. Did this occur? "Our expectation was . . . confirmed," MR writes in *Hypnosis and ESP.* "Selected outstanding cards gave a significantly better result than new cards."

In his monograph on PS, JGP makes a more modest claim. "There was some difference in the predicted direction, but this was statistically significant at only the modest level of P =.05. This result is of doubtful validity since the color hits are not statistically independent of the strong ESP focusing effects shown on the envelopes as well as sensory responses made to some of the covers."

The experiment took place in MR's apartment over a period of two days. MR was present at irregular times, only to give encouragement to PS. He played no role in the testing.

Each day there were 128 runs on eight covers, or 1,024 calls, making 2,048 calls for the entire two-day experiment. While PS was calling one run of eight covers, Barkema took the other set of eight to an adjacent room, where Barendregt randomized them for the next run. Evidently the experimenters were not satisfied (as well they should not have been) by the lack of a formal randomizing procedure in earlier tests. Barendregt used a table of random numbers, selecting an entry point by tossing a die. He then followed the numbers in the table, skipping 0's and 9's, and duplicate digits, until he obtained a random number of four distinct digits from 1 through 8. The number 2368 is cited as an example. Barendregt would reverse the envelopes in the four covers at positions 2, 3, 6, and 8 in the stack. This was a marked improvement over the previous crude randomizing in which we are never told how the envelopes to be turned were selected.

PS's calls, as well as the labeling of each envelope, were recorded in his presence. After every twelve runs (96 calls), Kappers and Barkema went to the adjacent room, where Kappers read aloud PS's guesses, along with the matching envelope labels. Presumably this was done outside of PS's hearing, though we are not told this. Barendregt, who had the code cipher for the target cards, then recorded the color hits and misses. When Kappers returned to where PS was sitting, PS was told in general terms how well or how poorly he had done for the twelve runs.

On the first 512 trials the hits were 286—a score of 55+ percent. On the next 512 trials there were 303 hits, or a score of 59+ percent. On the third set of 512 calls there were 322 hits, a score of 62+ percent. And on the last 512 calls there were 305 hits, a score of 59+ percent. Altogether there were 1,216 hits out of 2,048 calls, a highly significant positive success rate of 59+ percent.

As in earlier tests, PS showed a preference for green calls. In this experiment the preference was extreme—more than twice as many green calls as white. There were 1,410 green calls, and only 638 white. Green calls scored more hits than white, but percentagewise the white scores were better. There were very strong focusing effects for both hits and misses.

Is there a nonparanormal strategy PS could have adopted to achieve these remarkable results? Before making a conjecture, let me call attention to a procedural change that seems hard to understand unless PS had requested it. On the previous test, when PS scored such astonishingly high percentages of hits on certain cards, he had not been allowed to touch any covers. In this experiment the Dutch group tightened controls by adopting a good randomizing procedure and by stapling the sides of covers near the open end to eliminate flaps. On the other hand, for some inexplicable reason, they loosened controls by allowing PS to handle the covers.

The procedure was this. Kappers and Barkema sat opposite PS at a large table. Barendregt remained throughout the experiment in the adjacent room where he would randomize one set of eight targets while the other eight were being called by PS. Barkema would pick up a randomized set from Barendregt, carry it to the table, and hand it to PS. We are not told whether PS kept the stack in his hand or on his lap, or put it on the table. He picked up the topmost target, presumably with both hands, made his call, and put the cover on the table. This formed a stack of covers in reverse order to what they had been before.

The calls were independently recorded by Kappers and Barkema. After the run they went through the stack (reversing it again) to record the labels at the top of each envelope. Barkema would then carry the stack back to Barendregt for randomizing, returning with a randomized set of eight for the next run. The process of reversing four envelopes at positions indicated by the four random digits would reverse a stack for the third time. There was never a shuffling of covers, or turning over of covers. They always remained in the same sequence with their same sides up.

In view of PS's fantastic successes without touching the covers, why would he now be allowed to handle them? MR writes in *Hypnosis and ESP* that this was done to speed up the calling and recording procedure, though it is hard to see how this would be faster than having an experimenter hold each cover up to PS's gaze while he made a call. Again, it seems as if experimenters, when they close one loophole for an attempted replication of an extraordinary result, unconsciously open another.

Focusing effects were so strong that the Dutch parapsychologists wondered if some physical property of the targets provided unconscious sensory cues. The most promising conjecture was that green and white surfaces have different heat absorptions. However, careful tests were later made that ruled out infrared radiation as a sensory influence. A well-known Dutch magician, Fred Kaps, was consulted. After the experiment was explained to him he said he could think of no way PS could have used trickery.

My conjecture assumes that PS had no knowledge of the top colors in any envelope at the start of the experiment. It also assumes no fudging of data by the researchers, no secret peek moves, and no opportunity for PS to be alone with the targets. Scenarios can take many forms, of which I will outline only one. Three techniques are involved.

1. Memorizing covers by the imperfection principle.

2. The asymmetric marking principle explained in Chapter 3.

3. A simple strategy by which PS could deduce, from information given to him as the test proceeded, the orientations of colors in certain envelopes.

The authors make clear in their paper that the covers were handled throughout in such a way that they were always presented to PS with the same side of each cover uppermost. Unlike previous randomizing procedures, after four envelopes were turned there were no reversals of covers. This surely made PS's task much easier. It would have been necessary for him only to memorize one side of any cover containing an envelope he decided to track.

Although PS could have applied asymmetric marking in any of the ways explained in Chapter 3, this may not have been necessary. Charles Akers, reviewing Pratt's monograph on PS in the *Journal of Parapsychology* (Autumn 1974, pp. 89-91) mentioned that "in unpublished research Dr. Pratt had found a physical difference in a set of envelopes which probably served as a basis for extrasensory 'evaluative judgments' by PS."

In reply to my inquiry, Akers said that the differences involved the manner in which tape had been applied to the sides of the envelopes, though he could not recall exactly what these differences were. However, he kindly let me have two sample covers, with their envelopes, that had come into his possession. Both had been used in later testing of PS, but were constructed in exactly the way described in the paper on the Dutch experiment. On both envelopes the difference between the left and the right sides of the closed edge—the edge that would be on top when the envelopes were inserted open ends down in the covers—was instantly obvious.

Figure 3 is a photograph of the two covers, and Figure 4 shows the two envelopes. Note how the plastic tape closing the sides of the envelopes has on one side of each envelope been cut on a slight bias. The bias causes a corner of the tape to project beyond the folded edge. Figure 5 is a closer look at a corner. The projecting point is as sharp as a needle. In both cases, no asymmetric marking by PS would have been needed. He could instantly have distinguished one end of the top edge from the other by running a finger or thumb along the edge.

I did some experimenting with cardboard envelopes and found it difficult to tape the sides all the way from top to bottom without providing a tactile way to distinguish one side of the taped edge from the other. This suggests that in some cases it would not have been necessary for PS to put a mark on the folded edge of an envelope in any of the ways explained in Chapter 3. It would only be necessary for him to feel a blemish already there. To JGP such differences in the tape were taken as something PS may have perceived clairvoyantly. The thought that he could insert a finger or thumb and feel a difference never occurred to JGP or any other experimenter. From our perspective, the differences are easy to perceive nonparanormally.

At this point you may wonder how asymmetric tactile cues could be of service to PS unless he somehow could learn how certain cards were oriented inside their envelopes. This brings us to the third technique cited above.

We are told that after every twelve runs (96 calls) Kappers and Barkema took the targets and their records to the adjoining room where Barendregt did the randomizing. There the three men would check the record of calls and envelope labels against Barendregt's record of how the cards had been randomly oriented. This was done by Kappers reading aloud the calls and the matching labels on the envelopes. The envelopes were never opened for an actual check of the colors. We are not told whether Barendregt responded out loud by saying whether each call was a hit or miss, but we will assume he did not. If he responded out loud, then of course PS, alone in the adjoining room, would hear the response and know at once when he had hit and when he had missed. Indeed, after the very first run he would know the top color in any envelope he had chosen to track.

I will assume that the experimenters were not so careless as to allow PS to overhear the checking procedure. If they were that careless, then we need go no further in accounting for PS's scores. Is there a way he could have obtained information about certain card orientations even if he did not overhear the checking?

Here we encounter a major flaw in the experimental design. After each checking we are told that "JK [Kappers] gave PS an account of the scoring." This was done only in a general way: "It was good," or "It was very good," or "There was a decline," and so on. Thus after each checking PS learned whether he had scored high in hits, very high in hits, low in hits, very low in hits, the same as before, better than before, worse than before, or similar general evaluations.

Let's see how PS could have used this feedback to learn early in the game how certain cards were oriented with respect to asymmetric marks on their envelopes. On this point it would be enormously helpful if we knew exactly how PS's calls were distributed on the 32 sides of the 16 envelopes. A chart provides the totals of hits and misses on each side at the end of each of the two sessions, but it contains no information on how calls were distributed throughout the runs of a day's session. In the absence of such information, it is impossible to know what strategies PS may have adopted.

Consider the first run through the eight envelopes that were labeled with capital letters. These were targets containing envelopes and cards on which PS had scored high in previous tests. We can assume that PS was thoroughly familiar with these envelopes. Either he had already placed asymmetric marks on them—if our conjectures are correct—or he knew of asymmetries in the taping at the closed ends.

Here is one scenario. PS arbitrarily selects a cover, puts an asymmetric mark on its envelope (or feels one already there), and calls green. At the end of the first twelve runs (96 calls), with the two sets of eight alternating, he will have held that same cover six times. If he calls green each time the envelope's mark is on the same side as before, and white each time the mark is on the other side (indicating the envelope has been turned), he will be certain of either six hits or six misses on that envelope's card. He need make the tactile move only when that cover is in his hands. Recall that the covers were never turned over, making it easy for PS to know when he held the cover that contained the envelope he was tracking. On all the other fifteen covers he need make no move, calling each cover any way he likes.

Now let's see what happens when the envelopes are checked for color hits after the twelve runs. If PS hits six times on the tracked envelope, his expected hits will be $6 + 45 = 51$ out of 96 calls—a success rate of $51/96 = .53+$. Accordingly, he will be told by Kappers that he did well. If he missed all six times, his psi-missing score will be just as high and he will be told he did not do well. In either case, PS will have learned the orientation of the card inside the envelope that is permanently inside the cover he was tracking. Remember, the cards never altered their orientations inside envelopes, and the envelopes, though randomly reversed, always stayed in the same covers. From now on, PS can, if he wishes, hit on every subsequent call on that cover if he decides to make the tactile move.

During the next run, so goes our scenario, PS could continue to score high on the same cover, but track a second cover by the same technique. If he made six hits on the second cover, his expected score would rise and he would be told it had improved. If he missed all six times, he would be told there had been a decline. In this way he would learn the orientation of another marked envelope inside another memorized cover. Or, to give a different strategy, he might simply focus his calls on a second envelope and make random calls on all the others, including the one whose card orientation he knew. He would then be told, after the next run, that his score continued to be good or that it had declined.

It is easy to see that by adopting such strategies (I am just guessing, of course; PS may have followed no strategy at all, making all his scores paranormally) the feedback from Kappers would soon provide PS with knowledge of how certain cards were turned with respect to their marked envelopes. If he learned the orientation of five or six cards in this way, he would be able to score fantastically high on color hits. But we must bear in mind that he would have to acquire this information slowly, and there would be times in which he might be too carefully watched to make a tactile move. Moreover, he may have intentionally held scores down to avoid suspicions that would arise if scores were too high. As I have said, a complete account of exactly how he called each side throughout the test would provide clues that would tend to support or refute our conjectures. Unfortunately, this data has not been preserved and we have only the totals to go by.

These totals tend to support our conjectures by showing incredibly high focusing on certain envelope sides. On envelope AB, for example, out of 73 calls on side A, PS correctly called it green 69 times. Calls on side B were close to chance. This suggests (from our perspective) that on this envelope PS concentrated green calls on one side only, making random calls on the other. Out of 128 calls on each envelope he had 102 hits on AB, 93 hits on EF, 98 on $1/2$, and 100 on $11/12$. On these and other envelopes there are bizarre focusing patterns—sometimes high in hits or misses on one side, and at chance on the other.

Sometimes there are high hits on one side, and high misses on the other. On MN, for example, PS had 48 hits to 3 misses on side N, and 68 misses to 9 hits on side M. These extremes resulted from the fact that during the first session he called both sides of this envelope green 55 times out of 64 calls, and during the second session he called both sides green 61 times out of 64 calls. From our point of view this suggests that PS made no tactile moves on this particular cover, but each time he held it he decided (with few exceptions) to call green. Because its envelope was randomly turned thoughout the experiment, naturally he scored fantastically high on side *N*, which actually was green, and fantastically low on side *M* which was white.

The focusing effects revealed by the paper's chart are truly weird. Without more detailed information it is impossible to make even plausible guesses as to just what strategies PS may have followed in the course of the two-day experiment. What is surely clear is that if PS had opportunities to track envelope orientations by tactile moves, this together with feedback information and the memorizing of covers could easily account for the peculiar focusing effects and for the overall success rate of almost 60 percent.

The Dutch team is to be commended on two counts: an improved randomizing procedure for card turning, and the stapling of covers to eliminate flaps. The second precaution suggests that the group was aware of how easily peek moves could be made when covers had four-inch flaps. On the other hand, the experiment had three major flaws:

1. Not randomizing the cards after each run with respect to their orientations in envelopes, and not randomizing envelopes after each run with respect to the covers that held them.

2. Allowing PS to hold each envelope when he made his call.

3. Informing PS how he had done after each sequence of twelve runs.

In view of how easily PS could have boosted his score by tactile marking, we can dismiss this experiment as another weak support for paranormal claims.

ADDENDUM

After completing this chapter, I received two informative letters from para-psychologists in Amsterdam. Dick Bierman, a University of Amsterdam psychologist, informed me that J. T. Barendregt, another experimental psychologist (also, by the way, a Dutch chess champion) was a nonbeliever in psi phenomena. He was "embarrassed," Bierman wrote, by the outcome of the experiment in Prague.

Jan Kappers, who also participated in the experiment, replied to two letters. (He had been tipped off by Ian Stevenson, he told me, that I was "on the warpath.") Kappers confirmed Barendregt's disbelief in ESP. Barendregt's refusal for more than a year to allow his name on the paper had delayed its publication, much to the wrath of J. B. Rhine. Kappers said that the remark in the paper about Fred Kaps the magician not being able to think of how the test results could have been obtained by trickery, was added against his (Kappers's) objection. He did not want it included because the statement did not come directly from Kaps. Barendregt had asked Jan Blom (see Chapter 10), a friend of Kaps, to contact Kaps. But Kaps had provided no written statement.

The most surprising aspect of Kappers's letter was the disclosure that he and two associates were planning to bring PS to Amsterdam in the spring of 1989 for a new series of tests. In 1986 Kappers had made an experiment with PS by mail that convinced him that PS retained his clairvoyant powers. I found this surprising because, as I shall report in the last chapter, PS flatly stated in a 1988 letter to me that he had no interest in ever being tested again.

Kappers confirmed the fact that PS had been operated on to remove webbing between his fingers, adding that this certainly did not render him unfit for manual labor, as Ryzl states in *Hypnosis and ESP*. Kappers said that JGP strongly doubted Ryzl's integrity—most of his suspicions coming from Ryzl's sister.

Chapter 9

Prague, 1963

DATE: October-November 1963

PLACE: Miss R's apartment in Prague.

PAPER: "Preliminary Experiments with a 'Borrowed' Outstanding ESP Subject." J. G. Pratt, in the *Journal of the Society for Psychical Research,* 42 (September 1964), pp. 333–345.

JGP arrived in Prague in the fall of 1963 for a third series of experiments with PS. MR, then busy with his writing chores, proposed that JGP work entirely alone with PS. One purpose was to prepare PS psychologically for experiments that JGP intended to carry out in November with Jan Blom, a parapsychologist from Amsterdam. The work would also be significant in showing that PS could retain his powers in complete independence from MR. You will recall that in the previous testing by the Dutch group, MR not only planned the test but also was present during part of it. This time the tests would be made with no one present except PS and JGP. Miss R, a friend of PS, allowed JGP to use her walk-up apartment while she was away at work.

JGP decided on a small change in the target materials. Instead of cards that were white on one side and black or colored on the other, he prepared a new set of cards that were white on one side but either light green, dark green, or yellow on the other. The plan was this. Cards of two different colors would be mixed together. They would be sealed in envelopes, and the envelopes placed in covers, but the handling would be such that at all times the colored side of each card would be uppermost when PS made his call. This would eliminate the need for constantly altering the orientations of envelopes inside their covers. Also, half the cards would be one color, and half another color, greatly simplifying the statistical analysis of the results. PS had consistently shown a preference for calling green more often than white. JGP thought this preference would be less pronounced if PS had to choose between two different colors rather than between green and white.

Five series of tests were made during the first week of JGP's visit to Prague. They all used sixteen cards, half of which were light green on the colored side, and half of which were yellow. The cards were sealed in opaque envelopes, and the envelopes were inserted into eight covers made of thicker cardboard than had been used before. This was to remove any "lingering doubt" about infrared heat radiation being responsible for unconscious cueing.

The first series was set for fifty runs (800 calls). JGP randomized before each run by removing the envelopes from their covers, shuffling the envelopes and covers separately, then randomly putting envelopes in covers with the colored side always up. This was done with his hands behind an "opaque screen" so he could not see what he was doing, and therefore would have no knowledge of the colors inside any cover. During this randomizing, PS went to the entrance hall and closed the door. In the subsequent four series he sat in the same room, but with his back to JGP while the randomizing took place. The results of the first series (October 29) were disappointing. Of the 800 calls, PS scored 386 hits, a negative deviation of 14.

The second series (October 30) ended with exactly 400 hits out of 800. A check with a friend establishes the probability of this exact mean-chance-expectation score as .028+ or about three times in a hundred. Here again we have a strange anomaly, with no plausible explanation, that tends to cast suspicion on the reliability of the data. If JGP was aware of how improbable this score was, he gave no indication of it.

The third series (October 31) consisted of twenty-five runs, or 400 calls, on the same covers. This time the hits were 225, a plus deviation of 25, still at chance level.

The fourth series (November 2) went back to 800 calls. The hits were 416, again within chance range.

The fifth series, made on the same day, was a second short test of 400 calls. This time the hits were 187, a negative deviation of 13.

In summary, the first five tests, completed during the first week of Pratt's visit, were all failures. Presumably there also were no focusing effects, otherwise they would have been cited in the paper. JGP, puzzled by PS's loss of psi powers, offers three possible explanations:

1. PS was disturbed by being separated from MR.

2. He was disturbed by working in a different place.

3. He was disturbed by a change in the test procedure.

From my perspective, it is not hard to find simpler explanations, but I certainly do not know if they are correct—throughout this book I am only suggesting possibilities. Because the randomizing was done outside the range of PS's vision, there was no way he could follow arm movements that would aid in tracking envelopes. No checking of hits or misses was done until each test was finished, so there was no way PS could get feedback information from the checking. We can assume that JGP kept the targets carefully guarded, giving PS no opportunity to unseal any envelope to see its top color.

There is, however, one possibility that would have been open to PS for producing focusing. He could have marked the top edges of certain envelopes, in one of the ways previously described, or he could have used peek moves and then seen that his calls were consistently the same on the tracked envelopes. This assumes, however, that PS was allowed to handle the covers during each call. One of the infuriating blanks in JGP's extremely terse account of the five failed tests is that nowhere does he say whether PS was allowed to hold the covers. If he was not, then his two available ways to produce focusing would be ruled out. There would have been no way he could have scored better than chance on any of the five tests.

It is worth adding that even if PS had been allowed to hold the covers, marking envelopes in these tests would have been extremely risky. In previous tests, such marking would have seemed to JGP utterly useless. After all, the envelopes were randomized before each run as to their orientations, and being inside covers, JGP would have seen no reason to inspect the envelopes carefully for tiny nicks, crimps, pressure marks, and so on. But in the five new tests, it would have been obvious that any kind of tactile mark on an envelope would have provided a way of distinguishing one color from another. If PS had been allowed to handle the covers, JGP might have been wary enough to inspect the envelopes carefully after each run. My own guess is that PS was indeed allowed to hold each cover when he made his call (otherwise JGP would surely have mentioned the tighter control of not allowing this), but that PS did not want to take chances.

Over the weekend JGP discussed with MR the failures of the first five tests. MR believed that the chief cause of failure was the change in targets. He proposed that JGP return to the traditional green/white cards for the two days remaining before Blom was to arrive. JGP readily agreed. He prepared eight new target cards, white on one side, dark green on the other. These were inserted into envelopes, using a screen to conceal the random insertions from himself, and the envelopes were sealed and were not opened until the end of the test. JGP now discloses that the screen was 18 inches wide and a foot high. What was the nature of this screen? JGP does not tell us, and the screen is not shown in the photograph of the test materials. I suspect that it was JGP's briefcase because, as we shall see in Chapter 16, he used his briefcase as a "screen," giving the dimensions of the briefcase as a foot high and 17½ inches wide.

The series was set for 100 runs (800 calls). After each run JGP randomized with his hands concealed by the screen, while PS sat with his back toward him. As in the past, after each run JGP turned over half the envelopes in their covers, but as always, he does not reveal how he selected the four.

JGP also fails to say whether PS held the covers when he made his calls. I assume (as before) that he did hold the covers or JGP would have told us otherwise. This is strongly supported by remarks in the paper discussed in the next chapter. The authors there state that the experiment they describe was a replication of the one described here, using the same targets and the same procedures. PS sat at a table with the covers stacked in front of him, closed ends toward him. He picked up the covers one at a time, made his call, and placed the covers aside in another stack.

This series (November 4) was successful. Of the 800 calls PS scored 465 hits, a success rate of 58+ percent. There also were focusing effects, though not as strong as in previous testing.

What strategy could PS have adopted to boost his score? In view of JGP's brief description—it takes up about one page—we can only guess. First, it is important to realize that with only eight cards involved, it is necessary to be sure of only one or two cards to raise a score above chance. If hits are guaranteed on only two cards, the expected score rises to $5/8 = 62+$ percent, considerably higher than PS's actual score of 58+ percent. Here is one of several possible scenarios.

Assume that PS was allowed to hold each cover when he called. It would be tempting to suppose that, when JGP randomized after each run, he followed his usual practice of cutting and turning the top four envelopes, but we cannot assume this because he tells of a different procedure. Evidently he now realized the folly of cutting to determine which four to reverse. He explicitly says he "shuffled the covers with the envelopes still inside to conceal my starting point. Next I took exactly four envelopes out of the covers and turned them over."

Although PS could not have taken advantage of JGP's formerly flawed randomizing, the asymmetric mark principle could still be used for focusing.* A chart supplied in the paper shows that his high scores were made on five cards (the other three were at chance). My best conjecture, which could be entirely wrong, is that during the early runs PS either marked five envelopes or focused on five that already were marked asymmetrically by the way the tape had been placed on the sides. As the test proceeded, he tracked the five envelopes as best he could, making the same color calls when the mark was on the right, and opposite calls when it was on the left. Had he been able to track the five perfectly, it would have raised his success score to a whopping 81+ percent. His actual score of 58+ percent reflected the fact that conditions allowed only inefficient tracking, but accurate enough to give slightly positive scores on five cards.

Such tracking would account for focusing, but of course it would not explain success in hitting the right colors. It is hard to believe that JGP would have been careless enough to allow PS access to the targets *before* the test began, but (here I follow the suggestion of a parapsychologist friend who has always been strongly suspicious of PS) it is not hard to imagine that once the test was over, JGP would consider careful guarding of the targets no longer necessary. JGP had a long record of trusting everybody he ever investigated, and he certainly had total trust in PS. More than this, he knew he had a record of all the calls alongside the target numbers, although he did not know how any of the cards were oriented. From his point of view, not having thought of the possibility of asymmetric marking, there would be no way PS could raise his score on the colors even if he was allowed unattended access to the covers.

From our point of view, PS (knowing how he had chosen to call the five tracked covers) could have unsealed the five envelopes, made whatever adjustments of the cards were necessary, and resealed them. The paper says nothing about precautions taken to guard the targets *after* the experiment was over and before JGP unsealed the envelopes to check the colors. JGP and PS were the only persons present in the apartment. Given JGP's complete trust in PS, and his inability to see how guarding targets would be necessary at the end of the testing, I find it not far-fetched to suppose that when JGP left the room to go to the bathroom, or for some other purpose, PS would find himself alone with the targets.

Cheered by the success of this sixth test, JGP prepared a new set of eight envelopes, along with their green-white cards and heavy cardboard covers. On November 5, he made an attempt to replicate the previous

---

*Instead of tactile marking, PS also could have tracked envelopes by peek moves, but I am assuming that by now JGP was sufficiently aware of peek moves to make sure they could not occur. However, we are not told where JGP sat while PS made his calls. If he sat in front of PS, and allowed him to hold covers vertically, the use of peeks instead of tactile marks remain a possibility.

test. To his disappointment, the calls showed no focusing. When the envelopes were unsealed and the top colors checked, the hits were 410, a chance deviation of only plus 10. Why would PS have failed on this effort to replicate? Who knows? JGP describes the failed test in just twelve lines. It would have been significant to know the exact conditions under which this experiment was conducted, but no details of any sort are provided.

In an appendix, JGP describes one more experiment, which he conducted with the help of Ian Stevenson, an American parapsychologist and psychiatrist at the University of Virginia, best known for his research and books about evidence for reincarnation. Stevenson had come to Prague from Zurich. He and JGP prepared two sets of eight green/white cards that were sealed as usual in opaque envelopes and inserted into covers. Instead of coding the envelopes, however, they left them blank, and calls were recorded directly on the envelopes. On each of two days there were one hundred runs (800 calls). We are told nothing about the procedures that were followed. The overall results (hit scores of 401 and 430) were statistically insignificant.

From our perspective, the failure of this eighth test could be attributed to the fact that Stevenson insisted on precautions that JGP had ignored. With tighter controls, PS would have had no opportunity to raise his score by nonparanormal means. JGP closes his paper by listing three factors that he suspects were responsible for the test's failure.

1. The new variation in technique—that is, recording calls directly on the envelopes.

2. The presence of another stranger—Stevenson.

3. The fact that Stevenson subjected PS to a "battery of psychological and personality tests . . . before this experimental series began." These tests, JGP tells us, "taxed the subject's understanding of English and they likely put him under more strain than he showed on the surface."

In *Hypnosis and ESP* (p. 91), MR adds what he thinks was another cause of the test's failure. He remarks cryptically that for reasons "too private to be discussed here" PS intimated to him "that in this particular study he would not aim at obtaining a high overchance result." When I first asked MR in a letter what the private reasons were, he declined to answer. I also asked Stevenson. He replied that he had been only an observer in this test and had no inkling of what MR had in mind. He said he knew nothing about PS's trying to score negatively and that it seemed to him improbable.

When I asked MR a second time about the meaning of his cryptic remark, he agreed to answer. It was not that PS was annoyed in any way with Stevenson. Indeed, he enjoyed taking the battery of personality tests Stevenson gave him because it made him feel important. The reason

PS suppressed his ESP powers, MR wrote, was as follows. At the time, a conflict between Rhine and JGP had arisen—a conflict that eventually resulted (as we shall see in Chapter 16) in JGP leaving Rhine to go to work for Stevenson. Rhine strongly objected to letting JGP work with PS. MR, feeling a primary loyalty to Rhine, found himself walking a tightrope between this loyalty and the promises he had made to JGP. His way out of this delicate situation, he told me, was to suggest to PS that he deliberately lower his scoring with JGP to discourage further investigations! He said he now regrets this. Why? Because he is convinced that this stratagem backfired later (as I shall reveal in Chapter 15) when PS used the same tactic against him!

JGP adds in his paper: "No doubt other unrecognized possibilities for interference were also present, and the real factors may be among them." To me, this is his most perceptive sentence. Had he seen fit to give as detailed an account of the failure of the experiment in which Stevenson participated as he gives of successful tests, we might be in a better position to speculate about those "other factors."

I have already mentioned that PS declined to answer any of my questions on the grounds that he could not recall details about tests made so long ago, and I also mentioned Dr. Ryzl's failure to remember his efforts to replicate the test on which PS scored with 100 percent accuracy on fifty color cards. It seems that Stevenson has similar memory lapses. He wrote to me on August 30, 1988, to assure me he had never "participated" in any ESP testing of PS that yielded chance results. He said he had been an observer in a 1968 test at the University of Virginia (here covered in Chapter 25), and that when he joined JGP in Prague in 1963 he gave PS some psychological tests but took no part in any experiment.

I sent Stevenson a copy of the page on which JGP tells how he and Stevenson planned the two-day experiment, and how he (JGP) had randomized one set of targets "while Dr. Stevenson put the subject through a run with the alternate set." After each run the two men recorded the results. In a later paper (covered here in Chapter 25) JGP cites Stevenson and K. R. Rao as two "investigators" under whom PS had failed to show ESP, and spoke of how sorry PS was that "he had disappointed Dr. Stevenson and Dr. Rao through his poor results." Stevenson responded by saying he had completely forgotten about the Prague test, and that what JGP had to say about it was accurate. I intended to include a photograph of Stevenson in this book, but he asked me not to do so, and I have respected his wishes.

Chapter 10

Prague, 1963

DATE: November 1963.

PLACE: The apartment of Miss R in Prague.

PAPER: "A Confirmatory Experiment with a 'Borrowed' Outstanding ESP Subject." J. G. Pratt and Jan G. Blom, in the *Journal of the Society for Psychical Research,* 42 (December 1964), pp. 381–388.

This experiment, conducted by JGP with the assistance of Jan Blom,* took place immediately after the successful test described in the previous chapter. It used the same two sets of dark green and white cards, one with envelopes numbered 1/2 to 15/16, the other with envelopes numbered 17/18 to 31/32. Presumably the sixteen envelopes remained sealed after the previous test, and were not opened and the colors checked until the end of this test. As before, each envelope was inserted into a cardboard cover.

The experiment lasted two days. On each day there were 100 runs of calls on eight covers, making 1,600 calls for the two-day period. The covers were not labeled, a continuing flaw in the controls.

---

*I learned from the University of Amsterdam that Johannes G. Blom, as they called him, was on the staff of the Institute of Phonetics, and that he died on October 16, 1980. When I asked Ian Stevenson when Blom died, he replied by letter that he "distinctly" remembered Pratt telling him that Blom had died several years earlier than the date of their conversation. Pratt died in 1979. I mention this only to indicate how faulty Stevenson's memory can be.

Jan Kappers, writing to me in 1988 (see chapter 8) said that Blom's last years were deeply troubled by alcohol and unfortunate relations with women. Kappers had been his personal physician. He said he was not entitled to give details, but the events were sufficiently "hair-raising" to provide material for a U.S. bestseller. Blom died, he wrote, from a disease contracted while on a dangerous expedition to Africa.

Blom sat diagonally opposite PS in the "experimental room" where he handed the covers of one set of eight to PS, one at a time. After each call, PS put the cover on a stack on the table. Blom recorded the calls. While this was going on, JGP sat in the entrance hall, out of sight, where he randomized the targets of the other set of eight covers. We are told nothing about how he randomized beyond the fact that he followed the procedure described in the previous paper. JGP then brought his randomized stack to Blom, and the two "worked together" to lift cover flaps and record the envelope numbers beside Blom's record of calls. This was observed by PS. JGP would then retire to the hallway to randomize the just-called covers while Blom repeated the calling procedure with the set of covers JGP had left on the table. Two carbons were made of the records. The original was kept by JGP for his permanent files. One carbon was for Blom and the other carbon was given to PS.

PS scored 922 hits—a success rate of $922/1,600 = .57+$. There was evidence of focusing on some envelopes, including five on which PS had obtained high scores in the previous test. The experimenters say they are not sure whether PS was focusing his ESP on the colors of the cards or whether early in the test he associated colors with envelope numbers and thereafter focused on the numbers instead of the colors. They also leave open the question of whether focusing was a purely psychological phenomenon (as JGP believed)—that is, PS showed an unconscious ESP preference for certain sides of cards and/or envelopes—or whether some sort of physical change was made paranormally on the cards as MR always thought, and still does. In any case, they see the experiment as further proof that PS, unlike so many good ESP subjects, had retained his ESP powers, giving him a place of "unique importance in the history of parapsychology." They express their hope that other subjects can be developed with a similar ability to preserve their psi abilities. If so, they write, the "research gains would be incalculable."

PS was allowed to hold each cover while he made his call. (The earlier technique of screening his vision from the targets when he called seems now to have been permanently abandoned in spite of the fact that he had scored high when a screen was used.) He could, therefore, have used asymmetric tactile marking or peek moves to produce focusing, but the overall score of positive deviations on all but two envelopes suggests that more than markings would have been required to boost his score by nonparanormal means. It would have been necessary for him to have obtained access to the sealed envelopes, either during the testing process, or immediately afterward. The authors make much of the fact that there was no collusion between either of them and PS, but they say absolutely nothing about taking precautions to guard the test material.

Because JGP and Blom totally trusted PS, along with the fact that their envelopes were "sealed" on all sides with tape, I suspect it would never have crossed their minds that it would be important to guard the targets. Consider the circumstances. The testing covered a period of many hours, spread over two days. While JGP was randomizing covers behind a closed door, Blom was alone in the room with PS. There must have been occasions when Blom had to go to the bathroom. When he did, did he:

1. Take the eight covers with him?
2. Insist that PS accompany him to the washroom?
3. Ask JGP to come into the room to guard PS while he (Blom) was absent?

Any of these three precautions obviously would have been highly insulting to PS. Yet if none of them was adopted, it would take PS only a few seconds to pull out an envelope, peel back the tape on one side far enough to see the card's top color, then reseal it. If any of the three precautions was taken, it would have been important to say so in the paper. The fact that nothing was said about them is a strong indication they were not taken.

The first mention in a published report on the testing of PS that efforts were made to guard the targets at all times was by JGP in a 1966 paper discussed here in Chapter 16. See that chapter for the passage in which JGP speaks of taking the targets with him whenever for any reason he left PS's presence. That no such statement appears in any paper prior to 1966 suggests that no one found it necessary before that time to take such elementary precautions.

As I said earlier, it would have been even more important to guard targets *after* a test was completed, but there is no indication that the experimenters considered this necessary. Because PS was given copies of the sheets on which his calls and the top numbers of the envelopes were recorded, he would know precisely on which envelopes he had focused calls. If he had access to the targets *after* the experiment was over, when everyone was relaxing, it would be easy to adjust cards in certain envelopes to give positive hit deviations.

How many envelopes would he have to adjust? This depends on whether the sealed envelopes were opened and their cards randomized as to orientation between this test and the previous one. As I have said, the paper suggests that the envelopes remained sealed until the end of both experiments. We are told that the second test "made use of the same sealed green/white cards and opaque covers as was used in the previous successful series." In the previous test, PS scored high on five covers that continued to be high scorers in the second test. If PS had an opportunity to adjust some of those five cards (of course no adjustments would be needed for cards on which focusing produced hits) then he would know how to focus on those same five cards during the second test, and without having to give them any new tactile marks.

The five highest scores on the test with Blom were on envelopes 1/2, 7/8, 11/12, 23/24, and 31/32, with respective positive deviations from fifty of 18, 12, 21, 12, and 12. Each of these envelopes had 12 or higher deviations on the previous experiment (covered in Chapter 9) that used the same envelopes, except for 23/24 which had a deviation of 9. This suggests that PS, knowing the orientations of cards in the five marked envelopes continued to focus positively (with respect to colors) on all five. In the Blom test only two other envelopes had high positive deviations, 21/22 and 29/30, both with deviations of 10. On the previous series both of these envelopes scored at chance, with deviations of –1 and +1, respectively. From our perspective this indicates that PS added those two envelopes to those he marked and tracked. At some time during the testing he gained access to the targets and adjusted the two cards (if necessary) to obtain his overall score of 57+ percent on the colors.

Such speculations are of course of little value because we have such hazy information to go on. My main criticism is that most of the nine pages of the report by JGP and Blom are devoted to summarizing results and discussing their implications. The actual procedures and their controls are covered in less than one page. We have here another striking instance of an extraordinary result—establishing ESP beyond any doubt, provided the data are accurate and no nonparanormal techinques were used—is presented in a paper with an extraordinary absence of details about the controls that were in force.

Chapter 11

Prague, 1963

DATE: November 1963
PLACE: Miss R's apartment in Prague
PAPER: "A Second Confirmatory ESP Experiment with Pavel Stepanek as a 'Borrowed' Subject." J. G. Blom and J. G. Pratt, in the *Journal of the American Society for Psychical Research,* 62 (January 1968), pp. 28–45.

Although this paper was not published until 1968, it describes a final experiment conducted by JGP and Jan Blom in November 1963 when the Dutch parapsychologist joined JGP in Prague. Forty green/white cards were used, numbered 1/2, 3/4, . . . , 79/80. Odd numbers were put on white sides, even numbers on green sides.

The cards were sealed in cardboard envelopes after a complicated procedure in which JGP randomized the cards while Blom randomized the envelopes, each out of the other's sight. The two stacks were put under an opaque cloth. JGP would hand an envelope to Blom, who would insert a card. This was to ensure that neither man knew the orientation of any card inside its envelope. The envelopes were sealed at their open ends with paper tape "prepared in advance for this purpose." The envelopes were then put inside the usual opaque cardboard covers, stapled on their sides. Sixteen covers, none of them labeled, were used in two sets of eight each, which alternated throughout the test.

There were four sessions, each taking place in the afternoon in the sitting room of the apartment of PS's friend Miss R. At each session PS made 125 runs through a set of eight covers, or 1,000 calls per session.

Thus there were 4,000 calls for the four days. The envelopes remained sealed throughout each session. After the session, they were opened for checking by the two experimenters in JGP's hotel room. The next morning they repeated their randomizing procedure, and the envelopes were resealed for the next session. One assumes that the tape peeled away easily, otherwise the envelopes would have been rendered unsuitable for the next session.

All the calls were made in the presence of Blom only, who sat at a table to the left of PS. While the calling was going on, JGP sat in the hallway as before, behind a closed door, where he randomized the next set of eight envelopes inside their eight covers. He would bring the eight to Blom, and take away the set of eight that had been called. Blom would further randomize the eight covers he had just received by shuffling them below the table's edge.

PS took one cover at a time in his hands, made the call, and placed it aside in a reverse-order stack. Blom recorded the calls. At the end of the run, when JGP came into the room with a randomized stack of eight covers, the envelopes of the called stack were taken out of their covers and their numbers recorded while PS watched.

The results were as follows. There were 530 hits in the first session, 555 hits in the second, 509 in the third, and 560 in the final session. The respective success scores were .53, .555, .509, and .56. The overall success rate was 2,154/4,000 = .5385. The authors note the alternation of low, high, low, high scores, for which they say they have no explanation. The third session was at chance level, followed by the highest score (.56) of the experiment.

As in the previous test, the record of calls and envelope numbers was made in triplicate, one copy for each experimenter, and one for PS, who later gave it to MR. The opening of the envelopes for a check on the card colors was made, as I have said, in JGP's hotel room after the session was over. When they met PS the next day, at a streetcar stop, he was told in general terms whether he did well or poorly on the previous day's session.

The randomizing process put green uppermost in the envelopes 2,020 times, versus white on top for 1,980 times—a reasonable deviation from equality. PS called green 2,118 times versus 1,787 calls for white, a 55.4 percent preference for green. The authors found no strong focusing on cards, but there was a "general focusing" on envelopes that were consistently called the same way regardless of the orientation of their cards. There could have been focusing on covers, but since the covers continued to be unlabeled there was no way to tell.

As in all the papers about tests with PS, there is only a vague description of precisely how he handled the covers when he made his calls. We are told the stack was placed on the table with the closed ends toward PS and that PS called the color "while he lifted it [a cover] from the stack and laid it aside." We are also told that while he made his calls PS held the covers at their stapled sides, and that when he placed a cover aside he held it at the closed end between his thumb and index finger. As we saw in Chapter 3, the flaps of covers are open for several inches down the sides. This allows one to hold a cover at the stapled sides, and insert a forefinger invisibly between the flaps to contact the envelope's folded edge. The move can be made while in the act of picking up a cover from the table. Both hands can shift to a normal grip on the two sides, well below the flaps, while the call is being made. After the call, the grip can be changed again to holding a bottom corner of the cover as it is placed aside.

JGP did not witness the calling, so we have only Blom's memory to rely on; nevertheless, nothing in the description of how PS handled the covers is inconsistent with either peek moves or asymmetric marking. We see here the enormous value of making videotape records in the future when tests of this sort are made. Of course having a knowledgeable magician present is even better, but a videotape would at least preserve the kind of information needed for evaluating conjectures about how scores can be boosted by nonparanormal means.

PS's use of asymmetric marking or peeks would explain his focusing on envelopes, but would not explain positive scores on the colors. Here again my best conjecture is that during or after the first, second, and fourth sessions PS was allowed access to the targets. As in the previous test, we are told nothing about the care with which test material was guarded. Both experimenters totally trusted PS. Moreover, the fact that envelopes were taped shut would make it seem unnecessary to guard targets, especially at the end of a session after all the data had been recorded.

As in the previous test, there must have been times when Blom left the sitting room to go to the bathroom. It is hard to suppose he would take the eight covers with him or call JGP into the room to guard the covers. Parapsychologists feel strongly about not upsetting psychics, and strong measures to guard the targets would surely have been insulting. In the eyes of Blom and JGP, any emotional stress on PS's part would be sufficient to produce a temporary loss of his psi abilities. If PS had access to the targets during the three sessions on which his scores on colors were above chance, this combined with asymmetric marking would explain the results.

If PS had access to the targets *after* a session was completed, it would not even have been necessary to make use of asymmetric marking. PS knew what his calls had been during a session, not only because he watched the recording of envelope numbers but also because he was given a record of those results at the end of each session. He would simply note the envelope sides on which there had been chance focusing, then adjust (if necessary) a few cards to conform to his calls.

I have no way of knowing whether either of these conjectures is correct. Assuming that one is, we can speculate on why scoring dropped to chance during the third session. It would mean that PS had no opportunity during or after this session to be alone with the targets. His high score on the final session could be attributed to the fact that by then more asymmetric marks had been placed on the envelopes, enabling PS to increase his focusing, or PS could have made greater use of peeks. Recall that JGP did not witness the calling. There is no evidence that Blom, whose expertise was in phonetics, had much experience in the testing of psychics or that he had any inkling of how easily peeks could be made or a finger inserted to feel tactile marks.

One of the lessons that parapsychologists have been slow to learn is that, in testing psychics who display high ESP talents, it is essential to design controls "as if" a subject might take advantage of a loophole and that this should be done regardless of how strongly experimenters believe in the subject's honesty. The fact that this paper is silent on precautions taken to guard the targets, both during and after each session, is one of its major flaws. As I remarked in the previous chapter, the first disclosure in a paper that such precautions were taken is in JGP's 1966 report, covered here in Chapter 16. If such precautions were taken in the Blom-Pratt tests, they should have been mentioned. I take the paper's silence on this point to indicate that the experimenters did not think such precautions were necessary.

In his monograph on PS, Pratt speaks of this work with Blom as one of two that reached "the highest level of safeguarding and in providing conclusive evidence that PS was demonstrating ESP." The other report, which he considers equally conclusive, is the Pratt-Keil-Stevenson study which we shall consider in Chapter 25.

Chapter 12

Prague, 1963

DATE: 1963

PLACE: MR's apartment in Prague

PAPERS: *Hypnosis and ESP.* Milan Ryzl. Switzerland: Ariston Verlag, 1971.

Monograph About ESP Experiments with PS. Milan Ryzl. Unpublished typescript, 1965.

"Some Observations Bearing Upon the Mental-Impregnation Hypothesis." Milan Ryzl. An unpublished paper delivered at an annual convention of the Parapsychological Association, in Freiberg, West Germany, 1968.

In the three references cited above, MR describes a series of fantastic experiments with PS, all completed before the end of 1963, and all designed to test MR's theory of mental impregnation. None are described by JGP in his monograph on PS, though of course he knew about them. "It is known that Ryzl tried many things with PS," JGP writes in his monograph on PS, during the intervals between experiments made with visiting researchers. "He spoke to me about many such efforts that yielded highly significant results but which were not reported because they were mainly exploratory. . . ."

The most remarkable of these unpublished tests involved impregnation. Here is how MR puts it in the typescript of his 1965 monograph. "It seems as if the performed call would mark the target card in some way so that in the following calls the subject has the tendency to give information not on the real target, but rather on a trace clinging to the card as it arose in the preceding calls." This is, of course, a precise description of our conjecture about asymmetric marking (or the sensory detection of asymmetric differences in the way tapes were applied to the two sides of envelopes) except that in our conjecture the "traces" are not paranormal.

MR's first tests of impregnation, using all white and all green cards, are described at length in his 1965 monograph. I will not go into them here because of the more careful tests he describes in *Hypnosis and ESP*. These later tests used a hundred 3″ × 5″ cards that were white on both sides, and a hundred that were black on both sides.

The 200 cards were "impregnated"—half of them by MR, half by PS—in the following fashion. He (either MR or PS) would stare at one side of a card for about thirty seconds, "wishing this side to become white." The card would be turned over and the impregnator would stare at the other side for another thirty seconds, wishing it to become "black." This was done regardless of whether the card was white on both sides or black on both sides. The impregnated card then went into an envelope, its sides marked for future identification and a record kept of which impregnated color was up. The envelopes were sealed and inserted into 200 cardboard covers.

That was how MR, in *Hypnosis and ESP,* described the preparation of targets for this experiment, but in his 1968 lecture he gave a different account. No covers were involved. The targets consisted of what he calls "simple envelopes," and he adds, "so the former covers were no more used." The envelopes were not even sealed. "Between the individual runs the cards were always taken out of their envelopes, thoroughly shuffled, and again inserted into the envelopes." This was done behind an "opaque screen," the nature of which is not specified. PS's calls were recorded as he made them. After a run, the cards were removed from their envelopes, shuffled, and put back inside for the next run. It is easy to understand why MR would see no need for covers or for sealing envelopes. The cards would, of course, be labeled, otherwise checking calls would not have been possible.

Nineteen hundred sixty-eight, the time of MR's lecture, was closer to 1963 than was 1971, the date of *Hypnosis and ESP,* so I will assume that his memory was stronger then and that his earlier description of the targets is the more trustworthy. We are now, of course, back to MR's initial procedures in which controls were totally lacking. There is no description of how the envelopes were constructed, so we can assume they were like the ones MR used before, made of opaque cardboard and open at one end for ease in removing and reinserting the cards after they were shuffled. Of course this makes it childishly easy for PS to use either peek moves or asymmetric marking, or a combination of both techniques.

PS made his calls in sixty runs of 200 trials each, or a total of 12,000 calls. For 8,000 of the calls PS was asked to guess the impregnated color.

For 4,000 calls he was asked to guess the actual color. Both efforts were failures. PS scored at chance with respect to both kinds of colors.

There were, however, as one would expect, strong focusing effects. On certain envelope sides PS had had an unusually large number of hits with respect to both real and impregnated colors, but these hits were balanced by an equally large number of misses. MR sees this "great dispersion of scores toward extreme values" as the experiment's most significant result. In other words, PS seemed to have been focusing his ESP only on the sides of envelopes. Because this focusing completely ignored efforts to impregnate the cards, MR concludes that the focusing was not the result of "voluntary mental impregnation." It was not the impressing of a "permanent quality" on a target card by "normal voluntary waking concentration."

This abandonment of voluntary impregnation of the cards, before the experiment, for an involuntary focusing on the envelopes during the experiment must have been extremely puzzling to MR. From our viewpoint the results are surely unsurprising. We assume that MR was careful to guard his targets so that at no time, during or after a session, did PS gain access to the targets so he could check card labels. What could he do? The only strategy open to him was to focus on certain sides of cards by peeks or asymmetric marking combined with the imperfection principle to memorize envelopes. There would always be the possibility he might be lucky, and his focusing would show mostly hits. Perhaps PS even toyed with the notion that someday he might develop genuine clairvoyant powers that would turn his focusing into hits. Unfortunately, with such a large number of calls, his lucky hits were balanced by unlucky misses. The experiment was a whopping success with respect to focusing, but a failure with respect to "seeing" by ESP the stable "footprints" that he and MR hoped they had been able to plant on the cards.

MR next reports (in *Hypnosis and ESP*) on his analysis of the data in two former experiments—the ones discussed here in Chapters 6 and 8. Without going into the complex statistics, what he discovered was that in making calls PS did not alternate colors in a manner similar to the way heads and tails alternate when you flip a coin. PS tended to have long runs of identical calls on the same side of an envelope. As MR puts it, given an envelope side, the calls did not resemble a chance pattern such as *GWGGGWWGWG*, but rather a pattern like *WWWWGGGGGG*. Somehow PS remembered how he had previously called that side of the envelope, and tended to repeat the same call more often than he switched to the opposite color. Here is how MR expressed what he calls a "strange feature" of the calling:

The conclusion that can be drawn from these results is: There seems to exist some property in the target which stimulates the subject to give preferably the same response to the target as he did before. This property does not depend on material characteristics of the target (since the targets remained physically and chemically unchanged while this property changed). This property is not entirely stable; it is strengthened by consecutive identical statements and weakened by opposite statements. This property appears to be a kind of "footprint" of previous statements which clings to the target; which is created, strengthened or weakened by the subject's statements; which, according to its strength and polarity, stimulates the subject's ESP and increases, thus, the probability of his giving the particular corresponding response.

Since these "footprints" do not seem to possess any material characteristics in the physical sense; since they are associated with the mental activity of the subject during the process of ESP; and since they evidently bear some conceptual meaning, it seems proper to call them "mental impregnation."

A more detailed analysis of the same data is given by MR in his 1968 lecture in West Germany. There he considers two hypotheses concerning the nature of impregnation:

1. PS perceives by ESP some "nonmaterial" property of the target.

2. PS perceives by ESP a "material" property of the target, such as "identification marks, or slight differences between targets, irregularities or defects in the paper, scratches, etc., perhaps only of microscopic size."

MR rules out the second conjecture on the grounds that, if correct, PS would be able to score equally well on tests in which there were slight changes in the target, such as using ESP cards instead of bicolored cards. However, PS consistently scored at chance levels whenever there was the slightest alteration of test materials.

There are two other reasons for MR's rejecting the second hypothesis. For one thing, he thinks it is too complicated. More importantly, it does not explain why PS would alter his focusing in the course of an experiment. Since the material properties of the targets do not change, why should PS change his focusing?

MR is persuaded that his first conjecture is correct. However, he points out, experiments show that a nonmaterial "footprint" that somehow "clings" to the target is not a stable property as he first thought. It is a variable property, first created by PS at the beginning of a test, then later strengthened or weakened in the course of the experiment. If PS continued to call correctly it would strengthen the footprint. If he began to miss, it would weaken the footprint and change it to one of the opposite color, which would then be responsible for a greater-than-chance run of misses.

In a footnote to his 1968 lecture MR writes that to be "exhaustive" there are other hypotheses that could account for the long runs of identical calls:

1. PS used ESP to view the experimenter's records of previous calls.
2. PS "retrocognized" previous calls.
3. PS "precognized" future calls.
4. PS used psychokinesis (PK) to influence MR's randomizing of the targets between runs.

MR rejects all four conjectures as either too complicated or ruled out by PS's failures in all tests for precognition, retrocognition, and PK. This is the only indication I have come across that MR ever tested PS for PK.

Observe that MR never considers the simplest of all hypotheses, the one central to this book—namely, that PS was perceiving material properties by ordinary sensory means. From our perspective, which could be entirely wrong, the "footprints" were of two sorts: (1) imperfections on the outside of covers or on the outside of envelopes if no covers are used. (2) Asymmetric tactile markings on the top edges of envelopes inside covers or on cards inside unsealed envelopes when no covers were used. As we have seen, these could be marks placed there by PS, or marks already there by the way sides were taped.

MR's statistical analysis of long runs provides strong confirmation of the conjecture that PS had over the course of time become skilled in asymmetric tactile marking. It is the simplest available explanation of both focusing effects and the long runs of identical calls on the same side of an envelope. For example, suppose that during a run in which PS, following his asymmetric marks, makes five repeated green calls on a certain side of an envelope. After the run, he observes during the checking process that all five calls were misses. During the next run, he switches his calls on that envelope side to the opposite color and makes five repeated calls of white. Of the ten calls, five will be hits, five will be misses. The larger than expected frequency of long runs of the same color is indeed easily explained by what MR calls a property that "clings" to the envelope, but our suggestion is that the clinging property need not be paranormal. It could be an actual mark on the envelope. Go over the data of all the previous experiments, viewing them in the light of our conjectures, and you will not find it surprising that there are strong focusing effects as well as long runs of identical calls. PS could have been responding not to "footprints" of a psychic nature but to "handprints" of his own making.

Is it possible that PS could have produced focusing on envelopes by using peek moves? Yes, and this should always be kept in mind whenever PS has been allowed to hold covers vertically while he calls. I am assuming—it could be entirely wrong—that by now PS would have found tactile marking an easier way to produce focusing than by using peeks to track certain sides of envelopes. It would eliminate the need to keep many labels in mind. Moreover, the inserted-finger move would be invisible from three sides, and could be used in tests in which targets were held horizontally during calling.

In later reports we are never told why PS switched to holding targets horizontally. My guess is that JGP, criticized by colleagues for not having taken adequate steps to prevent peeking, had asked PS to keep the targets horizontal at all times. As we have seen, this made it even easier for PS to conceal an inserted left finger from anyone seated on his right. To an observer in front, the move is effectively screened by tilting the cover slightly downward at the far end while picking up the cover and making the move. Of course the left hand could then be withdrawn, leaving the cover held horizontally by the right hand while the call was made.

MR now returns (in *Hypnosis and ESP*) to his impregnation tests. The next test used twenty-four cards, white on both sides. One side of each card was marked with a small identification number. The cards were inserted into twenty-four envelopes. No covers were used. The envelopes were "presented" to PS (we are not told whether he handled them or not) for calls. After each run of twenty-four calls MR, behind an "opaque screen," took the cards out of the unsealed envelopes, shuffled them, and put them back. The cards were never turned, so at all times the numbered sides were down. In other words, the unlabeled sides remained up throughout the experiment. PS, MR tells us, was "left with the conviction" that the envelopes contained the usual white/green cards that had been used in most of the earlier testing.

There were 101 runs, or 2,400 calls in all. The first run was not counted. It served as an "impregnating run" during which PS did his best to imprint white or green on each up side of a card. From then on, he tried to give calls that corresponded to the impregnated colors.

Granting our conjectures, which could be mistaken, it is easy to predict that this experiment would be successful. PS had only to use peeks or to put asymmetric marks on some of the cards while he made his first run, then repeat the same calls on those cards. MR took this focusing as evidence of psychic imprinting. The test's success, about which we are given only the barest information (more is supplied in MR's 1965 monograph), inspired MR to follow with other kinds of impregnation tests using the same set of twenty-four blank cards. Descriptions of these tests are very brief in *Hypnosis and ESP*. I will supplement those descriptions with additional details from the 1965 monograph.

The idea behind the next series of experiments was to see if PS could imprint on the blank cards two different concepts, then show focusing effects on them in subsequent runs. The first test involved distinguishing "addition" from "multiplication" by imprinting either a plus sign or a multiplication sign. (When shown an ESP card with the plus sign, PS interpreted it as a "cross.") The next test was for PS to impregnate the *same* sign on the blank cards but to distinguish in his mind between the two interpretations: a sign of addition, or the cross as a religious symbol. (PS, you recall, is a Catholic.) Again, there were the usual focusing effects.

The next test was more complicated. On even runs PS was asked to impregnate the concepts of "love" and "murder." On odd runs through the same blank cards he was asked to imprint "man" and "woman." The imprinting was done during the first even and odd runs, thereafter PS tried to distinguish between the dichotomies. MR was struck by the fact that "love" was more strongly impregnated than "murder," and "woman more strongly impregnated than "man." He reminds us (in *Hypnosis and ESP*) that this correlates with PS being a "bachelor, with a normal attitude toward sex, but with aggressive traits." Hence his association of love with woman and murder with man. In his 1968 lecture MR correlates the symbol associations with these traits: "bachelor, at the time of the experiment 33 years old, lacking vigour and of a very shy complexion, however with a concealed aggressivity, indulging in day dreaming." In other words, MR thinks PS was using ESP unconsciously to express two suppressed emotions: his love of women and his hatred of men.

Using the same blank cards, MR continued his impregnation tests with more dichotomies. In each case PS sought to imprint the concepts on the cards, then try to focus on them to prove that impregnation had taken place. MR's 1965 monograph lists the following dichotomies: grass versus fire, green versus red, bird versus duck, tree versus poplar, and high versus low.

The results showed that PS did indeed focus on the concepts by concentrating similar calls on the same sides of cards, and with better than chance correlations with the sides he had impregnated. This proved to MR that PS's focusing was not on any physical property of the card, since all were blank, but on psychic properties that he somehow placed on the cards. From our point of view, PS did indeed place properties on the cards during his impregnation run, then by feeling the ends of the cards as he made his calls, he was able to produce the desired focusing.

MR's impregnation tests reached the ultimate in absurdity sometime in 1963 when he tried using envelopes that, unknown to PS, were entirely *empty!* In *Hypnosis and ESP* (p. 87) he tells of a test in which two envelopes on which PS had scored high in an earlier test were opened, their cards removed, and the envelopes resealed. The other envelopes in the test contained the usual bicolored cards. Sure enough, PS again scored high on the two empties (based on their former contents): 240 hits and 160 misses. This proved to MR that "the empty envelopes really carried some tendency to stimulate certain responses, which remained as a residue of the former tendency of the envelope-card combination." We are not told whether the envelopes were or were not in covers. If not, PS had only to use the imperfection principle. If in covers, asymmetric marking or peeks could account for the focusing.

Not content with using just two empty envelopes, MR reports in his 1965 monograph another experiment in which twenty envelopes, all empty, were used. Here is what he told PS:

> I have now removed all the cards from the envelopes. You will call these empty envelopes just in the same way as you did previously with the cards in the envelopes. We have recently learned that you have probably the ability of mentally impregnating the cards. This may be the case also with the envelopes. Yet this is not our concern here. You should definitely try to avoid exerting any influence of this sort on the envelopes. The only task you have is to "read" from these envelopes any trace which has possibly been left there by the cards or the experimental procedure we performed in recent weeks. Say—to ascertain which card has left the most outstanding trace there.

The empty envelopes were shuffled and turned between the fifty runs, or 1,000 calls in all. PS was allowed to hold the envelopes. No mention is made of covers. It is hardly surprising that his calls showed focusing on certain envelope sides.

Surely this is the most foolish experiment that MR ever made with PS. There was not even a need for asymmetric marking or for peeks. To produce the focusing, all PS had to do was memorize some of the envelope sides and concentrate similar calls on those sides. How did MR keep a record of the sides? He does not say. Presumably the envelopes were labeled on the inside of each envelope. If labeled on the outside, even the imperfection principle was unnecessary to invoke. PS would simply concentrate green calls on, say, side 7a, and concentrate white calls on, say, side 13b. MR describes his "controls" in these words:

> While preparing the targets, all usual measures against sensory cues were taken (screening of envelopes from the subject). During the experiment proper, the subject was allowed to touch the envelopes, but he was carefully watched. The experimenter's role as a recorder interfered only very little with this observation of the subject's behavior. In no case any intention of the subject was noticed to make use of his normal senses in discerning the colors of the cards, or to look for any sensory cues on the outer surface of the envelopes.

It is impossible to exaggerate the naiveté of the above quotation. Professional gamblers read subtly marked cards as rapidly as they are dealt. PS had years of practice in memorizing imperfections on envelopes and covers. To suppose he would look up and down each envelope, squinting his eyes as he searched for blemishes, reveals how totally MR was convinced that PS possessed remarkable clairvoyant powers and could be trusted not to boost his scores by any kind of sensory means. One can understand why JGP, in his monograph on PS, did not include any of MR's unpublished research on impregnation.

These tests seem to me a strong confirmation of our conjectures. Assuming as I do the honesty of MR, and the accuracy of his data, we have only two possible explanations of PS's focusing. Either he was impregnating psychic footprints, as MR continues to believe, or he was using the techniques we have conjectured. Since the testing of PS there have been no confirmations by reputable parapsychologists of psychic impregnation on cards or envelopes. Indeed, MR seems to be the only parapsychologist who still takes mental impregnation seriously, and he has published no experimental ESP work since he came to the United States. Which hypothesis is the simplest and most believable? Let readers make their choices.

MR describes a final unpublished experiment he made in late 1963 (1965 monograph, Part IV, pages 248–254). He calls it his "Time Factor Series" because it was designed to see if PS's impregnations would remain on cards or envelopes for periods of one or two hours to a month. The test was poorly controlled, using 1,200 white/green cards in unsealed envelopes and no covers. There were 13,200 calls in all, of which the first 1,200 were part of impregnation runs.

The results were unexpected. MR reports that although the number of color hits was above chance, PS's focusing ability had totally vanished. This was surprising because previous experiments tended to show strong focusing coupled with an absence of success on the actual colors. MR is rightly puzzled by this switch. He closes his monograph by wondering if the change will be permanent or whether PS's ability to impregnate will return. My best guess is that PS, confronted with color cards in unsealed envelopes, made no attempt at focusing. He simply boosted his score on colors by random peeks.

In his 1968 lecture MR stresses the great significance of his discovery of mental impregnation, a property that "cannot be perceived by normal senses" and "is probably not detectable by physical instruments." We have here a paranormal event comparable to the change of bread and wine during a Catholic mass to the actual body and blood of Jesus even though the change is "not detectable by physical instruments." MR was convinced that paranormal impregnation helps explain clairvoyance. It is not merely paranormal perception, but the result of "an interaction between the perceiving subject and the perceived object." It also helps explain, he argues, such phenomena as poltergeists and apparitions, and the ability of psychics to gain impressions from material objects like rings and watches. He also suspects it may underlie telepathy. "The trace of a thought fixed on a card is then surely a more objective and experimentally more easily definable target than the fleeting thought."

He concludes his paper by proposing that mental impregnation "could be used as a fundamentally new means of storing information. Similarly, bits of information could also be 'coded' into the impregnated trace—and such a parapsychologically coded information could never be decoded in a nonparapsychological way."

MR does not add here that he himself had supervised three failed efforts to replicate his most famous test for transmitting coded information (see Chapter 4). The third failure was halted in 1964 after negative results were obtained, and MR became convinced that PS was losing his psi powers. This loss became noticeable early in 1964, MR writes in *Hypnosis and ESP,* and was dramatically confirmed in July 1964 when PS was tested by John Beloff, one of England's best known parapsychologists. This famous failure is the topic of our next chapter.

Chapter 13

Prague, 1964

DATE: July 1964.
PLACE: MR's apartment in Prague.
PAPER: "Loss of Stability of ESP Performance in a High-Scoring Subject." Milan Ryzl and John Beloff, in the *Journal of Parapsychology,* 29 (March 1965), pp. 1–11.

Dr. John Beloff (henceforth JB), a psychologist at the University of Edinburgh and a former president of the Parapsychological Association, is one of Britain's most respected psi researchers. He is also one of the strangest personalities on the psi scene. This strangeness springs from two facts that are not easy to reconcile.

1. JB conducts carefully controlled psi experiments that uniformly produce negative results, nevertheless . . .

2. He enthusiastically endorses the work of other parapsychologists regardless of how wild and poorly controlled their work is.

A striking instance of the second fact is JB's high praise for the testing in the early 1970s of a self-taught card magician named William Delmore. In 1979 sociologist Marcello Truzzi asked JB to list the seven psi investigations he considered the most persuasive to skeptics. His list was published in Truzzi's *Zetetic Scholar* (Issue 6, 1980). One of the seven was the second Blom and Pratt test of PS, here covered in Chapter 11. Listing this experiment is understandable, but almost impossible to comprehend is his inclusion of the tests made of Delmore. At that time B. D. (as he is called in the published papers) was a young, long-haired dropout from Yale University's Law School, class of 1973. For several months he had been wowing parapsychologists at Dr. Rhine's laboratory and elsewhere with his supposedly psychic card tricks.*

When Persi Diaconis, a mathematician and expert on card magic, was allowed to witness a performance of BD at Harvard University in 1973, he was vastly amused by the standard techniques BD was using—shrewd estimations, key cards, forces, and (above all) the use of multiple endings not specified in advance: The latter is a powerful tool of card magicians. It means that the performer does not specify in advance what he is attempting to do, but decides on the trick's outcome as the trick progresses and he can take advantage of how the breaks fall. Magicians know such multiple endings as "outs."

Delmore has returned to Bismarck, North Dakota, where he was born in 1949 and where he was considered one of the brightest students ever to attend St. Mary's High School. An attorney, he works for the state's health department and in 1986 was the town's City Commissioner. An interview in the *Bismarck Tribune* (January 19, 1986) is headlined "Secret Psychic: Bismarck's Commissioner Talks at Last About His 'Gift.' " Delmore tells of receiving a grant from Harvard to be tested at Rhine's Foundation for Research on the Nature of Man, in Durham, N. C. The paper speaks of his having "done a few shows" in Bismarck "combining both ESP and Magic. He's also helped to find missing people."

In a long telephone conversation I had with Delmore in 1988, he freely admitted he used trickery to increase the probability of hits during his card demonstrations. He spoke with pride of being able to cut a deck precisely in the center. As card magicians know, this is a valuable ability because it provides the performer with knowledge of the twenty-sixth card. The "center card," as magicians call it, serves as a valuable key card in endless tricks of the ESP type. Delmore is firmly persuaded, however, that the number of hits in his magic shows exceeds what chance would allow, and he attributes this to genuine psychic abilities. He is especially adept, he assured me, in guessing the next song to be played on the radio.

To include reports of BD's psi powers on a list of the seven best "evidential experiments" is a splendid example of JB's bizarre ability to combine unbounded enthusiasm for dubious research by others with his own ability to conduct well-designed tests. JB actually writes: "Taken on

---

*See "A Subject's Efforts Toward Voluntary Control," by E. F. Kelly and B. K. Kanthamani, in *Journal of Parapsychology,* 36, 1972, pp. 185–187; "Card Experiments with a Special Subject. 1. Single-Card Clairvoyance," by the same authors, ibid; 38, 1974, pp. 16–26; "Awareness of Success in an Exceptional Subject," same authors, ibid; 38, 1974, pp. 356–383; and "On the Relation Between Visual and ESP Confusion Structures in an Exceptional Subject," by Kelly, Kanthamani, I. L. Child, and F. W. Young, in *Journal of the American Society for Psychical Research,* 69, 1975, pp. 1–32.

their own I would regard this series of experiments as, perhaps, the most evidential in the entire parapsychological literature! . . . It is only a pity that [BD] has done nothing further since then."

It is indeed a pity. The 1986 *Bismarck Tribune* interview ended as follows: "Delmore thinks more needs to be done in the field and says maybe some day he'll do more research. But for now, he'll do nothing more with his ability than perhaps guess what song will be played next on the radio." Now here is a splendid research project for Beloff. Surely the large grant by Arthur Koestler to the University of Edinburgh, for parapsychological research, could be drawn upon to finance Delmore's trip to Scotland to see how well he can do, under controlled conditions, in guessing the next radio song. Or does this work only when the psychic is at home or riding in his car?

JB's reluctance to believe that BD, or any other self-proclaimed miracle worker, is capable of deception extends even to the great Spiritualist mediums of the past. No magician, JB is persuaded, can explain how D. D. Home was able to levitate tables, or to float high in the air (always done in near total darkness) and leave a mark on the ceiling to prove he was really up there. (See our exchange of letters about this in my book *The New Age*.) JB is on record as having been thoroughly convinced of the metal-bending powers of Uri Geller, the thoughtography of Ted Serios, and other notorious claims. "It is just possible," he wrote in 1975, "that Geller may prove to be the most gifted all-round psychic subject that there has ever been, not excluding D. D. Home!"

Because JB is always eager to get positive results, his perpetual failures are a great puzzle to his colleagues. They cannot say skepticism biases his research, and of course no one dares suggest that his negative results could be caused by careful controls. They are left with only one possible explanation, which they frequently voice: For some reason, deeply hidden in JB's unconscious, he uses negative PK to bias experiments in the wrong direction!

As we shall see, his famous test of PS is a classic instance of how JB's experimental skill joins his total inability to believe that his expertise has any bearing whatever on his notorious failures.

When JB arrived in Prague, PS's scoring had been dropping so rapidly that MR was seriously concerned over the possibility that his star subject was losing his powers. This became particularly evident in January 1964, when Dr. K. R. Rao, who now heads Rhine's laboratory in Durham, visited Prague to conduct two experiments with PS in cooperation with MR. Both were designed to confirm MR's mental impregnation theory, for which MR had recently been finding so much confirmatory evidence.

As far as I know, the details of Rao's two experiments, both failures, have not been published. JGP, in his monograph on PS, sloughs them off in just one sentence. MR does not mention them in *Hypnosis and ESP*. When I asked him in a letter if he had any information about Rao's tests, especially whether they were successes or failures, he replied that he could not recall ever having had such information. I later obtained access to his unpublished monograph on 1964 testing of PS where I found four pages (26–30) devoted to Rao's experiments. The first one used all white cards on which PS endeavored to impregnate white on one side, green on the other. The cards were sealed in envelopes, which in turn were put inside the usual covers. Results were at chance. The second test used two sets of cards. The cards of one set were white/green, the other set consisted of all-white cards with the names of the two colors written on them. Again, all results were within chance expectation.

After Rao left, and before JB arrived from Scotland, MR tells us in the same typescript that he conducted an experiment in which PS tried to decide, after each call, whether his previous call had been correct. It was another failure. Much later MR says he discovered a "slight negative deviation" in this experiment.

Of course it never occurred to MR that the failures of Rao's test could be attributed to tighter controls. The purpose of JB's visit, as stated in the published paper by MR and JB, was to see whether JB's testing would revive "PS's flagging powers." PS is described as "eagerly looking forward to JB's visit," and MR adds that he maintained a "thoroughly friendly and cooperative attitude" throughout the testing.

The plan of the experiment, on which MR fully agreed, was to use thirty-six targets of cards, but instead of standard green/white cards, the cards would consist of six different kinds to see if PS's scoring would be affected differently by the nature of the cards. The six categories were as follows:

1. Six cards, each bearing a "full-face photo-portrait" of PS on one side, and blank on the other. This was to test PS's ability to identify himself by ESP.

2. Six cards, each blank on one side. The other side had a "full-face photograph, reproduced from a journal of plastic surgery, showing an elderly woman whose face had been partially eaten away by a disease known as *lupus*." This was to see whether PS would use his ESP to react to a horror image.

3. Six cards, each blank on one side. The other side was a "full-length photograph of a recumbent 'pin-up' girl with bare breasts and a bikini taken from the English magazine *Men Only*."* This obviously was to test

---

*I tried to obtain a copy of this picture, thinking it would brighten up the pages of an otherwise dull book. Beloff told me he no longer had a copy, but even if he had one he wouldn't send it because he considered the testing of PS too serious a matter to be treated with frivolity.

how PS would react to an erotic stimulus. We are reminded that PS was a bachelor in his mid-thirties and "rather bashful."

4. Six cards, each blank on one side. On the other side was a reproduction of one of Raphael's paintings of the Madonna with the infant Jesus. PS is called a "devout Catholic." The category was planned to test his ESP reaction to a religious stimulus.

5. Six of the standard green/white cards.

6. Six "joker cards," white on both sides.

All cards, except the jokers, were scored by designating the green sides of the standard cards equivalent to the sides with photographs. The white/white cards obviously could not be scored for hits, but they could be scored, as MR had done in earlier tests, for focusing on specific sides.

I think that anyone, believer or skeptic, would agree that this was an admirably designed experiment. Not only could PS's calls be checked for hits and misses, but variations from category to category might supply valuable new information about how PS's clairvoyance reacted to various stimulants.

JB prepared the targets in Edinburgh. There had been some speculation by skeptics that slight curvatures in cards may have been transmitted to slightly flexible envelopes—a conjecture I consider worthless. To eliminate this unlikely source of sensory information, JB sandwiched the cards between two sheets of stiff plastic material that sold in England under the trade name of "Tufnell." The "sandwiches" were tightly bound together with "strong cloth tape."

A table of random numbers was used by an assistant, outside of JB's presence, to determine the orientations of cards inside each pair of plastic covers. As soon as three cards of a given category were placed "up," the randomizing was stopped and the other three cards were placed "down." This ensured that each category had three up cards and three down cards. After this, all thirty-six sandwiches were mixed together and brought to JB, who coded them by writing labels on the cloth binding.

To further eliminate the possibility that card warping gave sensory cues, cardboard covers were replaced by two "long flattish" boxes made of plywood. Wooden strips divided each box into four compartments in which four sandwiches could be placed side by side in a row. The box was open along one edge to allow for easy insertion and removal of the sandwiches, but once inside they were totally shielded from PS's view. There was no way PS could touch the targets. He simply looked at the top cover of the box, and made his calls from left to right along the hidden compartments. The calls were recorded by MR.

The reason for having two "target cabinets" was so one could be loaded while the subject was still reading the contents of the other. The reloading was done by JB in an adjoining room. "The rate of calling was very brisk," the authors write, "so that progress was determined by the speed at which JB could load and reload the cabinets."

PS was not told the purpose of the experiment—only that "photographs would be used in addition to some green/white cards." He was instructed to call "black" to indicate he was sensing either the green side or the photograph side of a card. He was not told there were white/white jokers.

The experiment had two parts. The first part consisted of forty runs through the thirty-six targets, or 1,440 calls. Using the same sealed targets, this was repeated for Part II, only now PS was told in advance about five categories (the joker cards were not mentioned). He was shown samples of all the photographs and his reactions "duly noted." He was then asked to proceed exactly as before but to "be on the alert for any clairvoyant impression he might receive regarding the identity of the target card." This second part also consisted of 1,440 calls, making a total of 2,880 calls for the entire experiment.

To the astonishment of all three participants, PS scored at chance in all categories. The authors give a table that lists the hits and misses for the five categories on which hits and misses were possible. The joker cards are excluded. The table shows that of the 2,400 calls on the thirty targets capable of being scored, there were 1,197 hits and 1,203 misses. A breakdown by the five categories shows results uniformly at chance for each category.

"No focusing effect was observed as between photo-replicas within a given category," the experimenters conclude, "no sequential trends such as decline effects were apparent, and there was no consistency of calling on the white/white jokers. We may conclude, then, that this experiment had yielded a null result."

In *Hypnosis and ESP,* MR writes: "There was not the slightest doubt that another successful experiment was ahead of us. There seemed to be no reason why it should be otherwise. . . . This was a hard fact which hit us painfully and quite unexpectedly, and which we could not explain at that time. . . . After three years of continued success, this came like thunder from blue skies."

You might suppose that in view of PS's failure with ESP cards, and other variations in targets, MR would have been fearful of JB's changes. But consider the circumstances. He himself had conducted a variety of experiments, all successful, in which colors had been replaced by symbols and words. Moreover, PS had succeeded in impregnating totally blank cards. As for the plastic sheets and the wooden box, why would ESP have a harder time penetrating wood and plastic than two layers of thick cardboard? Besides, had not psi research established that ESP was independent of distance and capable of going through the walls of houses? Unlike the use of ESP cards, which involved five choices, JB's experiment continued to make use of choices between the two sides of a card. From MR's perspective, there was every reason to welcome JB's changes and see them as essentially trivial.

From our perspective, there was every reason to expect the experiment to fail. JB's tight controls offered no possible way for PS to use peek moves, asymmetric marking, or even the imperfection principle. No wonder he made his calls at such a brisk pace. He could not very well refuse to engage in such a test, or to protest against plastic sheets and wooden boxes. Unlike many other psychics, PS never tried to interfere with conditions imposed by experimenters. He went along patiently with any kind of test, always failing when the test did not involve binary choices between the sides of a card, or when controls did not permit him to see or touch targets. On guessing the sides of cards, he usually succeeded either in hitting the colors or displaying focusing effects. Sometimes he scored at chance, on rarer occasions below chance. It would have been inconsistent with his personality to object to JB's new conditions. All he could do was be as affable as usual, appear eager for any new exploration of his fantastic psi powers, make his calls at random (though his black calls slightly exceeded white), and hope for the best.

It never occurred to MR or JB that the experiment's failure could possibly be due to tight controls. Their unbounded confidence in PS's total honesty was unshakable. How then could his failure be explained? "We felt that we could safely exclude any explanation in terms of adverse psychological conditions," the experimenters write in their published paper. "As we said before, the subject entered wholeheartedly into his task and a good-humored, friendly atmosphere prevailed throughout." Two possibilities were considered. Either the modifications by JB had in some mysterious way interfered with PS's powers, or "like many previous high-scorers," PS had "at last reached the end of his tether and was truly 'played out.' "

To test the first possibility, the experimenters decided to go back to the tests on which PS had for so long been successful. Forty green/white cards were used. They were randomized, inserted into the usual cardboard envelopes, which then went into the usual cardboard covers. PS held a pile of covers, making his calls as he passed each cover to MR. "As before, calling was rapid and between sets of trials the subject chatted away gaily in Czech to MR. After the trials were over, however, and PS had gone away, MR remarked that he had observed a peculiar glazed look come over the subject during the later part of the experiment such as he had noticed during successful runs on earlier occasions. MR therefore wrote down in the record book a prediction to the effect that he expected the

Pavel Stepanek (circa 1971)   Dr. Milan Ryzl (circa 1971)

Gaither Pratt (*right*) and J. B. Rhine (circa 1960).

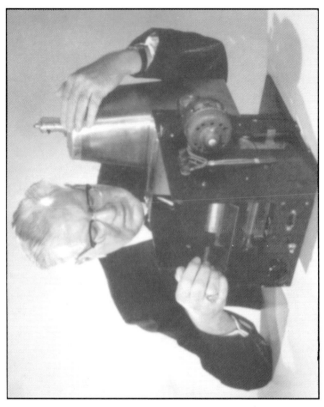

Chester Carlson, one of the nation's most generous benefactors of psi research, shown with an early model of the xerographic dry copier he invented and which made him a multimillionaire. Carlson's funds established the parapsychology laboratory at the University of Virginia, where many tests of Pavel Stepanek were conducted by J. G. Pratt and his associates.

John Beloff

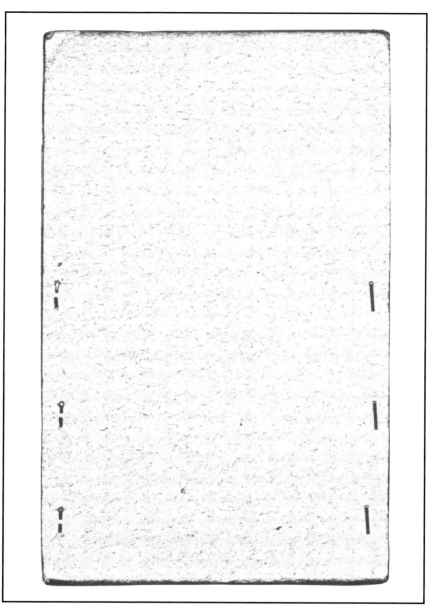

FIG. 1 This is a photocopy I made of a cardboard cover loaned to me by Dr. Ryzl. It is 9″ by 5¾″, made by folding a long strip and stapling the sides. The staples have been put through in opposite directions on the two sides to make the front and back of the cover look the same. Note that the three black spots at the bottom of the cover form a triangle that is easily memorized and seen from a distance of ten feet. The spots are part of the cardboard. Note also that the bottom staple on the right is noticeably out of line with the two above, and that the prongs of the top left staple are crooked. These are two other blemishes that make the side absurdly easy to memorize. (See p. 20.)

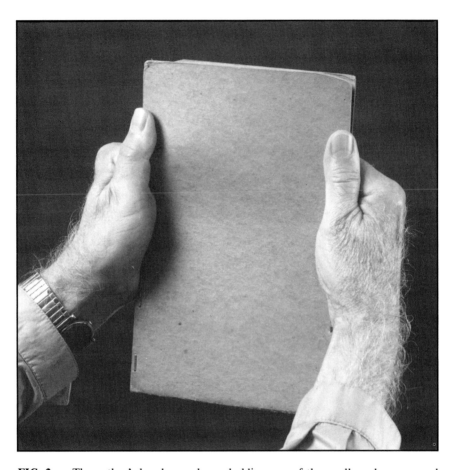

FIG. 2 The author's hands are shown holding one of the cardboard covers used by Pratt for testing Stepanek (see Chapter 8). The forefinger of the left hand has been inserted between the 4½-inch-long flaps. (The insides of the flaps are numbered 5 and 6. The edge of the interior envelope is 2½ inches below the top of the flaps.) The tip of the index finger is exploring the folded edge of the hidden envelope that in turn contains a color card. The right hand is keeping the flaps closed on the side where an observer sits. Of course if the observer is on the left, the right hand makes the move while the left hand closes the flaps. The insertion of the finger is not visible from the front, back, or right side of the cover.

Needless to add, if the only observer is sitting on the far side of the cover, the move is more easily made by the thumb. It is also possible, while holding a cover vertically, for the extreme tips of the forefingers, just above the top staple, to move a flap back about an inch. The flap's movement is invisible from the front, but allows the subject a quick glimpse of the color of a card, or a glimpse of the number at the top edge of an envelope if the card is inside an envelope. (See p. 39.)

FIG. 3   Photographs of two covers used by Pratt in testing Stepanek. The one on the left is number 7/8 (on the inside of each flap); the one on the right is number 5/6. On the 7/8 cover note the three dark spots that form a triangle at the lower left, the black spot between the prongs of the lower right staple (and another spot near it), the crooked bottom prong of the top right staple, and the damaged upper right corner.

On the 5/6 cover observe the two dark spots near the top, the even darker spot in the center of the lower part, the top left staple which is out of line, and the crooked prongs on the top right staple. The upper right corner of the cover is damaged, and there is a circular indentation at top right. The spots are not dirt marks, but permanent parts of the cardboard mottling. Similar blemishes are on the other sides of both covers, making each of the four sides extremely easy to recognize from a distance of many feet. (See p. 92.)

FIG. 4   Two cardboard envelopes (numbered 15/16 and 7/8) that were used by Pratt. Observe that the plastic tape sealing the right side of each envelope has been so carelessly trimmed that a corner projects almost 1/16 of an inch above the folded edge of the cardboard. The point is needle sharp and easily felt by a fingertip. These are examples of asymmetric tactile marks created by whoever prepared the covers. They make it unnecessary for Stepanek to put a mark on either envelope. (See p. 92.)

FIG. 5   A closer look at the top right corner of envelope 15/16 showing the projecting corner of the plastic tape. Note that the folded edge of cardboard is so uneven that with practice it can be identified by feeling its pattern of bumps without even touching the corner of the tape. (See p. 92.)

FIG. 6 This schematic drawing identifies the three participants and shows the aspects of the experimental setup more clearly. Explanation: ABCD = extension of horizontal screen. EFGH = briefcase serving solely as weight to hold ABCD in place. IJ = exposed end of large tray forming lower section of horizontal screen. KL = end of table visible to only JGP and NJ and on which they examined the target after each trial for making independent records. (See p. 194.)

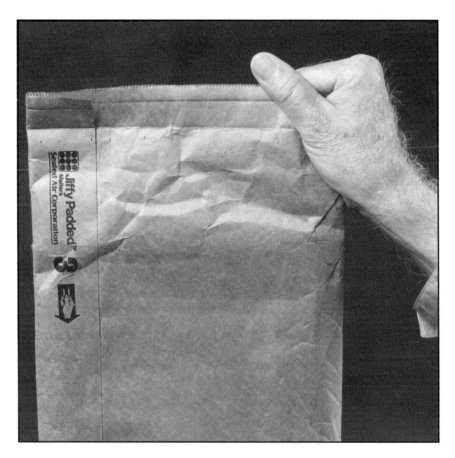

FIG. 7   The author is shown holding a Jiffy bag of the size used in the Series 23 test. The forefinger has been inserted in the opening and is feeling the folded edge of a hidden jacket that comes to within a half-inch of the bag's opening. The jacket contains an envelope that contains a color card. In this test Stepanek showed focusing only on certain sides of the Jiffy bag, and certain sides of the jacket. There was no focusing on envelopes or cards, both of which were beyond the reach of finger contact.

The inserted finger is not visible from the front, back, or right side of the bag. An observer in front assumes the finger is in back of the bag, and an observer in back assumes the finger is in front of the bag. Note also that the wrinkles at the top of the bag make it ridiculously easy to memorize and to recognize from a long distance. (See p. 218.)

subject's ESP ability to be operative at least during the second half of the experiment (i.e., during the last 600 trials)."

As in the previous experiment, a total of 1,200 calls were made. There were 535 hits and 665 misses, a negative deviation of 65. The deviation was –33 for the first 600 calls, and –32 for the last 600. Obviously PS's "glazed look" did not signal success.

"Only one conclusion can be drawn with any assurance," the authors write. "The subject had definitely lost his former ability." But all is not lost. The fact that PS had a significant negative score allowed for the possibility that "PS had not so much lost his ability as lost his *orientation*. In other words, information of a clairvoyant nature was still coming through, but at some stage of the process was being systematically distorted. Unfortunately, as no previous instances of psi-missing had been noted in PS's performance, we were not alerted to this possibility . . . although after [JB's] departure MR, going back to the results of experiments completed shortly before JB arrived, but left unanalyzed, discovered that psi-missing effects *had* figured even in these earlier experiments."

Although the negative deviation in this test may have resulted entirely from chance, it is also possible to account for it in other ways. With a careful experimenter like JB present, PS would have no way of discovering the orientations of any of the green/white cards, but he could have used peeks or asymmetric marking to focus his calls. As we have seen, such focusing produces a wide dispersion of scores which can be either in the direction of hits or misses. It is easy here to overlook the fact that a dispersion in either direction would have made the experiment a "success." Indeed, had PS been lucky in the hit direction, the experiment would have been an even greater success because it would have indicated a return of PS's psi powers.

Unfortunately, as JGP points out in his monograph on PS, the experimenters apparently made no effort to check on focusing. At any rate, they fail to report such an analysis, and the data given does not include a breakdown of calls by envelope sides. That unlucky focusing accounted for PS's negative score is, of course, only a guess. More likely, this was just one of those occasions, which so rarely get published, on which chance produced a lower than average score.

In his unpublished monograph on 1964 testing with PS, MR considers various explanations for the failure of JB's two experiments:

1. The stress on PS caused by working with assistants other than MR. In the monograph (p. 64) MR describes some of these tests. They were made by "less gifted assistants," both during and after the impregnation tests covered here in Chapter 12. These experiments, made without MR being present, involved "scores of thousands" of calls, all directed to obtaining

hits on actual colors rather than on psychic footprints. One assistant was a "lady friend of PS." MR says the tests were informal, monotonous, mechanized, and so dull that he thinks PS lost his desire to try hard. It was during these tests that his ESP showed signs of deterioration, and he began scoring at chance and below chance levels.

MR cites the long-drawn-out effort to obtain the signaling of a 17-letter sentence (see Chapter 4) as another instance of long monotonous testing that may have influenced PS's loss of ESP. However, in *Hypnosis and ESP*, he expresses doubts that monotonous testing was a factor on the grounds that PS had been successful in the past in many long, monotonous periods of testing.

2. PS became mentally confused by experiments in which it was not clear just what he was supposed to do. Should he concentrate on the actual colors, on focusing on envelope sides, on impregnating blank cards, and so on?

3. Beloff introduced too many novel departures: photos instead of color cards, plastic inner covers instead of cardboard, and plywood boxes instead of cardboard outer covers. "All these changes could in themselves be the reason for the experiment's failure."

After JB left, MR designed a series of tests to try to pin down which of the factors above was most responsible for the failure. The first test retained the plastic sheets and the plywood boxes, but replaced the photos with the usual green/white cards. The results were at chance, suggesting that plastic and wood were the disturbing influences.

The second experiment retained the sandwiches and the green/white cards, but the wooden boxes were replaced by the standard cardboard covers. This too produced chance results, although there was evidence of impregnation. The test suggested to MR that the sandwiches could be the chief hindrance to PS's ESP. It is possible, he speculates, that the subject's ESP was unable to penetrate the plastic, even though he could impregnate traces on the plastic. However, he adds, this "does not fit well into the framework of our ideas of the abilities of ESP." I take this to mean that psi research had provided strong evidence of ESP going easily through hard materials.

A more plausible explanation for PS's loss of ESP, MR believes, is that PS had developed "inner doubts" about whether he could use his ESP under the new and rigid conditions imposed by Beloff. From our viewpoint, PS did indeed develop doubts, but they were doubts about how to use his nonparanormal techniques.

To test this "autosuggestion" theory for the loss of PS's powers, MR carried out two more series of experiments: one was "to study the influence of autosuggestion on the subject's performances when altered sandwiches were applied," the other was "to study the influence of autosuggestion on the subject's performances when targets covered with an aluminum foil were used." Both series are covered at length in the monograph (pp. 64-84).

To MR's amazement, these test failed to corroborate the autosuggestion hypothesis. "No basis was then found for the notion that the failure with Dr. Beloff was caused in consequence of autosuggestion. On the contrary, it appears that an ability appeared meanwhile in the subject to manifest ESP even when sandwiches were used."

What was MR's final conclusion? It was a startling one. He decided that PS had been persuaded by JGP on his last visit to Prague, that he should no longer work with MR, but should continue working with JGP. As a consequence, PS was deliberately refusing to use his psi powers! We have already mentioned (Chapter 9) MR's explanation for this refusal, and will return to it again in Chapter 15.

After JB left Prague, and while MR was still brooding over the causes of PS's failure, his first reaction was to try to reactivate PS's abilities. He first thought of going back to training under hypnosis, but "PS was no longer hypnotizable. His ESP was fully under control, and every new training influence was ineffective" (*Hypnosis and ESP,* p. 103).

However, as MR tells us in *Hypnosis and ESP* and in his monograph on 1964 testing, he persisted in daily efforts to get PS back into shape. PS was instructed to keep testing himself at home, under relaxed conditions, and to report back as soon as he found his powers returning. After a while, PS phoned MR to give him the good news. His ESP powers were back and he was now confident of success. MR at once gave him an informal test, using green/white cards inside cardboard envelopes—no covers were used—on which PS scored 46 hits in 60 trials, a huge success rate of more than 76 percent.

Encouraged by this sudden return of PS's ability to hit on actual colors, MR prepared a "confirmatory experiment" using ten white/green cards prepared and sealed by an unnamed assistant who also participated in the experiment. In his monograph (p. 48ff.) MR refers to the assistant throughout as "he," but in *Hypnosis and ESP* (p. 103) the assistant is called "she." PS scored 1,114 hits out of 2,000 calls, a success rate of .55+. There were focusing effects, though less strong than on previous tests.

This return of PS's powers proved, as we shall see, to be temporary, but by the end of 1964 PS had convinced MR that he was again capable of scoring high on the actual colors of cards, and in "cognizing the mental impregnation sticking to the card (i.e., the past call to the given target). Yet the subject for the time being is not able consciously to direct his ESP ability exclusively to one or to the other of both alternatives. His ESP performance is sort of a mixture of the manifestations of both these aspects."

I have been quoting from MR's monograph on the 1964 testing of PS. In *Hypnosis and ESP* he writes: "Now the time was ready to invite new foreign visitors to Prague to witness PS's revived talents." The first of these new tests by outsiders is the topic of our next chapter.

Chapter 14

Prague, 1964

DATE: September 1964
PLACE: MR's apartment in Prague
PAPER: "A Confirmatory ESP Test with Stepanek." Milan Ryzl, John Freeman, and B. K. Kanthamani, in the *Journal of Parapsychology,* 29 (June 1965), pp. 89–95.

In September 1964 two researchers from Rhine's Institute for Parapsychology, at Durham, North Carolina, arrived in Prague to test PS. They were John Freeman (now deceased), of the United States, and B. K. Kanthamani, an East Indian parapsychologist who continues to be on the staff of the Durham institute. As we learned in the previous chapter, the failure of Beloff's experiment had been an unexpected, crushing blow, and MR had also been obtaining poor results from assistants to whom he had delegated work with PS. Freeman and Kanthamani mention "insignificant results in some of the unpublished work carried out by two of Ryzl's assistants." On the other hand, as also reported in the previous chapter, after PS worked on his ESP alone at home, his powers seemingly revived. The purpose of the visit by Freeman and Kanthamani was to confirm this revival, and to determine whether PS's clairvoyance would once more manifest itself when he worked with outsiders.

The two researchers adopted essentially the same protocols that had been used in 1963 by the visiting Dutch committee (see Chapter 8). The targets were ten green/white cards in sealed and coded envelopes, in turn placed inside the customary cardboard covers. The covers are described as made of heavy cardboard. There is no description of the envelopes, but

Kanthamani told me in a letter that Ryzl had supplied the target material, and that cards, envelopes, and covers were the same as those he had used in earlier research. She could not recall how the envelopes were sealed.

The targets were prepared in Ryzl's apartment, out of PS's sight. We are told that at the start of the first session Kanthamani "inserted each of the 10 cards in separate envelopes." Presumably the cards were randomized as to which side was up before they were inserted, but nothing is said about how this was done. I asked Kanthamani by letter which of the following three procedures she followed:

1. Five envelopes were inserted green side up, and five white side up.
2. All envelopes were put in covers with the same color up.
3. A randomizing procedure of some sort was used to determine which color was up in each envelope.

She could not recall which procedure she adopted. She said she would be hesitant to try to pull any details from her memory.

After sealing the open ends of envelopes, presumably with cloth tape, Kanthamani shuffled the envelopes and turned some of them over. The envelopes were again shuffled by Freeman before he labeled them on both sides and put them into unlabeled covers. Between each run of ten calls, the envelopes were removed from the covers and their code numbers recorded opposite each call. The covers and envelopes were placed on a chair, at the side of the table opposite where PS sat and out of his sight. The envelopes were shuffled, "turning some of them over," and replaced in the covers. The covers were then handed to PS for the next run. The envelopes remained sealed until the end of the day's session.

The experiment was divided into two sessions of 1,000 calls each. The first session occupied one afternoon; the second, another afternoon two days later. MR played no role in preparing the targets, nor was he present during the calling or recording. We are not told whether he stayed in his apartment throughout each session. I asked him about this. He replied that the situation was similar to what happens when you invite friends to a party, then leave them alone in a room. You may call upon them, or they may call upon you, but most of the time they remain alone in the room. If necessary, you may even leave the house for a while. The paper tells us that each afternoon Ryzl "came into the room with coffee for a short break." At the close of each session he helped in opening the envelopes and checking the cards to determine hits and misses on colors.

Nothing is said about checking envelopes for focusing. I find this mystifying because at this stage of the testing both MR and JGP looked upon focusing as the most remarkable of PS's psi talents. Why were the data not analyzed for focusing? Because envelopes were labeled, such an analysis would have been easy to make. Kanthamani told me this was not done because the main point of the test was to determine overall scoring on colors. The paper provides no data about how calls were distributed on the twenty sides of the envelopes. Unfortunately, this data seems not to have survived. At any rate, Kanthamani does not have the data, and Freeman is no longer living. She said she does not know whether Ryzl or anyone else later checked the data for focusing.

PS sat at a table, holding the stack of covers in his left hand, open ends away from him. We are told that he picked up each cover with his right hand, made his call, then placed the cover on the table. Of the 2,000 calls he obtained 1,158 hits for a success score of .579. On the first thousand calls he had 555 hits (score: .555). On the second thousand calls there were 603 hits (score: .603).

The authors admit that "allowing the subject to touch the covers containing the cards is a rather elementary way of testing." To justify this, they point out that on some previously published experiments PS did not touch the covers at all. In those tests, they write, the targets were sometimes hidden "by a large piece of cardboard resting on the subject's knees," and at other times MR held targets in front of PS for his calls. In view of the significant results in those earlier no-touch tests, one wonders why the experimenters did not again adopt a no-touch precaution. Here is how they explain this loosening of controls: "Since PS has also been able to score significantly without handling the cards, tactile impressions need not be considered as the basis of his success in the present experiment."

Test conditions, we are told, were "friendly and informal." PS chatted and smoked constantly, but the paper is brief and significant details are lacking. Nothing is said about taking precautions to guard the targets at all times before, during, and after each session. When I asked Kanthamani if she could be positive that PS was never left alone with the targets, she replied that she did not "think" he was. She and Freeman did not stay in Ryzl's apartment during the three-day span of testing. Kanthamani said she did not take the targets with her after the first session, and she cannot recall whether Freeman took them or whether he left them in Ryzl's apartment.

We are told that PS held the stack of covers in his left hand, open ends away from him. He picked up each cover with his right hand, made his call, then put the cover on the table. If this is an accurate description, it does not eliminate either a peek move or a tactile-mark move. In my description of how the peek move can be made by forefingers (see Chapter 1), I pointed out that it was not essential to do the flicking of the flap with both fingers. One finger can manage it just as easily, using only the fingernail to move the flap. However, if two observers are sitting opposite, such a move is more difficult to conceal than it is with one observer, because each observer sees the cover from a slightly different angle. My best conjecture, which could be totally wrong, is that while PS was holding and calling a cover he made the tactile move with his left hand on the top cover of the stack he was holding. The calling of a cover in his right hand would provide ideal misdirection for the move. For all we know, the stack of covers in PS's left hand may have been below the table top and outside the visual range of the two observers. (For details on the tactile moves, see Chapter 8.)

Here is one of many possible scenarios. At the start of the first session PS marked and tracked three of the ten envelopes. If he focused his calls consistently on all six sides, he had a fifty-fifty chance of being correct on at least two envelopes. An even split is not possible, and there is a probability of $1/8$ that all three choices will be right. If only two are correct, the expected score is .60. His actual score was about .58. This suggests that his calls were not perfectly consistent.

Focusing tends, as we have seen, to produce a wide dispersion of scores in either a positive or negative direction. Had PS been wrong on two or all three envelopes, his score would have been significant evidence of psi-missing. As we saw in Chapter 13, this is what happened in Beloff's second test, and it was cited as an instance of paranormal missing. As we shall see in Chapter 18, another strongly negative score (.561) was interpreted as paranormal missing. Other instances of psi-missing are in the published literature, and who knows how many such instances were never published?

The authors write: "After the first session was completed, PS remained in the room until all the data had been checked. He was quite pleased when the results showed a significantly positive deviation, and he left MR's home noticeably elated. At the outset of the second session he appeared to be much more cheerful and seemed to be more confident of his calls."

From my perspective I take this to mean that PS did not know, until the checking, whether he had been lucky or unlucky in his focusing. He was understandably elated to learn that the focusing showed psi-hitting rather than psi-missing.

We are not told whether the cards remained sealed in the same envelopes for the second session, or whether at the start of this session the cards were removed, shuffled, and some turned over before they went back into the envelopes or perhaps into fresh envelopes. Kanthamani's memory is not clear on this point, though she thinks that the cards were removed and randomized for the second session. If the envelopes were simply resealed after the colors were checked, without altering the positions or orientations of cards, then PS's task at the second session would be simple. He would merely repeat his correct calls on two envelopes, and switch his call on the third envelope if it had previously been wrong. Consistent calling on all three would raise his expected score to .65. His actual score was about .60.

Put yourself in the position of the two researchers. Why would it be necessary to remove all the cards at the start of the second session and randomize them? The envelopes would be shuffled, some turned, and inserted into covers where they would be completely invisible. Changing the orientations of cards inside envelopes would seem completely unnecessary.

It is possible that at the beginning of the second session Kanthamani pulled the cards halfway out of the envelopes and turned the envelopes so all the cards were green on top. She then removed the cards, shuffled them, and returned them green side up. This, of course, would leave the orientations of the cards unchanged with respect to asymmetric markings on the envelopes.

Let's assume that the old envelopes were discarded, and the cards placed in fresh envelopes at the start of the second session. If the fresh envelopes were ones that Ryzl had used in earlier testing, some of them may have been previously marked. If they were brand new envelopes, then of course new markings would be required. PS would again, according to our scenario, make consistent calls on the six marked sides. The probability of positive scoring on both sessions is 1/4, which certainly is not outside the bounds of chance. Remember, too, that had he scored negatively both times the experiment would have been hailed as significant psi-missing. If he scored positively on one session, and negatively on the other, it would have been considered psi-hitting on one, psi-missing on the other.

Here we see once more how extremely valuable it would have been if records had been published of how calls were distributed on the twenty sides of the envelopes. If our conjectures are close to being right, we would expect extreme focusing on a few envelopes with chance calling on the others.

Our scenario assumes that at no time was PS left alone with the targets. We know that each session lasted about six hours, with a coffee break in the middle. After each run of ten calls, the envelopes were taken from the covers so their top numbers could be recorded beside a record of calls. There were a hundred runs during each session. This means there were a hundred occasions on which uncovered envelopes were on the table where PS sat. Before the next run, the experimenters put the envelopes and covers on a chair opposite PS and did their randomizing of envelopes "out of the subject's sight." The covers were then stacked on the table for the next run.

Was there a time, during one of the hundred occasions between runs, when both experimenters left the room? Kanthamani thinks this never occurred, but without explicit protocols for target guarding, how trustworthy is her memory about events of almost 25 years earlier? Not suspecting asymmetric tactile marking, the experimenters would see no way that PS could boost his score even if he opened some of the envelopes and resealed them. Perhaps one of them went to the bathroom, and the other to the kitchen for a drink of water. Perhaps they both went to where Ryzl was working to confer with him about something or to report on how the experiment was progressing. Such trivial events are the sort that would quickly fade from their memories.

If PS had been left alone with the targets, it would take only a few moments to peel back tape and reverse one or two cards if necessary to assure that his focusing was in a positive direction. If this did not occur, then our scenario must rely on the assumption that PS was either lucky in the sense of flipping heads twice, or lucky the first time and repeated his focusing the second time. Unless told otherwise, PS would assume that the envelopes would remain sealed for the second session. Even if he suspected that their orientations would be randomized, he would have nothing to lose by repeating his calls on the marked envelopes, taking advantage of his knowledge (obtained during the first checking) of how their cards were oriented.

All this is, of course, mere guessing and could be entirely off the mark. PS may have exhibited a genuine renewal of his lost ESP. What we *can* say with assurance is that the extraordinary results of this experiment are reported with an extraordinary lack of significant information. Here are the paper's leading lapses:

1. We are not told how Kanthamani randomized cards at the start of each session.

2. We are not told that protocols included a careful guarding of targets at all times.

3. We are not told how calls were distributed on the twenty sides of envelopes.

4. No analysis of focusing patterns was made.

5. We are not told if fresh envelopes were used for the second session, or whether there was a new randomizing of card orientations.

6. No good reason is given for allowing PS to handle covers while he called.

A second confirmation of the renewal of PS's flagging powers was made by another visitor to Prague. It is our next chapter's topic.

Chapter 15

Prague, 1964

DATE: September 1964
PLACE: MR's apartment in Prague
PAPER: "An Experiment in Duplicate Calling with Stepanek."
Milan Ryzl and Soji Otani, in the *Journal of Parapsychology*, 31 (March 1967), pp. 19–28.

A few days after the experiment discussed in the previous chapter, Soji Otani, identified as an assistant professor of psychology from Tokyo (no university is named), visited Prague to conduct an almost identical experiment with PS. It had two aims:

1. To corroborate the renewal of PS's ability to score high on the actual colors of cards.

2. To check on PS's tendency, as frequently observed in earlier tests, to repeat his previous call on the same face of a target card (or what amounts to the same thing, the same side of an envelope) even though the cards were constantly being randomized as to their covers and orientations inside the covers. Otani gives an example. A given envelope side could have, as a typical series of consecutive calls: *GGGGWWWWGGGG*. In other words, identical calls would tend to bunch together far more often than they bunch in a random sequence of heads and tails obtained by tossing a coin. As we have seen, MR viewed this as a mental impregnation effect. PS would put on the card (or envelope) a psychic "footprint" which would become strengthened each time he made the same call, but would evaporate when he made a different call, to be replaced by a footprint of the opposite sort.

The targets of Otani's experiment were ten green/white cards, sealed inside envelopes that in turn were inside cardboard covers. As in the previous paper, the envelopes are not described. Presumably they too were of opaque cardboard, sealed along the open edge with cloth tape. The procedure was exactly as before. The test had two parts, each of a thousand calls (100 runs through ten covers). Between runs the envelopes were randomized by shuffling, turning some over, and replacing them in the covers. As was customary, the covers were open at one end, and the envelopes were coded on both sides. The randomizing was done in another room by one of the experimenters (we are not told who) while the other sat at the table with PS and recorded his calls and also the label on top of each called envelope. The experiment was completed in a single day (September 17). The first part, consisting of 1,000 calls, took place in the morning. After a lunch break, the second part, another 1,000 calls, took place in the afternoon.

As in the prior test, PS held the stack of ten covers, picked up one cover at a time, made his call, then put the cover on the table where he sat. During the first session he scored 574 hits—a success rate of .574. Curiously, as in the previous test he did better on the second session with 613 hits—a score of .613. His overall score—1,187 hits out of 2,000—gave him a success rate of .5935.

In the morning session PS was asked to concentrate solely on card colors. In the afternoon he was asked to forget about the colors and concentrate instead on impregnation; that is, on repeating for each envelope side his previous call on that same side. However, as the authors recognize, the two tasks are not independent. For example, if PS had learned by ESP that the top color of a particular card was green, he might continue to use ESP to call it green. If he did this every time, he would have what the authors call a "perfect score for duplicate calls." When the authors made adjustments for this interlocking of the two tasks, they found that there was no significant change in results from the first to the second part of the experiment. Indeed, PS's score on the actual colors went *up* during the second half of the test. They conclude that the test failed to provide evidence for impregnation as an effect acting independently of ESP on the actual colors. They also observe that no "fatigue factor" was present, since PS did even better in the afternoon than in the morning.

My best conjecture is the same as for the previous chapter. Because PS was allowed to handle each cover, he could have selected a few envelopes for asymmetric marking, concentrating his calls on both sides, while mixing a few calls of the wrong sort into the right ones. The envelopes were not opened and the calls analyzed until the end of the day. This would mean that PS needed only *one* occasion to open the envelopes he had marked, adjust any cards that needed turning, and reseal.

Did he have an opportunity to do this? It is impossible to know. It seems unlikely that MR would remain in the sitting room throughout the entire day. Nothing is said about who observed the calling, but MR has informed me that it was Otani alone. It seems likely that MR, as in the previous experiment, spent the day working in another room, interrupted only when Otani brought him covers for randomizing.*

Again, try to put yourself in Otani's place. Like MR he had complete confidence in PS's honesty. Moreover, he would not be able to see how PS could profit even if he secretly opened a few envelopes. Because the envelopes were periodically shuffled and turned, what good would it do PS if he knew the orientations of *all* the cards inside their envelopes? There must have been a time, before the day was over, when Otani excused himself to go to the bathroom. If he took the precaution of carrying all the covers with him, the authors do not tell us so. I find it plausible that he did not, and that in the few moments PS was alone with the targets, he had time to adjust a few cards (if necessary) in the few envelopes he was tracking. It is worth adding that hearing the toilet flush would be a cue to PS that Otani was about to return.

If this guess is correct, PS's calls would show strong focusing on just a few of the envelopes, perhaps on both sides, perhaps on only one side. Again, for reasons hard to fathom, the paper gives no data on how the calls were distributed on the envelope sides, although the experimenters had those records.

This was the last significant experiment before PS again seemed to lose his ESP powers. MR devotes several pages (104–107) of *Hypnosis and ESP* to explaining why. It is a fascinating but sad story. Headed "End of Cooperation," MR begins by writing: "The revival of PS's ESP ability in the fall of 1964 was destined to be of short duration only. Soon after the departure of Mr. Otani, his performance grew unstable again, and, therefore, we could not pursue any new signficant research project."

MR goes on to say that at first nothing seemed to change about PS except his performance. He continued to attend experiments regularly, for which he continued to receive payment. He "behaved in his usual friendly

---

*After obtaining Otani's Tokyo address, I wrote to him on July 7, 1988, to ask if he would be willing to answer a few questions about his experiment with PS. There was no reply. I wrote again on September 4. Again no reply. A third letter (September 22) raised three questions: Did the data for his test still exist? If so, could it be analyzed for focusing effects? Did Ryzl witness the calling, or did he work in another room to which you took covers for randomizing? This produced an answer (October 2) in which Otani said he could not respond to my questions until he checked his records, but he was not sure where he had stored them. He promised to get back to me as soon as possible. I never heard from him again. I mention this only because parapsychologists often accuse their critics of failing to contact them for accurate information.

way." To provide him with additional income, at a time when he much needed it, MR even gave him some clerical jobs.

As the experiments continued to fail MR began to notice slight changes in PS's behavior. He started to name colors in a "slovenly, haphazard way, without due attention to his task." He turned "into a kind of prima donna." It seemed to MR that PS was deliberately supplying his ESP "in doses" so that he would remain "interesting enough to encourage the continuation of experiments, but refusing to give any results of value."

In one informal test PS had a hit rate of .697, but when it was followed by a controlled test the score dropped to chance. On another occasion, he scored .76 in an uncontrolled exploratory test, but again the score dropped to chance when the test was followed by a formal experiment. The thought that the controls MR had perhaps now learned to impose in formal testing may have caused the drop in scores never crossed MR's mind. Nor did it at first occur to MR that his star subject may have been deliberately holding back his powers in the formal testing. No details of these failed tests, by the way, are provided.

MR's first thought was that PS might be afraid his rising fame would come "into the focus of unwelcome attention" by Czech authorities. However, MR discarded this explanation on the basis of what he later learned from "mutual friends, and other indications from events of a too private nature to be reported here."

MR's final conclusion, forcibly stated in his book, is that "PS had developed a definitely hostile attitude toward the author—which he had succeeded for years to conceal. What the reason for this hostility was could only be guessed. The most probable explanation is that he grew too self-conscious and overproud of his ESP ability, and imagined that his contribution was not sufficiently rewarded (in terms of fame as well as in terms of finance)."

MR goes on to say that PS, throughout all his testing, "received a regular remuneration for his cooperation, which was very good in Czechoslovakian standards. But as a matter of principle I insisted that he should conceive of his ESP ability as a gift which should be placed to the service of scientific research and not commercially exploited."

> Apparently this conception was not realistic enough, since ESP is subject to the same laws of supply and demand as anything on the market. PS's ability was too unique, and the demand for a person with ESP too great. In his contacts with foreign parapsychologists, PS realized that cooperation with them could bring him advantages which the author was unable to offer him at that time. And since he had learned long ago how to use his ESP independently, he felt that he could, henceforth, use it entirely

according to his own discretion. So he was hiding his hostility, making his own plans, and continued attending the author's experiments as if nothing had happened. Externally, there was no change in his behavior; but internally, he had no more any desire to bring his ESP in operation in these experiments.* Finally, in October, 1966, PS informed the author of his decision to stop cooperation with him entirely and to cooperate with other investigators instead. This is the end of the history of PS as MR's ESP subject.

Later on, PS's ESP ability reappeared again, and he continued to give (with changing success) the former type of ESP performance in experiments with other researchers with whom cooperation was more desirable for him.

The asterisk refers to a footnote in which MR writes: "I am in possession of PS's statement, dated September 9, 1966, in which he states: '[Mr. X] told me that in his opinion it would be better for our results if I discontinued experiments with Dr. Ryzl and that I should experiment only with him. I have promised [it]. . . . [He] told me also that in case the quality of my performance would be permanently high, he could consider my coming to visit [him in the United States] at some future time.' "

In correspondence, MR told me that the Mr. X of this footnote was Joseph Gaither Pratt. That PS, eager for higher pay and fame, would choose to stop working with the man who had discovered and trained him, and who had brought him his initial fame, is worth emphasizing for the light it throws on PS's character and motives.

I have been told by parapsychologists, totally convinced of PS's honesty, that he would have had no motive for boosting his scores by nonparanormal means. On the contrary, he had two strong motives. His growing fame around the world as a psychic was the one colorful episode in what otherwise was a dull, unproductive life. Moreover, he continued to be poor, and the steady income from those who tested him was not something he would want to terminate. I find MR's diagnosis convincing. PS saw an opportunity to make even more money, to become even more famous, by switching his allegiance from MR, an obscure Czech parapsychologist, to Dr. Rhine's noted assistant. As we learned in Chapter 9, MR became convinced that at this time PS deliberately stopped scoring positively in tests with him, as he had once urged PS to do with JGP.

Whatever the reasons, PS abandoned MR completely. The rest of our book will deal entirely with JGP's testing of PS, starting in 1966 and continuing for about five years until PS again lost his psi abilities. So far as I have been able to learn, he has not been tested since.

Chapter 16

Prague, 1966

DATE: July 1966
PLACE: Miss R's apartment in Prague
PAPER: "Further Significant ESP Results from Pavel Stepanek and Findings Bearing on the Focusing Effect." J. G. Pratt, in the *Journal of the American Society for Psychical Research,* 61 (April 1967), pp. 95-119.

From now on the career of Pavel Stepanek is in the hands of Joseph Gaither Pratt (1910-1979), or Gaither, as his friends called him. Because PS's reputation as a psychic rests mainly on JGP's experiments with him, it seems appropriate to pause for a brief account of JGP's life and personality.

Pratt was born on a farm near Winston-Salem, North Carolina. He had three brothers and six sisters. His parents were Methodists, and as a young man JGP seriously considered a career as a Methodist minister. In later years he abandoned his Christian beliefs to affiliate with a Unitarian church in Charlottesville. Jürgen Keil, in his essay on JGP in a book he edited. (*Gaither Pratt: A Life for Parapsychology,* McFarland, 1987—the chief source for what I write here) gives his opinion that JGP had "no strong expectations about his personal survival of death. He had great respect, though, for research on the survival question."

Shortly before his death Pratt set the combination of a padlock so it could be opened only by knowing three two-digit numbers that he had selected from a table of random digits. He memorized the combination by coding it into a six-word mnemonic sentence. This was done in his head. Nothing was written down, nor did he tell anyone the key. Each year he would lock himself in his office and silently test his memory by opening the padlock. He challenged anyone to discover the key by telepathy, and in 1975 he wrote: "In the event that I find myself surviving death, I intend to communicate the sentence that will open my lock. If I succeed, that will be evidence that I have survived." At the time I type this (1989), the lock remains unopened.

JGP graduated from Duke University in 1931 and later obtained his doctorate there. He was on the research staff of Rhine's laboratory at Duke from 1937 through 1961. More than a hundred papers bear his name as author or collaborator, and he wrote eight books about parapsychology. During World War II his career was set aside for four years of service in the Navy. In 1970 he and his colleague Jürgen Keil (we will consider their work in later chapters) received parapsychology's McDougall Award for their testing of PS.

Pratt's break with Rhine in 1963 stunned the psi community. For twenty-five years PS had faithfully served Rhine as his man Friday, obeying every command, and never disagreeing with Rhine's decisions or pronouncements. A friend of both men described JGP (in a private phone conversation) as a "masochist" in his relationship with Rhine.

Keil, in the book he edited on Pratt, paints an unflattering portrait of Rhine as a harsh autocrat with an inflated ego:

> For many years Gaither Pratt loyally helped to build and maintain a picture of Rhine as the great man, assisted by lesser mortals like himself. When Gaither Pratt left the Duke Laboratory in the 1960s he was over 50 and had worked for Rhine for more than a quarter of a century. During long periods they had daily discussions related to the Laboratory and to parapsychology in general, yet Gaither Pratt was never invited to address Rhine by his first name and he never succeeded in initiating such a move.

When the day approached for Rhine to retire, it was widely expected by most workers in his laboratory, including JGP himself, that Rhine would name JGP as his successor. But tensions between the two men had been surfacing. JGP's wife Ruth had become openly hostile to Rhine, and he had reciprocated the hostility. In addition, JGP was convinced that the laboratory would have a brighter future if it would reaffiliate with Duke University—not with the psychology department (which never had any respect for Rhine), but with the philosophy department. He had even started quiet overtures in that direction. But Rhine, whose laboratory was now heavily funded by wealthy patrons, wanted to preserve total control. He was fearful that his organization would become dominated by any university willing to accept it. As Ian Stevenson puts it in the book edited by Keil: "Gaither had decided that J. B. Rhine was flying his airplane in the wrong direction—away from universities instead toward them—and Gaither jumped out of the airplane. He did this and opened his parachute without knowing where he might land."

It would be more accurate to say that JGP was pushed out of the plane. Rhine established his Foundation for Research into the Nature of Man (FRNM), of which his laboratory became a part, and made his daughter the temporary head. A few years later he groomed a young parapsychologist on his staff, Walter Levy, to be his successor. Levy's promising career came to an inglorious end when his associates caught him flagrantly cheating.

In 1965 JGP was rescued by Chester F. Carlson, one of the nation's top funders of psi research. Born in Seattle in 1906, the son of an itinerant barber, Carlson obtained a bachelor's degree in physics at Caltech, and later was licensed as a patent attorney. After being fired from Bell Laboratories, he began an intensive study of photocopying processes, and in 1937, in a makeshift laboratory at his home in Astoria, New York, he invented xerography. This was the dry electronic process that revolutionized photocopying around the world. It led to the establishment of the Xerox corporation and made Carlson a multimillionaire. When he died in 1968, of a heart attack in a Manhattan movie theater, he was sixty-two and living in Pittsford, the suburb of Rochester where Xerox is headquartered.

Tributes to Carlson by his wife and by four parapsychologists (Gertrude Schmeidler, Gardner Murphy, Ian Stevenson, and Karlis Osis) appeared in the *Proceedings of the ASPR* (28, May 1969) and is available from the American Society for Psychical Research as a booklet. The former Dorris Hudgins, Carlson's second wife, was and is a passionate believer in reincarnation, Hindu mysticism, and psychic phenomena. "Looking back," she declares, "it seems to me as though I were 'used' as an instrument to draw my husband into the field of parapsychology." It started, she relates, with a series of paranormal events in their home. She began to hear "clairaudiently" the names of persons and places, and to see images of persons and events. On one occasion when her husband was trying to produce a paranormal sound, they both heard a noise like that of a paper bag bursting after being filled with air. The two began to have similar dreams on the same night. One day she heard the word "Lilliput" spoken. Six weeks later, at a Toronto hotel, she found on sale a magazine called *Lilliput*. Inside was a story about a man and woman who had simultaneous dreams.

It is hard to know the extent to which Carlson shared his wife's strong beliefs, but according to Stevenson (in a tribute to Carlson that appeared in the *JASPR,* 63, 1969, pp. 115-122), Carlson did believe in reincarnation and was fascinated by Zen Buddhism and the Hindu Vedantic tradition.

On many occasions, Stevenson writes, he heard Carlson recite as grace before dinner a passage from the Bhagavad Gita that is directed toward Brahman. His funeral service, at his wish, was a Vedanta ritual, and a Zen monk spoke at the memorial service held later in Rochester.

All who knew Carlson speak of him as shy, gentle, kind, and modest, with a reverence for life strong enough to include insects. Osis tells us that Carlson wept when he attended *Man of La Mancha* and heard "The Impossible Dream." Inventing xerography had been an impossible dream. Osis thinks Carlson's second impossible dream was helping parapsychology find firm empirical support for life after death. Carlson provided funds for a revived ASPR in 1962 and was a lifelong member of its board of trustees. He also gave liberally to the United Nations Society and to Robert Hutchins's Center for the Study of Democratic Institutions. Stevenson calls him the "greatest benefactor [of psi research] of recent years or perhaps of any time."

A professor of psychiatry at the University of Virginia, Stevenson is the world's leading researcher on evidence for reincarnation. It was Carlson who established a parapsychology division in the University of Virginia's department of psychiatry and made Stevenson its head. After Rhine dumped JGP, Carlson offered additional funds to the university's laboratory if it would hire JGP. Stevenson readily agreed, and soon obtained JGP's appointment to the Department of Psychiatry, of which he (Stevenson) was then chairman. Until that time JGP's papers on PS had appeared in Rhine's journal. Henceforth they would appear in the *Journal of the ASPR.*

JGP believed in every aspect of psi—poltergeists, the psi powers of Nina Kulagina in Russia, ESP, PK, precognition, metal bending, and animal psi. He was convinced that homing pigeons navigated by ESP. For many years he raised such pigeons, studied them, and wrote about them. His paper with Stevenson on their investigation of Ted Serios, the Chicago bellhop who projected photographs from his memory onto Polaroid film, is reprinted in *Gaither Pratt.*

This paper must be read to be believed. Ted's simple method of producing Polaroid pictures by secretly palming an optical device with transparencies into his "gismo" (a rolled-up piece of black paper that he held in front of the Polaroid camera lens) had been fully exposed by Charles Reynolds and David Eisendrath.* It is hard to comprehend the mind-set a of para-

---

*"An Amazing Weekend with the Amazing Ted Serios," Charles Reynolds and David B. Eisendrath, Jr., in *Popular Photography,* 61, October 1967, pp. 81ff. Reynolds is a skilled magician and one of the world's leading designers of stage illusions. The late David Eisendrath (he died in 1988) was a well-known photographer and also an amateur magician. Persi Diaconis, another knowledgeable magician who is now a noted Harvard mathematician, accompanied Reynolds and Eisendrath to assist in the investigation. The report is carefully worded to avoid threatened legal action by Ted's mentor, Jule Eisenbud. Ted's PK powers vanished after the investigation and have not returned since. Eisenbud's *World of Ted Serios*

psychologist who, after this was published, could still accept Ted's "thoughtography" as genuine.* Stevenson and Pratt sit on the fence in their paper, one of the most naive ever to appear in the *JASPR,* but on page 194 of *Gaither Pratt,* Stevenson discloses that "both Gaither and I privately believed that Ted was producing his effects on the photographic film by paranormal means; but we also both realized that we had not demonstrated that conclusively, Unfortunately, Ted lost his ability before we reached the decisive experiment in this respect, and our report of 1968 had to be appropriately guarded in the conclusions we published." John Beloff informed me by letter (1988) that neither Pratt nor Stevenson ever wavered in their belief that Ted was genuine. He said he had met Stevenson in London in October 1988 and Stevenson assured him that he knew of no reason to change his mind on this score.

Stevenson goes on (in *Gaither Pratt*) to tell how much Pratt brooded over Ted's outrageous claims. JGP was then working with Jule Eisenbud, who had written a book about Ted, but their investigations were cut short by JGP's sudden death in 1979. Stevenson completed their report on this project. It ran in the *JASPR* in 1981 (vol. 75, pp. 144-153) under the title "Distortions in the Photographs of Ted Serios" and the byline of Eisenbud, Pratt, and Stevenson. It was JGP's last published paper.

Very few parapsychologists today take thoughtography seriously. Until the end, however, JGP and Ted remained (in Stevenson's words) "attached in warm friendship." When JGP died, Ted wrote to Stevenson: "God bless Dr. Pratt. . . . I shall miss him." Let me add that any parapsychologist capable of supposing that Ted is not a charlatan is incapable, in my opinion, of supposing any self-styled psychic a charlatan unless there is a smoking gun and a full confession. Even then history has shown that true believers are capable of dismissing both smoking guns and confessions as unconvincing.

Almost all his associates seemed to have liked JGP, not least because of his sense of humor. We learn in *Gaither Pratt* that he could do a "very convincing" imitation of Stan Laurel, that he was fond of making jokes,

---

(Morrow, 1967) has become an undisputed classic of gullibility and wild pseudoscience. For more on Ted and the exposure of his technique, see my *Science: Good, Bad and Bogus* (Prometheus, 1981), especially Chapter 12.

*Parapsychologists who continue to defend Serios—John Beloff for example—argue that Ted would have been incapable of making the optical device constructed by Eisendrath and shown to be capable of producing all of Ted's pictures. But it was not necessary for Ted to make one. On sale at the time throughout the United States were tiny plastic viewers, attached to key chains, through which one could peek to see an unclothed woman. Any transparency, substituted for the pin-up, would produce a "thought" photograph on Polaroid film when the device was inside Ted's gismo. The gismo had no conceivable purpose except to conceal the device while light from the Polaroid flash bounced off Ted's face and clothing to go through the gismo and the camera's lens.

and that in Prague, "during pauses in the card-calling" of PS, he would entertain those present with "relaxing melodies on his mouth organ." After his death, PS wrote to Stevenson: "We could always believe each other, we always could say [to] each other everything what we think, what we feel. . . . He always was so modest in his personal needs, but very great in his spiritual qualities and opinions."

At about the same time that Rhine was dumping Pratt, PS was dumping Ryzl. JGP writes in the paper discussed in this chapter:

> After my first visit to Prague in late 1963, I had no expectation of returning there for further work with PS. In February of 1964 I received a friendly letter from PS expressing a wish that we should keep in touch with each other by correspondence. I welcomed this idea first of all because of the bonds of friendship we had formed during my three visits to Prague. Also I wanted to encourage PS to continue to do well as a subject in any ESP tests with Dr. Ryzl and other investigators. I especially emphasized that he might be the first to prove that an outstanding subject need never lose his ability to succeed in ESP experiments.
>
> For a short period during the late summer of 1964, a simple daily test of ESP at a distance was attempted between Prague and Charlottesville with the knowledge and approval of Dr. Ryzl. This gave no significant results, and when I learned of the renewed success of PS in the tests in Prague in September of that year, I suggested that the distance tests should be terminated. A letter from Dr. Ryzl suggesting the same thing crossed mine in the mail.
>
> Early in 1966, however, Dr. Ryzl informed me that he had almost completely stopped working with PS in ESP experiments and he stated that I might work with him again if I should so desire, especially if it seemed to me worthwhile to try some more experiments at a distance.
>
> In the spring of 1966, both Dr. Ryzl and I accepted an invitation from Dr. K. R. Rao to attend a seminar on parapsychology to be held at Andhra University in India. I wrote to PS that I would like to stop in Prague for a day to get a detailed floor plan of the room in which we had worked in 1963 and to take some photographs showing the experimental arrangements.
>
> In India Dr. Ryzl told me that PS was looking forward to my visit and was expecting to try some experiments with me. Dr. Ryzl also said that he had not been able to obtain any further significant results in ESP tests with PS after the visit of Dr. Freeman and Miss Kanthamani (September, 1964). He had therefore abandoned ESP work with PS and had no further plans for using him as a subject. Dr. Ryzl said that PS had developed a strongly sympathetic attitude toward me personally, and expressed the opinion that if the subject could again succeed in ESP tests at this time it would be most likely to occur with me.

It would be of immense value to science, JGP continues, if PS could be shown to have regained his ESP. In addition, the discovery of the focusing effect was an "unusual and challenging" feature of his work that cried out for further investigation. "This peculiarity of his performance was first recognized as a tendency to concentrate his ESP success upon particular card faces more than upon others." In other words, his overall positive deviation of hits on colors was concentrated on a small number of cards, sometimes on one side only, sometimes on both sides. On other card faces his number of hits dropped to chance. JGP suggests that this type of focusing henceforth be called "specific focusing"

From our perspective it simply reflects PS's use of peeks or asymmetric marking, or mixtures of the two techniques, to track a small number of cards or envelopes. If he used tactile marks, sometimes they would allow him to repeat hit calls on both sides of a target. At other times his marks would allow repeated hits on only one side of a target. As we shall see, JGP was now insisting that PS hold targets horizontally while he called. For this and other reasons I will assume that from here on PS abandoned peek moves for the tactile move, and eventually even abandoned tactile marking.

JGP now introduces a new term, "general focusing." By this he means a tendency to repeat the same call on the same face of a card or envelope regardless of whether it hits or misses the color; that is, a focusing on particular sides of cards or envelopes combined with chance scoring on the actual colors. Past experiments with PS, JGP continues, display a mixture of both specific and general focusing. The primary result of the tests reported in this paper is showing that for some reason, which JGP cannot fathom, PS has shifted his focusing from specific to general. Indeed, as we shall see, from now on general focusing predominates in PS's performances.

From our point of view this shift to general focusing is easy to understand. By adopting the policy of sealing envelopes, and not opening them until the end of an experiment, the possibility of PS discovering the orientations of certain cards was made difficult. The best he could do was mark the envelopes and track their sides, not knowing whether he was hitting or missing on the colors. To raise his score above chance it would be necessary to obtain access to the targets, at some time before the envelopes were officially unsealed, and adjust cards to conform to chance focusing. But beginning with this experiment, JGP has decided to close this loophole. For the first time in the history of the testing of PS there is an explicit proviso about guarding targets. Here is how JGP puts it:

> I was careful always to keep the materials in my possession, under direct surveillance, throughout the entire period of my visit. Even if I had only to turn my back upon the subject momentarily or to leave the experimental

room briefly, I followed the rule of taking the covers and the enclosed targets with me. Thus there was no time when the subject could have handled the covers in such a way that he could have turned some of them over to allow the possibility of his associating marks on opposite sides.

Observe that it has not occurred to JGP that if his subject were left alone with targets he might actually unseal an envelope, turn over a card, and reseal. He is adopting the new controls only to prevent PS from turning over a cover so he can associate imperfections on one side with those on the other. Even so, the statement signals a significant tightening of controls. Earlier experiments with PS had been criticized for not having included steps to guard the targets at all times, and I suspect that this was the main reason JGP adopted such a policy. It also implies that in earlier testing of PS, careful guarding had not been part of the protocols.

The new tests with PS took place over a five-day period in July 1966 in the apartment of PS's friend, still identified only as Miss R. The tests were divided into five series, one conducted on each day. The targets consisted of ten white/green cards, four by six inches, their sides numbered 1 through 20—odd numbers on white sides, even numbers on green. For both envelopes and covers, JGP says he used thicker cardboard than used before—not that the earlier cardboard was inadequate, but to remove all questions about PS's obtaining normal sensory information from the cards.

It is amusing to note that at the same time JGP went to considerable lengths to tighten certain controls, he simultaneously weakened others. For example—we will see other instances later—he adopts his briefcase as a "screen." The briefcase, he tells us, "sits vertically upright and measures 12 inches high and 17½ inches across. I gave particular attention to using it in a way that insured getting the desired shielding. There were no reflecting surfaces in the room that permitted the subject to see what was going on in back of the screen."

The main purpose of this "screen" was to hide the targets while JGP randomized them in PS's presence. As we have said before, it is hard to imagine a more inadequate screen than MR's vertical piece of cardboard that PS held on his lap, but a briefcase standing on a table is surely not much better. It may conceal the experimenter's hands, but not his arms and elbows, and it is easy to obtain peeks over the top and around the sides. However, as we shall see, observing JGP's randomizing was probably not necessary for PS to boost his scores.

Each day's session lasted three to six hours, "depending upon differential demands imposed by variations in the procedure and upon occasional intervals taken for rest and relaxation." With the exception of Series 4, in which ordinary playing cards were used, each series consisted of 100 runs through the ten targets, or 1,000 trials per session. I will consider each series in turn.

SERIES 1

The purpose of this test was to determine if PS could still score positive on the colors. No envelopes were used! The cards were simply placed in open covers. PS and JGP sat at a table about four feet from each other, with PS on the right of JGP. At the beginning of each run of ten calls JGP randomized the cards behind his briefcase, then placed the covers in front of PS. He picked them up one at a time, holding each cover "by its edges." We are told that PS kept each cover in a horizontal position while he made his call, then moved the cover to a stack on his right. As he made his calls, JGP recorded them.

After PS finished the stack of ten covers, JGP slid the stack over in front of himself, then raised the top flap of each cover far enough to see the card's number and color. He recorded the number beside the respective call, and if the color agreed with the call, he circled both call and number. Next he counted up the hits and wrote this number at the bottom of the column.

It is hard to believe, but all this was done while PS watched! Thus after the first run through ten covers, PS knew exactly which calls were hits and which were misses. "The subject was able to observe my recording," JGP writes, "but he was not asked to take any responsibility for checking my accuracy. Indeed, he made no effort to see the cards in the covers nor the numbers on the cards, and he appeared to be interested only in the progress of the test as shown by the number of hits made on the runs as the work progressed."

This paragraph, with its naive use of the word "appeared," proves that the idea of asymmetric tactile marking never entered JGP's mind. All PS needed to do under these loose controls was to mark a few cards at the start of the test, observe whether his calls on those cards were hits or misses, and from then on, whenever a marked side presented itself, he would know what to call if he wanted a hit. Of all JGP's experiments with PS, as reported in formal papers, I nominate this one as having the flimsiest controls.

It is worth recalling that JGP sat to the right of his subject. PS normally picked up covers by holding them at their top corners. By keeping the cover horizontal, the back of his right hand would effectively screen the entrance of a left finger or thumb into the open end of a cover. It is also worth observing that if PS marked, say, two cards, it would not be necessary to feel the top edges of a card each time he picked up a cover. Since the cards never changed covers throughout the session, it would be easy to memorize the covers that held the two marked cards, then feel for the mark only when he held one of the memorized covers. At all other times he could hold the covers in such a way that his hands were far below the top edge. This way of holding the covers would be what would stick in JGP's memory.

JGP describes his randomizing procedure (after every run of 100 calls) as follows. Behind the briefcase he would cut the stack of covers "at least once, and as a rule two or three times," then reverse five cards. As usual, he does not reveal how he selected the five, and of course his arm movements behind the briefcase would reveal the number of cuts he made. Amusingly, after reversing the five cards, he would "cut the stack eight or ten times." Not only were these later cuts irrelevant, but apparently JGP was still unaware that any number of cuts is equivalent to a single cut. Why he would limit his cuts to one, two, or three when random cutting was crucial, then later achieve a truly random cut by cutting eight to ten times, is surely puzzling.

The result of this first session was a positive deviation of 31 hits. Thus the success score was a mere $531/1,000 = .531$. If our hypotheses are correct, PS could have scored much higher. I will outline one possible scenario.

PS marked and tracked a few cards, as suggested earlier. JGP does not provide a chart showing how hits and misses were distributed on the twenty sides. He does give a chart for "general focusing"—one that shows the ratio of green to white calls for each card. On card $3/4$, for example, PS made 69 white calls to 31 green. On three other cards he made 60 or more calls of a certain color to 40 or fewer of the other color. It would have been enormously helpful in trying to deduce PS's strategy if this chart also showed how these calls were distributed on the two sides of each card, but such data are not provided.

My best guess is that PS marked and tracked about four cards, but was careful not to make too many correct calls. It had been almost three years since he had last been tested by JGP. For all PS knew, during those years JGP may have become aware of subtle techniques by which PS could boost his score. Indeed, as we have seen, for the first time he adopted a policy of carefully guarding the targets at all times. From my perspective, PS was being extremely cautious in all five sessions. He would raise his score by just enough to show that his clairvoyance had returned and that he deserved further testing, but not enough to arouse suspicion and run the risk of having his "move" detected.

SERIES 2

For this day's session JGP put the ten color cards in ten cardboard envelopes. Each envelope was sealed by a piece of adhesive tape over the open end.

(This is the first mention of "adhesive tape." It is possible that the cloth tape used in earlier tests for sealing envelopes was the familiar adhesive tape sold for medical purposes.) The envelopes were numbered on both sides and inserted taped-end first into the covers. JGP tells us that he prepared the targets in his hotel room, his hands screened from his vision by his briefcase so that he would not know the orientation of any card inside its envelope. The test procedures were the same as in Series 1 except that the envelopes were not opened and the colors were not checked until the end of the session.

In the light of JGP's stated policy of guarding the targets at all times, there was no possible way PS could have elevated his score by asymmetric marking. As we would expect from our perspective, PS's scores on the colors in this test would drop to chance, and that is exactly what happened. You will perceive, as you continue reading this book, that when experimenters close all loopholes, PS's ESP vanishes.

PS was, of course, aware of MR's and JGP's intense interest in the focusing effect. Although we are given no data on how hits and misses were distributed on the faces of the envelopes, a chart shows that on six envelopes (or on the covers, which amounts to the same thing) PS called the same color more than sixty times. On one cover the split was 71 to 29. To explain this focusing is simple. There would have been no need for PS to mark any envelope. All he had to do was memorize one side of six covers. Whenever one of those sides presented itself he would tend to repeat the same color call. The result would be precisely the general focusing recorded in the chart. Had JGP taken the time to shift envelopes to other covers when he randomized, this general focusing on envelopes (and covers) would have been rendered impossible. Of course PS could still have focused on covers, but there would have been no focusing on envelopes.

SERIES 3

The procedure for this session, we are told, was "identical with that of Series 2 except that the envelopes were not taped shut." JGP writes that in randomizing between every ten runs, the briefcase shielding his hands from PS, he noticed that in two envelopes the card had slid down to the opening so that when he recorded the number on the envelope's top face he could glimpse the color of the card. For this reason, he recommends that in future testing the open ends of all envelopes be sealed.

This time PS had 553 hits out of the 1,000 calls, giving him a success rate of .553. On the assumption that JGP, true to his word, carefully guarded the targets at all times, how can we account for this significant display of ESP on the colors?

The description of this series is so brief—less than a page—that we can only guess. JGP does not tell us that, after checking colors at the end of the previous session, he removed all the cards from their envelopes, randomized their orientations, and reinserted them. He would see no reason to do this because between runs he always randomized the orientations of the envelopes inside their covers, and since the envelopes could not be seen, how could PS have any knowledge of their top colors?

I suspect that after checking colors at the end of Series 2, JGP left the cards and envelopes as they were. He simply pushed the cards back down in their envelopes and left the envelopes in the same covers. He did not trouble this time to tape the envelopes shut. "This did not appear to be necessary," he writes, "since the envelopes stayed so tightly closed and since, in the randomizing procedure, each one to be turned over was slipped out from its cover only far enough to permit it to be changed and reinserted."

As in the previous series, the cards kept their orientations inside their envelopes throughout the series, and the envelopes were never moved from cover to cover. We are told that at the beginning of the third session PS was informed of the results of the second day's testing. If he was allowed to look over the records, and there is no reason why he would not be so allowed, he would see exactly how he hit or missed on the six covers he was tracking. And if JGP had not reoriented the cards before the start of the third session, PS would know which colors were now up in the envelopes inside the covers he had been tracking by the imperfection principle. He could now mark the envelopes inside each of the six covers as soon as he came to them. (Of course if he had marked the six on the previous series, it would not be necessary to do so now.) Thereafter, by feeling for the marks when those covers came into his hands, he could raise his score much higher than .553.

Here again a chart showing the distribution of hits and misses for each envelope side would be invaluable. As it is, the chart shows only the distribution of green versus white calls on each envelope, but even this is revealing. I mentioned earlier that the table for Series 2 shows high general focusing on six envelopes. In series 3 all six of those envelopes once more show high general focusing. On five of them the calls for one color are 68, 63, 69, 68, and 59. On envelope 17/18 the calls of one color went from 62 to 73. Two other envelopes also show high focusing—72 green calls on one, and 63 green calls on the other. This suggests that PS may have been tracking more than six envelopes. If my conjecture is correct, it would mean that PS was continuing to play it cool by holding his score on colors down to a level just high enough to warrant continued testing.

Obviously we have no way of knowing, and doubtless will never know, whether JGP bothered to reorient the cards before starting this series. If he did reorient them, this detail should have been in his paper, and its omission alone would be a serious defect. My opinion is that if he reoriented the cards he would have said so. Let me again remind the reader that throughout each session that used envelopes in covers, the envelopes never changed covers, nor were the cards turned inside their envelopes. I see no reason why it would seem necessary to JGP to reorient the cards between one day's session and the next.

SERIES 4

This was a novel departure. As always, when there was a significant change in targets and/or procedure, PS's clairvoyance mysteriously failed to operate.

Ten playing cards, ace through ten of clubs, were the targets. Behind his briefcase, JGP shuffled the packet and held it face down in one hand. One at a time he dealt a card to the table, arbitrarily dealing it face up or face down. Since JGP randomized in his head, this test was equivalent to the child's game of guessing which hand of an opponent holds a penny. (Why, I wonder, did no parapsychologist think of giving PS such a simple binary test?)

PS's task was to guess which way each card was dealt. Results were at chance. It would not be appropriate, JGP writes, to discuss this series until Ryzl has "reported his own data out of which the suggestion arose. Accordingly, nothing further will be said regarding Series 4 in the present paper." This is the only indication I have come across that MR ever made a test with playing cards. Is it not curious that PS could apparently "see" through two thicknesses of heavy cardboard, but could not "see" through JGP's briefcase?

SERIES 5

For this final session JGP decided to abandon covers. The same ten green/white cards were now sealed inside ten envelopes. PS and JGP took their accustomed places at the table. Behind his briefcase JGP picked up an envelope and tapped it on the table to indicate he was holding it up for a call. PS then named a color. Envelopes called green were put in one stack, those called white in another stack. JGP then recorded the results, shuffled the envelopes behind the screen, and repeated the process for another run.

As JGP rightly says, this procedure made for rapid testing. It was not necessary to record each call when made—the stacking of the envelopes took care of that—nor was it necessary after each run to remove half the envelopes from their covers so they could be reversed. As JGP puts it, "Much of the strain caused by the old testing procedure was lifted from the experimenter. The procedure adopted in Series 5 is one to be greatly preferred." JGP must have soon forgotten those words, because he never used the procedure again.

As in the first three series, 1,000 calls were made. PS had 528 hits on the colors, a success rate of .528. This is almost at chance. General focusing, judging from the chart, seems to have vanished. On only one envelope did PS make more than sixty calls of the same color. It was envelope 17/18, on which he had shown high general focusing in Series 1, 2, and 3. Indeed, in Series 3 he made 82 white calls on that envelope as against 18 green. In Series 5 his split was 61 green to 39 white. This is not an extreme ratio, and could have been entirely accidental. Most of the other splits were very close to 50/50, so one stronger deviation from chance could be expected.

JGP concludes that the series "did not show any evidence of general focusing." He believes that "the novelty of the situation in Series 5 was sufficiently distracting to eliminate the ESP general focusing effect, even though it did not eliminate the positive scoring."

JGP is right to be puzzled by the fact that "specific focusing has for the time being petered out or become too faint to follow." From our point of view, the petering out is not hard to understand. At any rate, JGP feels that the new type of focusing is of great importance for further investigation. "If PS can continue as a successful ESP subject, this fact alone could become one of growing significance for parapsychology. It would, first of all, show that not every experimental subject must inevitably lose his ability to score well on ESP tests."

Although the low score of .528 could have been accidental, let us speculate on two ways PS could have raised his score above chance. It is possible that JGP would once more have seen no reason to remove cards from their envelopes and randomize their orientation after finishing Series 3. In any case, he says nothing about having done so. If he left the cards as they were, PS would have known the orientations of many of them. The envelopes were numbered on the outside, so there would have been no need to memorize imperfections. PS would simply recall, for example, that green was up in envelope 7/8. During the 1,000 times that JGP held an envelope behind his briefcase, it is possible that on many occasions PS would obtain a glimpse around the side or over the top of the briefcase while JGP was in the process of picking up an envelope from its stack. No doubt JGP was careful to see that each envelope was hidden from PS's gaze *when a call was made,* but was he equally careful when he picked up an envelope and moved it to the center?

How do we know the envelopes were labeled on the outside? JGP does not describe the envelopes in this paper, but he does remark that they were the same as those used in the experiment we discussed in Chapter 9. In the paper for that chapter JGP doesn't describe the envelopes either, but he says they were the same as those used in the experiment we discussed in Chapter 6. Turning to that chapter's report, we read (page 165) that each envelope was labeled on its "upper side." Moreover, I own two envelopes and covers that were used by JGP. The covers are labeled inside their flaps, but the envelopes are numbered in black ink on each side of the folded edge, where they could be easily seen by lifting cover flaps.

Let us assume, however, that JGP took the precaution of removing all the cards and randomizing their orientations before he began this test. He makes a point of saying that for Series 2 he did his initial preparation of targets in his hotel room, but he does not tell us where he prepared the targets for *this* series. (What is not said in a report is often the most important clue to what actually happened.) Assume that he did this preparation in PS's presence, at the start of the session, but with his briefcase hiding the process. If so, PS may have observed some of the cards while they were being inserted into envelopes. JGP would not have considered it important to take extreme precautions to hide this target preparation because he knew he would be shuffling the envelopes later and would be concealing each one behind his briefcase while PS made his calls. From JGP's point of view, even if PS saw how some of the cards were oriented it would serve him no purpose during the actual calling. PS would not, of course, obtain glimpses of those memorized envelopes every time one was held up behind the briefcase, but perhaps often enough to provide a small excess of "right" calls. JGP writes that "the briefcase served as a screen to conceal all ten of the envelopes from the subject throughout each run." For all we know from this brief statement, the stack of envelopes may have been on one side of the briefcase where PS could see the top envelope *before* JGP picked it up for the calling.

It seems to me that the first conjecture is the most likely. Indeed, there is nothing in JGP's paper to suggest that the cards *ever* changed orientations in their envelopes after JGP prepared them in his hotel room. In his monograph on PS he writes: "The parts of the target packets remained together throughout each series as they were assembled at the start. That is to say, the W/G card alone (Series 1) or the envelope-card combination (other series) was kept inside the same cover throughout each series; its position in relation to the cover was varied by turning it over or not doing so on a random basis before each run. . . ." The wording is ambiguous as to what is meant by "at the start." If "at the start" meant his preparation of the envelopes in his hotel room before starting Series 2—and this seems the most reasonable interpretation—then the cards retained their orientations within their envelopes throughout Series 2, 3, and 5.

There are other possible explanations of the mild positive score in Series 5. It is always dangerous for a test to be made by one experimenter working alone because there is no way to guard against an unconscious "experimenter effect." We have to rely on JGP's scrupulous accuracy in providing data. Whether the raw data are still on file among Pratt's papers I do not know. If so, they would be worth exhuming to see precisely how hits and misses were distributed on each envelope side. This of course applies also to the other two tests that used color cards inside envelopes.

The overall results of the four sessions (Series 1, 2, 3, and 5) can be summarized as follows. Of the total of 4,000 calls, hits on colors were 2,126, an overall success score of .5315. JGP gives an analysis which shows that specific focusing, so dominant in earlier testing, had been replaced by general focusing—that is, focusing with almost no regard for actual colors. It was not possible, as JGP recognizes, to say whether general focusing related to the cards, to the envelopes (or covers), or to both cards and their containers. "Until the matter has been pursued further, therefore, it is necessary to reserve judgment regarding whether we are dealing here with two separate general focusing effects that only overlap to some degree, or whether there is only one effect that is being examined from the two related points of view." JGP devotes several pages to analyzing general focusing in earlier tests, but without reaching any positive conclusions.

JGP was aware of the possibility that PS's focusing could have been based on memorizing the outsides of targets. Here is what he has to say about this in discussing the five-day series in his monograph on PS:

But it could equally well have been a matter of calling preferences shown for the exposed covers, since each one of them was used with the same target throughout the series. In the published report I recognized that sensory responses to the covers *could* explain the focusing results, but (as I have already said) the main emphasis of the research was on using ESP to identify the hidden envelopes and cards. Now I think, in the light of later findings that clearly showed that PS was "calling" the exposed covers, that he was almost certainly doing this in the mid-1966 research as well.

If the patterning of responses was linked with the exposed covers and if this effect was psychologically similar to (or perhaps of the same nature as) the earlier patterning of responses on *concealed* objects, then it would appear that by 1966 PS was no longer able to control his attention and focus it successfully on the concealed aspects of the target packets. Rather, the results suggest that his attention was at that time being captured by the surface aspects of the outside containers and that he was responding to them in essentially the same manner as he had earlier been responding to the inner, hidden ESP targets.

Of course there is a ridiculously easy way to eliminate memorizing of the outsides of targets. Simply use a large fixed, opaque screen that will completely conceal the targets during both randomizing and calling. In view of the fact that in earlier tests PS seemingly had no trouble seeing through cardboard "screens," and in these tests seemingly had no trouble seeing through a briefcase, it is one of the mysteries of JGP's investigations of PS that the idea of using an adequate screen seems never to have occurred to him. True, such a screen would be cumbersome to transport, but large folding screens are readily obtainable in furniture stores and easy to construct even if one is not a skilled carpenter.

Why were such screens never used? If ESP can penetrate cardboard and briefcases, surely it can penetrate a large cloth screen. Think, also, of how greatly this would simplify procedures. There would be no need to prepare targets in hotel rooms or behind closed doors, or even to guard the targets. Everything could be handled behind the large screen as efficiently and rapidly as JGP handled things behind his briefcase in Series 5. Since PS's ESP easily penetrated cardboard, another simple procedure would have been to put a cardboard carton over PS's head, then hold up targets without letting him touch them. Why is it that psi experiments are so frequently designed in such complicated ways that endless loopholes invade the picture? I can only conclude that deep in the recesses of JGP's unconscious, as in the unconscious of many another parapsychologist, lurk strong impulses to leave loopholes open.

I close with a paragraph from JGP's paper that suggests how trusting and naive he was. "The subject's manner [during a run] did not suggest that he was at all alert to visual details which he might pick up by scrutinizing the appearance of the upward face of each cover. He seemed rather to go into a state of abstracted attention in which, while his eyes were open, his thoughts appeared to be elsewhere than upon visual details of his immediate environment or of the target material in particular."

From our point of view, PS was indeed not concentrating on visual details. He was concentrating on tactile details. No wonder he had an abstracted expression on his face!

Chapter 17

Prague, 1966

DATE: October and November 1966

PLACE: Miss R's apartment in Prague

PAPER: "Seeking the Trail of the Focusing Effect: Part I. An
Exploratory Investigation of Pavel Stepanek in Prague."
J. G. Pratt, in the *Journal of the Society for Psychical
Research,* 62 (April 1968), pp. 158–170.

J. G. Pratt returned to Prague in October 1966 for another series of tests
with PS. They were made as before in Miss R's apartment in Prague while
she was away during working hours. JGP again was the sole experimenter.
The main purpose of the new series was to see if PS could regain his
earlier ability to score high on concealed colors.

The Prague visit lasted three weeks, with tests made on fourteen days.
A thousand trials were made on each of the first thirteen test days. On
the last day, two series of a thousand calls each were made.

The targets were ten white/green cards for all the tests except the last
two. In Series 1, 2, and 3 the cards were inside unsealed cardboard envelopes
with no covers. JGP shuffled the envelopes behind a "screen." The nature
of the screen is nowhere described in the paper, but in the next paper
JGP reveals that his briefcase was the screen, "as in previous experiments."
This time, however, if I read JGP's terse description right, throughout the
entire first three series the targets were kept behind the briefcase where
they were hidden from both men.

PS was asked to call the color uppermost on the top envelope of
the stack. JGP recorded the call (both envelopes and cards were numbered

on both sides), then reached behind his briefcase "and laid the target aside." After each run of ten calls, he shuffled the covers by reaching around his briefcase so that neither he nor PS could see the shuffling. After every fifteen runs he removed the cards and randomly replaced them. This was done "out of sight of both subject and experimenter," so I assume he again did the randomizing by reaching around his briefcase.

Even though the "screen" was far from adequate, it is easy to see that PS would have had no chance to mark the cards or even to focus on individual envelopes. As we would have expected, he scored chance on the card colors (the deviation from the expected 500 hits was a negative 24), and there was no evidence of focusing on envelopes. Thus the first three tests were in all respects failures.

In Series 4 the ten cards were inside unsealed envelopes as before, but this time the envelopes went into the usual cardboard covers. The briefcase was abandoned. The stack of covers was placed on the table. PS called the color he thought uppermost inside the top cover, then picked up the cover and put it aside. Before each run of ten calls JGP randomized envelopes inside covers. After every fifteen runs he removed the cards and randomized them inside the envelopes.

Asking PS to make each call *before* he picked up a cover was an enormous improvement in controls, although JGP may not have been aware of it. PS had no way to use peeks or asymmetric marking, nor was there any way he could know the orientation of any card. Again, as we would have expected on the basis of our conjectures, PS scored at chance on colors (the positive deviation from 500 was a mere 7).

For the first time in the history of PS's testing, JGP tells us, the covers in this fourth series were labeled (on the inside of their flaps) and a record kept of the sides that were uppermost each time PS made a call. Because under the circumstances the best PS could do would be to focus on covers, we would expect strong focusing of this sort, with no signs of focusing on envelopes or cards. This is precisely what took place.

JGP recognized that since PS saw each cover, "the covers were clearly distinguishable on the basis of blemishes; and there was no way to exclude the possibility that the subject had associated particular blemishes with either white or green and that he simply recognized some of the covers and called them consistently in a large majority of the runs." In any case, PS showed a strong tendency to focus on specific covers. JGP calls it "specific focusing" on covers, though of course it was "general focusing" with respect to actual colors. We are told that on one cover the ratio of white to green calls was 43 to 0 on one side. In other words, each time PS saw that side he made the same color call! On the other side of the same cover his ratio of white to green calls was at chance. This suggests (on the basis of our conjectures) that PS had memorized only one side of the cover.

Only open covers were used for the ten green/white cards in Series 5 through 8. We are given no details about procedures beyond the fact that JGP randomized the covers behind his briefcase, and that PS made his calls "as he handled the covers in the usual way." JGP thus abandoned his sensible practice of having PS call before he picked up a cover. We are now back to the loose controls in which it is easy for PS to use peeks or asymmetric marking.

JGP also loosened controls by checking for hits in PS's presence at the end of each run of ten calls, rather than at the end of the day. He writes that he believed this "might provide more favorable motivation and thus help PS reach a period of successful ESP performance." It helped him all right. From our perspective it gave PS a chance to mark a few cards early in the game, then learn whether his calls were hits or misses as soon as those cards were checked. It is no surprise that on this poorly controlled test he scored 550 hits on colors for a success rate of .55.

On Series 6, which presumably followed the same procedures as Series 5, PS's score dropped to a negative deviation of 19. Was there some variation in the procedures that accounted for this low score? It also occurs to me that PS may have been reluctant to mark more cards, and also reluctant to show focusing on the same cards on which he made his above-chance hits in the previous series. This could have aroused suspicion. PS may have deliberately called at random, or even intentionally lowered his score below chance.

JGP justifies his extremely brief descriptions of procedures—in some cases no description at all—by saying that this "seems especially appropriate for those series that yielded only chance results." He couldn't have been more wrong. In reporting failed tests with psychics, a careful, detailed account of the controls can provide valuable clues as to whether the psychic was using nonparanormal techniques in experiments where certain controls were lacking.

Although JGP says nothing about how procedures were varied for Series 6, he does tell us some of the variations he made for Series 7 and 8. "The covers with the enclosed cards remained out of sight of the subject," in back of the briefcase, "until after he had made his calls. I handled the targets, and I laid each cover out where the subject could see it as soon as he had made his guess." This procedure of course prevented PS from feeling for marks, although JGP was oblivious to this aspect of his controls. As we would expect, scores on colors were at chance. The deviation for Series 7 is given as zero—another one of those remarkable anomalies that tends to cast suspicion on the accuracy of JGP's data. The probability of getting exactly 500 heads in a thousand tosses of a coin is about .03, or three times out of 100 attempts. For Series 8 the deviation was +9, also at chance.

Envelopes continued to be unused for Series 9 and 10. On these tests the ten cards were "sealed" inside covers, though we are not told how they were sealed. Adhesive tape? Evidently they were easily unsealed because after each run of ten calls JGP removed the cards, randomized cards and covers, and reinserted the cards. The sealing would have prevented PS from using marks. Again he scored at chance. Series 9 followed the same procedures as Series 7 and 8, with chance results. Series 12 and 13 used cards sealed in envelopes, but now the envelopes went into covers. We are told nothing about the testing procedure. Because JGP was soon to leave Prague, he did not have time to check on hits, nor could this be done later because the envelopes got "merged with a general stock of material and their identity had been irretrievably lost." However, an analysis of the calls for focusing showed that there "could not have been any appreciable deviation on the color score."

The last two tests, Series 14 and 15, used twenty envelopes, each holding a white card with a green dot in the center of one side. JGP held each envelope behind his briefcase while PS called. In Series 14 JGP sorted the envelopes into two piles as calls were made. In Series 15 he handed the stack to PS who sorted as he called. Both tests, JGP writes, "gave nothing of significance from any point of view."

Because scores were not checked for two of the series, only 6,500 calls could be evaluated. If the +50 deviation on the poorly controlled Series 5 is included, the overall deviation for the entire experiment was +18, or 6,518 hits out of an expected 6,500. If the +50 is left out, the overall deviation was a negative 32. The entire experiment was, therefore, a colossal failure. As JGP put it: "It is evident that there is no outstanding success represented by the scores for total hits on the fifteen series. . . . PS was not successful during this visit in scoring significantly on the task to which he was primarily committed: the naming of the color presented upward on the concealed card."

From our point of view, which could be entirely mistaken, the failure of these tests sprang from the controls that prevented PS from adopting any of his usual tactics. But parapsychologists are fond of blaming failures on psychological disturbances. Had these tests been a whopping success, we probably would have never learned that PS was undergoing a psychological crisis. It was such a crisis that both JGP and PS believed was responsible for the failures.

Do the results given in this paper mean that PS had finally lost his ability for successful ESP test performance with me, as he had previously apparently done with Dr. Ryzl? Or were there special circumstances which might account for the poor results and which might therefore justify the hope that PS would again be successful on later occasions?

Both PS and I thought while we were together in Prague that the latter was the case. As I mentioned near the beginning of the paper, before I went there I knew that the subject had been going through a particularly difficult crisis. The details regarding this difficulty are personal and need not be mentioned here; but the fact that the crisis existed *is* relevant, for it may well account for the absence of successful scoring during this period. Indeed, the matter became more serious in the mind of the subject after my arrival, and at one point it seemed to endanger our plans to such a degree that I had serious doubts about whether we would be able to continue our work. Not until the end of my visit, when it had become apparent that we were not going to be successful, did the subject specifically mention the possibility that perhaps his personal difficulties had been responsible for his failure. I agreed with him that this was likely the case, and I assured him that therefore we did not need to feel discouraged regarding the prospects for his being successful on future occasions.

I asked Dr. Ryzl about this crisis. He replied in a letter that he believed it was a mixture of two elements. PS was concerned over the wisdom and ethics of his break with MR so he could continue testing with JGP, and he was fearful that his relationship with JGP might bring him to the attention of the Czech Secret Service. PS had a strong desire for contacts with the United States, to further his career as a famous psychic, but this was combined with strong apprehensions about how the authorities would view such contacts.

Although PS had no way of hitting on colors (except for Series 5), it would have been easy for him to focus on the outsides of targets (envelopes or covers). "Since these areas of significance occurred in those series in which the covers were visible to the subject, it is obvious that the results cannot be interpreted as excluding a sensory interpretation," JGP writes. He immediately adds: "But just because a sensory explanation of the results is possible is no reason for saying that it is the correct one. It is easily conceivable that PS, who has repeatedly demonstrated ESP under conclusive conditions, may have been using this ability to respond consistently in relation to the sides of the covers."

In other words, JGP is suggesting that although PS could easily have accomplished his focusing by memorizing the outsides of targets, it is equally possible that he ignored the outsides and used ESP instead to focus on them! It is statements like this by some parapsychologists that magicians find so incredible. How many times have they heard it said that just because a psychic could have used an invisible thread to move an object across a table, it doesn't follow that the psychic did not move the object by PK. To bolster his view that PS did all his focusing by ESP, JGP cites later experiments in which PS achieved high focusing under conditions in which observing blemishes or labels were excluded. (We will consider these tests in forthcoming chapters.) Another argument he gives is that analysis of PS's focusing showed a strange lack of agreement on his "favorite" covers from one test to another. JGP concedes, however, that it would be equally hard to explain such shifts on the ESP hypothesis:

> Perhaps it might be said with equal logic that this lack of agreement regarding the "favorite" covers in the two series is also strange from the point of view of ESP. But we know very little about how ESP operates, and I suggest that any judgment about how strange it may be that ESP should reveal such a contrast would only reflect an intuitive judgment that ESP ought to work like memory.

Here is how JGP, in his monograph on PS, described the "migration" of PS's clairvoyance from actual colors on the cards to the outsides of targets:

> If the patterning of responses was linked with the exposed covers and if this effect was psychologically similar to (or perhaps of the same nature as) the earlier patterning of responses on *concealed* objects, then it would appear that by 1966 PS was no longer able to control his attention and focus it successfully on the concealed aspects of the target packets. Rather, the results suggest that his attention was at that time being captured by the surface aspects of the outside containers and that he was responding to them in essentially the same manner as he had earlier been responding to the inner, hidden ESP targets.
>
> A series of experiments carried out in Prague in November, 1966, was unsuccessful in producing unequivocal evidence of ESP. In some of the series, however, the subject's responses to the sides of the opaque covers presented upward were recorded for the first time. This record made it possible to localize the focusing effect precisely. The results showed that highly consistent calling preferences were indeed shown for particular covers. These findings underscored again the importance of seeking the further facts needed to distinguish between two questions. Was the migration of the focusing effect to the surface aspects of the target packets only a sensory imitation of the subject's earlier successful ESP performance? Or had a new kind of response emerged from the long experience of PS as a subject that might be pursued in further research and that could possibly open the way to a new stage in his ESP performance?

These quotations reveal how powerfully JGP's mind was set against admitting even the possibility that star subjects like PS could be boosting their scores by nonparanormal means. This mind-set reached an incredible high in 1978 when Betty Markwick published a sensational paper proving that S. G. Soal, England's most respected parapsychologist, had deliberately fudged data in a famous experiment with Basil Shackleton. Markwick showed that in Soal's list of the random digits he used in testing he had later inserted dummy digits that correspond to target hits. Remove the fake digits, and Shackleton's score dropped to chance.*

JGP, who had been one of the loudest voices in protesting earlier evidence that Soal had cheated, was allowed a comment following Markwick's paper. He called her work "exemplary" and agreed that for the time being all of Soal's work, including work done with JGP himself, would have to go on the "dump heap." But he could not resist offering his own theory as to what had happened. Soal, he suggested, could have "used precognition when inserting digits into the columns of numbers he was copying down, unconsciously choosing numbers that would score hits on the calls the subject would make later. For me, this 'experimenter psi' explanation makes more sense, psychologically, than saying that Soal consciously falsified for his own records."

One can only marvel at the kind of mind JGP must have had to advance such a preposterous hypothesis. If he was unable to accept incontrovertible evidence that his friend Soal had cheated, it is easy to understand why the possibility of PS's boosting his hit scores by clever dodges would never have entered JGP's mind. He was one of psi's true believers. Although his reputation among many parapsychologists continues to be high, I find him one of the most gullible and least competent of the researchers who worked for Rhine. JGP believed everything—poltergeists, metal bending, thoughtography, levitations, even the mind-reading ability of dogs. As we shall see in the chapters to come, JGP never performed a successful experiment with PS that did not contain loopholes through which PS could maneuver.

Although extremely simple experimental designs were readily available—designs that would have closed all loopholes tightly—JGP was consistently unable to use them. Whenever by accident the loopholes were closed, and PS's scores fell to chance, the failures were always attributed to something psychological that disturbed the operation of PS's psi powers. Instead of continuing with tight controls, JGP invariably managed to design

*"The Soal-Goldney Experiments with Basil Shackleton: New Evidence of Data Manipulation," Betty Markwick, in the *Proceedings of the Society for Psychical Research,* 56, May 1978, pages 250–277.

a new experiment in which an old loophole reappeared. On no occasion did he seek the advice of a magician knowledgeable about card magic. Had he done so, he would have learned about asymmetric marking and, if our conjectures are correct, PS would never have made it into *The Guinness Book of World Records.*

Chapter 18

Charlottesville, 1967

DATE: May 1967
PLACE: University of Virginia, Charlottesville
PAPER: "Seeking the Trail of the Focusing Effect: Part II. The First Stage of ESP Research with Pavel Stepanek in Charlottesville." J. G. Pratt, in the *Journal of the American Society for Psychical Research,* 62 (April 1968), pp. 171–189.

Although the tests described in the previous chapter failed to revive PS's ability to guess concealed colors, JGP did not despair of achieving this goal. With the help of a special grant from an unidentified friend, JGP was able to bring PS to Charlottesville, Virginia, for a period of five weeks in May and June 1967. The first nine series of tests took place in May, with JGP again serving as the sole experimenter.

Series 1 used the same ten white/green cards and the same ten covers used in the previous series of tests in Prague. JGP's briefcase continued to be the "screen." One would have thought the University of Virginia could have afforded to provide a more suitable screen, but apparently not. Here is how Ian Stevenson, JGP's boss at the University, described the difficult conditions under which JGP was forced to work. (I quote from *Gaither Pratt,* edited by Jürgen Keil, McFarland, 1987, p. 242.)

> The experiments with Pavel at the University of Virginia also took place under difficulties. In the 1960s our only available "laboratory" was a former bedroom in the interns' quarters of the University Hospital. It was so small that many persons would have scorned it as a cupboard for a room of ordinary size. Yet Gaither managed to conduct numerous ex-

periments with Pavel there. In some of them three experimenters were squashed into their proper positions around Pavel. There was not much chance of diversion there, either, but Gaither humorously exploited the otherwise annoying discharge of steam noisily emitted by the University's power plant, often just in the middle of an experiment. As the power plant was less than a hundred meters from our tiny "laboratory," the noisy steam could not be ignored, but it could be turned into a joke, and Gaither did this.

JGP did his usual randomizing behind his briefcase. Before each run of ten calls he would cut the stack of covers, reverse five cards (presumably the top five), shuffle, and cut once more. Apparently he had abandoned the excellent practice of cutting ten or more times and was back to cutting just once. PS picked up the covers one at a time, holding each horizontally while he called. After finishing the stack, JGP pulled the stack to his side of the table, lifted the flap of each cover, and recorded the number on the card. This was done while PS watched.

We are told that the procedures were the same as in Series 5 of the previous experiment. You will recall that this had almost no controls, and was the only test on which PS had a significant positive hit score of .55. To remind the reader, the lack of controls allowed PS to mark cards, then observe during each checking whether his calls had been hits or misses.

Now for a surprise. After thirty runs, PS "noticed that the score had been running fairly consistently below mean chance expectation. At that point, the total deviation was −17. The subject asked if it would be just as significant if he continued throughout the series scoring below the chance level. I answered that it would be, and thereafter he was hoping for a negative score instead of a positive one."

Sure enough, after six hours of 1,000 calls, PS obtained only 439 hits, a deviation of −61 below the expected chance score of 500. Expressed as a success rate on *misses,* it was .561, slightly better in its negative way than the positive score on Series 5 in Prague. Assuming that PS marked and tracked some cards, how can we explain the negative score? Note that all of JGP's shuffling and cutting was irrelevant because there were no envelopes; once a card was marked, and PS felt the mark, he would know what call would raise or lower his score. My guess is that PS, who of course knew well by now that an unusually large number of misses was just as significant as "psi hitting," simply switched his goal to "psi missing." Perhaps he was inspired to do this by the fact that his first few guesses on the cards he was tracking all turned out to be misses. Enormously pleased, JGP congratulated his subject for having "been successful on his very first day of working at the University of Virginia." Why

PS, who had been trying hard to guess the colors right, found his ESP suddenly shifting to misses, remains one of those mysteries about the variability of ESP that parapsychologists have always been at a loss to explain.

For Series 2, a new set of ten numbered white/green cards were used, along with ten new numbered cardboard envelopes. The targets were prepared by Dr. B. M. Smith (not identified), out of sight of JGP and PS, and sealed with "white tape" (adhesive tape?). Smith kept a record of how the cards were oriented, a precaution that (as we shall see) JGP failed to adopt later in the series. The envelopes remained sealed throughout the test.

No covers were used. The envelopes were stacked behind JGP's briefcase, shielded from PS until he made his call. After each call JGP moved the envelope to one side where PS could see it, but was not allowed to touch it. As we observed in the previous chapter, having PS make his call *before* he saw the target was an excellent plan because it completely eliminated the use of asymmetric marking.

JGP now makes a curious error. He writes that the procedure he adopted here was the same as in the successful Series 5 test of the previous experiment in Prague. He remembered wrong. It was another test that had PS make his calls before he saw a target. The previous paper tells us that in Series 5 PS made his calls "as he handled the covers in the usual way." I assume this was just a careless mistake on JGP's part. However, it doesn't matter because when the data of this well-designed test were eventually analyzed they "revealed nothing of interest."

Disappointed by the failure of Series 2, JGP tried the same experiment again for Series 3, using the same unopened envelopes. This time JGP made the controls even tighter by keeping the envelopes completely out of PS's sight throughout the entire run. (In the previous series each envelope was put aside where PS could see it immediately after his call.) Thus if PS had memorized all the envelopes, he could not even deduce the identity of the last envelope after calling nine of them. As to be expected from our point of view, when the calls were checked (apparently against Smith's record of card orientations) the results were again at chance. "At this point," JGP writes, "we appeared to have slipped backward to a level of monotonous failure, and we both welcomed the next day as a day of rest."

Series 4 was a weird departure from customary protocols. Procedures were the same as in Series 2 and 3 except that while JGP was handling the envelopes prepared by Smith (still sealed) behind his briefcase, PS was allowed to handle ten *empty covers* on his side of the "screen." In other words, when JGP picked up an envelope behind the briefcase, PS picked up an empty cover at the same time and made his call. The idea was to let PS get his usual "feel" by handling empty covers! It is hard to think of a more ridiculous variation in experimental design. Of course PS did *not* get his usual "feel." The results were again at chance, with nothing of interest in the way of focusing. How could he focus on envelopes when he couldn't even see them when he called?

For Series 5—"still groping for a way that would allow PS to be successful"—JGP decided to alternate runs under two different conditions. Series 5a (even-numbered runs), involved the same ten cards sealed by Smith. Series 5b (odd-numbered runs) used ten color cards in covers without envelopes—the same covers used in Series 1. Both 5a and 5b each consisted of 1,000 calls.

For 5a a new modification, almost as whimsical as the modification in Series 4, was introduced. JGP attached a piece of cardboard to the top of his briefcase "in such a way that it projected approximately six inches horizontally beyond the edge of the briefcase" in his direction. JGP held each envelope under this little shelf, pressing it up against the shelf while PS put his fingers on the shelf and pressed down. The idea was to let PS "feel" each target through a thickness of cardboard, the way he felt an envelope inside a cardboard cover. However, as JGP correctly perceived, "letting PS be aware of the 'presence' of the envelope from the pressure it exerted through the cardboard could not, of course, provide any sensory cue to the color on the upward face of the sealed card."

Yes, and of course it also eliminated (though JGP was unaware of it) tactile markings. The score on colors once more was at chance, although in Series 5b, in which PS was allowed to see and handle the envelopes, there was evidence of general focusing—that is, a tendency to repeat calls on specific sides of envelopes regardless of whether they were hits or misses. It would, of course, have been absurdly easy for PS to memorize covers (if he had not already done so during the thousand calls of Series 1) and focus on some of the sides. Nevertheless, JGP was encouraged by this appearance of general focusing.

Series 6 was a replication of Series 5b. JGP strongly urged PS to try to hit on colors, not just focus on covers. General focusing on covers was about the same as before, however, while hits on colors continued to remain at chance. From our point of view, this reflected the fact that PS had no inkling of how the cards were oriented inside the covers, and JGP was careful not to allow him access to the targets after the test was over.

Series 7 used cards (without envelopes) in covers. It differed from the previous tests of cards in covers, we are told, in that after every run of ten calls JGP randomized the orientations of the cards and shifted them about in covers. After completing the usual thousand calls, the total deviation from chance was −1, another anomaly improbably close (the probability is about .08) to an even split. There was the usual focusing on covers. "I was at that time still limited to thinking of the outer covers as the screens for the envelopes/cards," JGP confesses, "and I was reluctant to concede that it might be necessary to admit that the general focusing effect could be in the covers, and could conceivably therefore be a sensory-plus-memory effect. It was only later . . . that the simple idea arose of putting the target packets (including the covers) into larger opaque jackets."

To this remark JGP appends the following remarkable footnote:

> Looking back, this change seems so simple and so obvious that it seems amazing that it took so long to think of it. The history of science is filled with instances of this sort which illustrate how limited or incorrect ways of thinking persist under circumstances that afterward seem surprising if not amazing. In the present instance, I must confess that the delay in coming to the use of opaque jackets to hide the covers is made even more surprising by the fact that it was I who had, in early 1963, first suggested to Dr. Ryzl the practice of using opaque covers to conceal the sealed envelopes containing the W/G target cards. And the parallel between the two situations leading to these similar steps is very close: the covers were introduced to conceal the envelope and were required to remove an ambiguity regarding whether the specific focusing effect was due to ESP; the jackets were introduced to conceal the covers and were required to remove an ambiguity regarding whether the general focusing effect was due to ESP.

JGP's brilliant idea of putting cards in envelopes, envelopes in covers, and covers in larger covers marks the point at which the saga of Pavel Stepanek takes a wild and hilarious turn. It is like putting a rug on top of a rug to protect the bottom rug, then putting another rug on top to protect the second rug. Perhaps a better analogy would be to put a blindfold on a clairvoyant, then a second blindfold over the first one, and finally a third blindfold over the second one.

As we have seen, with only cards inside covers, PS could mark and feel the top edges of a few cards. With cards inside envelopes inside covers, he could mark and feel only a few envelopes, hence the "migration" of his ESP from focusing on colors to focusing on envelopes. As we shall soon see, when the covers went into still larger covers—henceforth we shall call them jackets—PS's technique migrated again, moving outward from envelopes to covers, since only the covers were now accessible for marking. But we are getting ahead of our story. At the time of the first tests in Virginia, JGP had not yet thought of jackets. Let us return to his nine-test series.

For Series 8 the ten envelopes prepared by Smith were put inside covers. PS randomized as usual behind his briefcase. Although after each run the envelopes were changed from cover to cover, and half of them inverted, the cards remained sealed in their envelopes throughout the test. Because PS still had no way of knowing how any card was oriented, his score on colors remained at chance. There was the usual general focusing on covers.

PS handled the covers while he called, but was not allowed to turn over a cover to see the other side. "Whenever I needed to leave the experimental room," JGP writes, "the subject went out with me, and if we were not to be together constantly, the laboratory door was always locked." JGP is to be commended for continuing to guard the targets, though he makes clear that these precautions were not to prevent PS from unsealing an envelope to check a card (to JGP this would have been unthinkable) but only to prevent him from turning covers so he could associate blemishes on one side with blemishes on the other, and thereby intensify his general focusing!

Up until now PS had struggled to score on colors, but had succeeded in this only in the first test in which his ESP manifested itself as psi missing. "We appeared to be stalled insofar as our primary goal for the cards prepared by BMS [Dr. Smith] was concerned. We had not yet opened the envelopes, because we had not obtained sufficiently good results to infer anything regarding the positions of the cards in the envelopes."

JGP now decided to make a fresh start. He made a new set of envelopes, while PS watched, by folding ten strips of cardboard and taping the edges with red tape to distinguish them from Smith's envelopes, which used white tape. Ten new cards, taken from JGP's reserve supply, were randomized and inserted in the envelopes by Joyce Morgan, a secretary, who did this alone in a room. Unfortunately, she kept no record of how the cards were oriented. After receiving the envelopes from Morgan, JGP sealed the open ends (he does not say how) and numbered the envelopes. Ten new covers were also prepared and labeled inside their flaps.

PS made the usual thousand calls by picking up a cover, calling, then putting it aside. After each run JGP presumably did the customary randomizing behind his briefcase, although this is not explicitly stated except as something he did before the experiment started. JGP quotes from his notes about the mood that prevailed during this Series 9 test. PS was so exhausted that he had to "force himself to continue." There was no "sparkle" in his conversation and he seemed to make no effort to succeed. When the day ended, JGP's mood was "bordering on despair." However, when the results were eventually analyzed for focusing JGP was amazed to find that focusing was unusually strong. JGP dismisses the memorizing of cover blemishes on the ground that the covers were new and PS had never seen them before!

The envelopes were not opened and checked for colors, we are told, until "several days later." The reason for this delay is not given. The checking showed a positive deviation of 48 hits on the colors, giving PS a respectable ESP score of .548.

The cover focusing is not hard to explain. Memorizing blemishes on covers is extremely easy, and PS had had five years of practice. How can we explain the sudden revival of PS's ability to score on colors? Naturally we can only guess on the basis of the scanty information supplied in the paper. I offer the following tentative hypotheses:

1. We are told that when Morgan brought the envelopes and cards to JGP, he sealed the open ends in PS's presence, but was careful not to let PS see any of the cards inside. How careful was he? Assume that PS glimpsed just one card, recalled the envelope's number, and later was able to place a tactile mark on that envelope. If PS consistently called correctly the two sides of that envelope, it would raise his score to .55+. No breakdown is given of how calls were distributed on envelope sides, though a chart does show that PS called white 86 times (out of 100) on one cover, and green 83 times on another cover. If he had glimpsed two cards and marked their envelopes it would have been easy to distribute his calls in a way that would raise his score to .54+. Let me add that I consider this the least likely of my four conjectures.

2. PS marked one envelope early in the calling, without knowing its color, and consistently called green for one side and white for the other. His chance of being right was 50/50. Had he been unlucky, he would have repeated his significant score of psi missing on Series 1, and JGP would have considered this a great success. As it was, he was lucky and scored on psi hitting.

3. We know from JGP's notes how desperate he was to finish this experiment with a successful test. When someone checked the cards several days later, did the "experimenter effect" take over? Did he or she make recording errors that favored JGP's intense hopes? Because JGP in the past always identified himself as the person who checked sealed envelopes after a test, his failure to tell us who did the checking in Series 9 is worth pondering. My guess is that this task was turned over to someone in the laboratory on such a low level that JGP did not consider it necessary to mention the person's name. I find it within the bounds of possibility that an underling, eager to please the boss, consciously or unconsciously fudged the data on one or two cards to give PS a positive score. This may not have happened, but JGP's failure to say who opened and checked the colors is another instance of how important it is, when extraordinary results are claimed, to provide all relevant details.

4. How carefully were the targets guarded during the "several days" that elapsed before the envelopes were unsealed and the cards checked? Recall that JGP's precautions in guarding the targets was to make sure PS could not see both sides of covers and so learn to associate them. But once the test was over, from JGP's point of view such guarding would

be entirely unnecessary. Guarding targets during the course of a test may have seemed essential to JGP, but guarding them *after* a test would have seemed irrelevant. We know nothing about the informal conditions that prevailed during PS's five-week visit to Charlottesville. I find it not impossible that during those several days PS found his way to the targets and was able to adjust one or two cards to fit his focusing. Had Morgan kept a record of card orientations after she randomized, as Smith had done, this hypothesis could have been falsified. That she kept no such record is another example of how carelessly JGP set up controls.

I must say again, in spite of how repetitious such remarks are, that I put these four conjectures forward only as conjectures. For all I can be sure of, all four may be false. In spite of PS's exhaustion and depressed mood, he may have found his clairvoyant powers mysteriously returning, giving him the final score so desperately needed by JGP to justify the time and cost of further testing.

Had JGP seen fit to provide a breakdown of exactly how PS's calls were distributed on each envelope side, we would be in a much better position to analyze his guessing strategy and make deductions about what occurred. Because the covers too were labeled, data on how the calls were distributed on cover sides would also have been enormously helpful. Apparently JGP did not even make a record of the cover sides that were up each time PS made a call. The absence of this data, not just for Series 9 but for all the tests in this series, is one of the paper's most obvious flaws.

Chapter 19

Charlottesville, 1967

DATE: May 1967
PLACE: University of Virginia, Charlottesville
PAPER: "Confirmation of the Focusing Effect in Further ESP Research with Pavel Stepanek in Charlottesville." J. G. Pratt and W. G. Roll, in the *Journal of the American Society for Psychical Research,* 62 (July 1968), pp. 226–245.

William G. Roll, who coauthored this paper with Pratt, was and continues to be the director of the Psychical Research Foundation, in Durham, North Carolina. JGP continued to work alone with PS, at the University of Virginia, until Roll arrived, after which the two men collaborated on two more tests. As in the previous chapter, the new research further confirmed the fact that PS no longer was able to score high on colors. His ESP had mysteriously "migrated," as JGP liked to put it, to envelopes and covers. Roll was enormously impressed by this migration. Both he and JGP believed it arose from "some unknown quality connected with the targets instead of purely psychological or motivational factors within the subject."

This marks a turning point in JGP's beliefs about focusing. He earlier attributed it solely to psychological factors; now he thinks it is a psychic quality within the targets similar to what Ryzl had always maintained. There is, however, an important difference. For Ryzl the quality is put on the targets by PS in the course of calling; in JGP's theory it is a mysterious property already there. In a footnote on the paper's opening page, Roll writes that focusing has "important implications not only for card tests but also for mediumistic studies with 'psychometric' objects and other situations where the subject seems to respond to unknown stimuli from the target."

In summarizing PS's history the authors introduce a terminological change. What JGP had earlier called specific focusing (focusing on card colors with an above-chance score of hits) is now called "side focusing." The term is broadened to refer not just to colors, but specific focusing on the sides of any concealed part of the target—cards, envelopes, covers, or jackets. What JGP had previously called general focusing (focusing on cards, envelopes, or covers, but with only chance hits on colors) is now called "object focusing." The term is again generalized to refer to focusing on entire containers without reference to interior parts or individual sides. The tests in the previous chapter and in this one showed that PS had shifted his ESP from the "innermost core of the target packets" (the cards) to the exteriors of packets. The purpose of the new tests was to determine if this new pattern of focusing was an ESP phenomenon.

From our perspective, the shift reflected the fact that PS, no longer able to learn the orientations of cards or to gain access to targets, could do no better than track envelopes or covers regardless of how cards were oriented. Naturally he could do this only when he could see or feel the packets. Whenever the packets were kept behind a screen, even this kind of focusing vanished. Here is how the authors say it:

> As the number of completed test series increased, it became apparent that the object focusing effect was only present when the targets (cards or card/envelope combinations) were hidden inside the individual opaque cardboard covers, but not when the sealed envelopes were concealed from the subject in back of a screen.
>
> The fact that the covers were visible to the subject and were handled by him during the test suggested that his tendency to call certain ones of them white and others green might be based upon sensory cues. But certain features of the test procedure made it difficult to suppose that this was actually the case. At least the results justified continuing the research and suggested the direction to take in further investigation of the focusing effect.

Series 10 (continuing the numbering of the previous tests) used the ten targets of Series 9, designated the "red set" because red tape was used for sealing envelope sides. The cards remained in the sealed envelopes throughout the test, but envelopes were shifted to different covers without telling PS. For example, the packet on which PS had called white 86 times out of 100 in Series 9 was cover q/r, which contained envelope 1/2. The packet on which he called green 83 times out of 100 was cover a/b, which contained envelope 11/12. These two envelopes were exchanged in the two covers. Other shifts were made of covers that had shown strong focusing, while the four covers closest to chance calls were left in the same covers.

As in earlier testing, JGP randomized behind his briefcase. The stack of covers was placed on the table. PS picked up each cover, held it horizontally, called, and laid it aside. JGP recorded the calls as well as the top labels of both envelopes and covers. PS clearly had no way of knowing how the targets had been prepared. It would have been dangerous to track previously marked envelopes and make the same calls on them, so from our point of view he would confine himself to focusing on covers. By now he was thoroughly familiar with their blemishes, having made a thousand calls on them in Series 9. It is not surprising that the results showed only object focusing; that is, focusing on covers irrespective of the orientations of cards or envelopes. "Since the envelopes were systematically shifted among the covers . . . ," the authors write, "it is obvious that the object focusing effect followed the *covers* instead of the *card/envelope inserts.*" Was this a sensory effect (memorizing of cover imperfections) or was it ESP?

In an effort to decide, JGP decided to put the red set of targets inside opaque jackets, which he made by stapling together three edges of cardboard cut from ordinary manila file folders, leaving one side open for ease in removing and inserting interior parts of the packet, and in recording labels on those parts. Following earlier practices, half the staples faced one way, half the other way, to make both sides of the jacket look the same. This was a naive precaution because not only do manila sheets show the usual unavoidable blemishes, but the staples also provide additional imperfection clues. Apparently the jackets were not labeled.

The previous experiment was now repeated exactly as before with PS handling the jackets in the same way he had handled covers. Before Series 11 began, and after each run of ten calls, JGP randomized the targets in his customary manner by inverting five covers and shuffling the jackets. To test the influence of jackets, ten runs with jackets were alternated with ten runs without jackets. There was no evidence of ESP hitting on the colors. As usual, there was object focusing. In the runs when PS handled the covers, the focusing on covers was the most striking— as naturally it would be because by now PS knew all the covers by heart. Focusing was also significant, however, when the covers were inside jackets. From our point of view this meant that PS was using tactile marking, only now the only hidden parts of the targets accessible to his finger or thumb were the covers.

Following Series 11, the ESP tests were interrupted for several days during which JGP took PS on a sightseeing trip to Washington, D.C., and New York City. The testing resumed on May 15 with a brand new set of ten targets. To distinguish the new set from the red set, the sides of the envelopes were sealed with blue plastic tape. As before, both envelopes and covers were labeled on both sides. Ten new white/green cards were also used. This time the initial randomizing of cards inside envelopes was done by Ian Stevenson, head of the parapsychology laboratory where JGP was now the number-two man. Together the two parapsychologists sealed the open ends of the envelopes, though we are not told how.

The previous test was now repeated in all respects except that no jackets were used. The results were as before—object focusing on covers, no focusing on envelopes or colors.

For Series 13, two new sets of jackets were prepared, one to enclose the red set, the other to enclose the blue set. They were like the jackets made before except that now each side consisted of *two* manila-folder sheets to make the screening material twice as thick. It still had not entered into JGP's head that PS could be using tactile markings; he was thinking entirely of screening off visual perceptions. The jackets were labeled with letters inside their flaps.

A hundred runs were made with each set, the blue for odd-numbered runs, the red for even-numbered runs. Roll, who had now arrived on the scene, did the randomizing on a table, using a "large suitcase" (his own?) for a screen. While PS was calling one set of jackets, Roll randomized the other set. Again, PS failed to score on colors, but scored high on cover focusing. His focusing was stronger on the red set, with which of course he was more familiar—a fact that the researchers found mystifying. They attributed it to a "function of some other difference, as yet unknown, between the two sets of targets or in the subject's attitude toward them." Neither researcher, it seems, considered the possibility that PS's ESP may have preferred red to blue.

For Series 14 the experimenters selected the five targets that in Series 13 had shown the strongest focusing on covers—four from the red set, one from the blue. The five targets were mixed with five newly prepared targets. Roll again did the randomizing behind his suitcase, preparing one set of five targets while PS made his calls on the other five.

There were strong focusing effects on the five covers of the red set. Among the new targets only one showed focusing—cover o/p. PS strongly favored green for the o side, white for the p side. The other four targets showed no departure from chance except for PS's customary tendency to prefer green calls to white. Roll's account is contradicted by JGP's account of the same test in his monograph on PS. There he writes (p. 15): "Of the five used objects selected on the basis of earlier outstanding results, four gave significant focusing effects in this series; but none of the five new objects did so." Why would JGP's memory fail him on this point? Perhaps he was unconsciously trying to suggest that PS's ESP was familiar with mysterious properties on the old covers, but not yet able to pick up properties on the new set.

The focusing on covers in this test, in contrast to earlier focusing, showed strong specific focusing on *sides* of covers. Of course this is easily explained by our hypothesis of tactile marking, the marks being precisely the occult properties that the researchers were trying to understand. To the experimenters, this kind of focusing was a profound mystery.

We are not told when the envelopes for this test were unsealed and the colors checked, or who did the checking. Indeed, no data are given for any of the tests showing how hits or misses were distributed on colors. We *are* told that in this last test there was a small positive deviation on colors, but the amount of deviation is not given. The big question was how PS managed to focus so strongly on covers. "Does PS prefer particular targets for purely motivational or other psychological reasons, or is there something about certain targets that makes it easier for him to make contact with them by ESP?"

Our conjecture is that there is indeed something, namely, tactile markings. To the authors of the paper, the evidence points strongly toward some "peculiar quality in the targets themselves":

It is difficult to imagine that any subtle and unidentifiable psychological motivation in the subject toward these pieces of cardboard could have remained so stable over this period of time and under these different conditions of working. But it is equally difficult to identify any quality or qualities associated with the targets themselves that might account for the consistent patterns of response shown.

What is needed, the authors conclude, is a long-range program in which targets and conditions can be varied "in ways that might help us solve the puzzle." These variations form the content of papers yet to be covered in this book.

Chapter 20

Charlottesville, 1967

DATE: June 1967
PLACE: University of Virginia, Charlottesville
PAPER: "An ESP Test with Aluminum Targets." W. G. Roll and
J. G. Pratt, in the *Journal of the American Society for
Psychical Research,* 62 (October 1968), pp. 381–386.

Of all Pratt's experiments with Stepanek, this is one of the most absurd
and the most poorly designed. W. P. Bentley, in a paper on "Research
in 'Psychometry' in the U.S. and England" *(International Journal of Parapsychology,* 3, Autumn 1961, pp. 75-98), had made a bizarre conjecture.
Psychometry is considered a form of ESP. A psychic handles a watch,
handkerchief, bracelet, or some other object, feels its "vibrations," and obtains
information about persons and events associated with the object. Bentley
suggested that organic objects, because they are made of substances also
in the human body, might work better than inorganic objects. This view
was supported by G. Pagenstecher, in "Past Events Seership: A Study in
Psychometry" (*Proceedings of the ASPR,* 62, July 1968, pp. 226–245). His
theory was that organic objects work better not because they have substances
in common with human bodies but because metals are less porous. This
porosity of organic objects makes it easier for them to soak up the vibrations
that psychics pick up with their ESP.

Bentley's proposal, the authors write, is consistent with W. G. Roll's
psi field theory, as outlined by him in "The Psi Field" (*Proceedings of
the Parapsychological Association,* No. 1, 1957–1964, pp. 32–65). According
to this conjecture:

The physical state of an ESP target is copied in its psi field and this, in turn, affects the psi fields of objects in its environment, including living ones, the process terminating in the physical change in these objects which results in an ESP response. According to one of the psi field hypotheses, the probability of ESP interaction increases with the similarity ("isomorphism") between the two psi fields. Since an object's physical state is (according to this theory) reflected in its psi field, objects that are physically alike should work better as source and transmitter than those that are unlike.

Additional support for the superiority of organic objects in holding psychic impressions came from two papers by A. A. Cochran: "Life and the Wave Properties of Matter" (*Dialectica,* 19, September-December 1965, pp. 290-312), and "Mind, Matter, and Quanta" (*Main Currents,* 22, March-April 1966, pp. 79-88). Here is how Roll and Pratt describe Cochran's wild theory:

> He suggests that particles of matter "have a rudimentary degree of life as one of their fundamental properties." Using the analogy of Niels Bohr between the dual aspect of man as mind and matter on the one hand and the dual aspect of the fundamental particles of matter as being both particles and waves on the other, Cochran goes on to write, "If one suspected that a rudimentary degree of life were possessed by all matter, he would naturally suspect that the dual aspects of man are a direct result of the dual aspects of the matter from which he is made, and that the mind of man and the wave properties of an electron are two extremes of the same thing: the mind properties of matter." This leads Cochran to predict that elements with the greatest wave predominance should be abundant in living matter. Carbon and hydrogen, which together constitute about eighty per cent of protein, have the greatest wave predominance of all the elements at room temperatures and nitrogen and oxygen, which constitute about nineteen per cent of the proteins, are in the fourth and seventh position respectively.
>
> If the wave or "mind" properties of substances are related to or identical with their psychical properties, several interesting consequences follow, one of which would be that cardboard cards, which in large part are made of carbon, ought to possess a greater wave and "mind" predominance than, say, aluminum cards and consequently should work better as a source of ESP signals.

To test these conjectures, Roll and Pratt designed the following experiment. Eight new covers were made by putting one manila folder inside another, stapling the sides, but leaving the top open. The folders were not labeled. Into four of these covers were inserted four cardboard cards (cardboard being organic) of the usual white/green sort. They were in fact the four on which PS had the highest positive deviations in the previous test (Series 14.) They were already numbered, but in this experiment the numbers were considered irrelevant.

Into the other four covers went aluminum "cards." The aluminum was obtained from the Reynolds Metals Company, who assured the experimenters that the metal had a purity of 99 percent. The foil was silver colored on one side. This was designated the "white" side. The other side was coated with vinyl containing a yellow pigment that gave it a gold color. This was designated the "green" side. "Presumably the subject could have responded by ESP to this 'organic' plastic coating," the authors say in a footnote, "but failed to do so for psychological reasons."

The aluminum cards were not marked in any way because the marks "might provide a basis of distinction that could vitiate the inorganic quality of the aluminum cards. For the same reason WGR used rubber coverings on his fingers when he handled the cards."

Pause a moment to reflect on how painstaking the experimenters were on matters related to chemistry. To keep the aluminum cards free from any organic molecules rubbing off Roll's fingers onto the metal, Roll actually covered his fingers with rubber! Contrast this with a total absence of precautions that would prevent PS from putting and feeling tactile marks on cards.

Two hundred runs were planned with each of the two packs of four covers, or a total of 1,600 calls—800 on cardboard cards, 800 on aluminum cards. While PS called one set, Roll randomized the other behind his suitcase by inverting two cards, then shuffling the folders. We are told that PS held the covers in his "usual way" while calling. I take this to mean that he kept them horizontal. As we have seen, JGP had introduced this control, probably to meet objections from critics that PS may have been using peek moves.

PS was shown a sample of the aluminum before the experiment began. He understood the purpose of the test, but was not told which set of covers held the aluminum cards. In a footnote the authors admitted there was a difference in weight between the organic and metal folders, and that "this and other differences could be perceived through the folders by special methods of handling." They decided, however, it was unlikely that PS could detect these differences. "We can therefore say with reasonable assurance that the subject was not *consciously* aware of the difference between the two kinds of targets." It is hard to imagine a more naive conclusion. It still has not occurred to either experimenter that in the process of calling all PS need do is insert a finger to tell the difference. Of course he need do this only once because the two sets of targets remained separate and were alternated throughout the calling.

As in the previous tests in Charlottesville, the authors tell us (for the first time) that there was a coffee break in the morning and a pause for tea in the afternoon. The radio, they add, "was on most of the time with PS's favorite program of country music."

Because the aluminum cards were not labeled, and the numbers on the cardboard cards were ignored, it was not planned or possible to record scores on individual cards. The checking —and this is almost unbelievable— was done in PS's presence immediately following each run of four calls. JGP would open the flaps of the covers enough for him and Roll to see and record the actual colors.

This procedure of course made it extremely easy for PS to boost his scores. Assuming our conjectures are correct, all he had to do was mark one or two cards in each set. In the aluminum set, if the vinyl side had a different feel than the uncoated side, no marking would even be necessary. PS would observe during the checking whether his first calls were hits or misses, and thereafter focus his calls any way he liked. Since he knew the purpose of the test, it is no surprise that on the aluminum cards his hits were 419 out of 800 calls, a low success rate of .52+. On the cardboard cards his hits were 456 out of 800, a high success rate of .57. The overall positive score was $875/1,600 = .54+$. The only surprise is that he did not do better on the cardboard cards. Perhaps Roll was watching too closely and he had infrequent opportunities to feel for marks.

Roll and Pratt viewed the results as follows:

> The total results and the results on the cardboard cards are well beyond chance expectation. Since there appears to be no ordinary way in which PS could have perceived the color of the targets through two layers of manila cardboard, the most reasonable hypothesis is that he did so by ESP.
>
> The failure of PS to score significantly on the aluminum cards is consistent with the theories of Bentley and others discussed above. However, it can be explained in another way as well. The selection of four cardboard cards on which PS had previously succeeded may have provided a favoring condition for the cardboard targets. For some reason, as yet unknown, with this subject certain cards become endowed with a special stimulating property which is absent from other cards, though these seem physically similar to the favored ones. We chose the favored cards to provide optimum conditions for the subject's ESP abilities. If we had not done so and if PS had failed to score on either cardboard or aluminum targets, this failure might have been due to an absence of favored cards rather than to anything having to do with the ordinary physical properties of the targets.
>
> In experiments on this problem in the future, in addition to the preferred cards, a series of new cardboard cards could be used. If the subject also scores better with these than with the aluminum cards, this would give

stronger confirmation of the hypothesis that the chemical composition of the targets affects their stimulating properties than has the present series. Or preliminary tests could be done with a larger number of aluminum cards in the hope of finding favored ones to compare with the favored cardboard cards.

In whatever way the problem is approached, the possibility that the stimulating properties of ESP targets is related to their chemical composition deserves to be fully explored.

In his monograph on PS, JGP speaks of "chance results" on the aluminum cards. Because of the organic dye on the aluminum, he writes, "the conditions did not clearly distinguish between organic and inorganic targets. This lends a degree of support to the interpretation that the failure to get significant results on the aluminum targets was attributable to psychological factors." I'm not sure just what JGP is getting at. It seems to me that the very low score on the aluminum targets provided strong support for the hypothesis he was testing.

I know of few ESP experiments in which results this extraordinary are combined with such an amazing absence of controls. One would surely have expected follow-up experiments along the lines called for, to confirm or disconfirm the organic-versus-metal theory. As far as I know, this was the first and last time any such experiment with PS was made. One of the many ways in which parapsychology differs from other sciences is that experiments like this—which, if valid, would revolutionize physics—are performed, written up, then forgotten and never replicated. Parapsychologists simply move on to other kinds of experiments, equally extraordinary and revolutionary, which in turn are never replicated and soon forgotten.

Chapter 21

Prague, 1967

DATE: September 1967

PLACE: Miss R's apartment in Prague

PAPER: "A Transitional Period of Research on the Focusing Effect: From Confirmation Toward Explanation." J. G. Pratt, N. Jacobson, J. G. Blom, and G. L. Meinsma, in the *Journal of the American Society for Psychical Research,* 63 (January 1969), pp. 21–37.

Stepanek returned to Prague in June 1967. This was the year that Ryzl and his wife escaped from Czechoslovakia to settle eventually in the United States. Ryzl has had no contacts with Stepanek since, except by correspondence.

JGP visited Prague in the fall of 1967 to conduct further tests on focusing. (Efforts to replicate the previous test showing cardboard to be superior to aluminum in absorbing psi qualities apparently was abandoned.) The testing took place in Miss R's apartment over a period of ten days. Three men assisted JGP on the first test: J. G. Blom and G. L. Meinsma from the University of Amsterdam, and Dr. Nils Jacobson, a Swedish friend of JGP who had spent the summer as an extern at the University of Virginia's medical school. He is now a psychiatrist at a clinic in Fjalkinge, Sweden.

Three sets of ten targets were available, all used in testing at Charlottesville: the white set, the red set, and the blue set. (The color names were derived, as we have seen, from the color of the plastic tape used to seal the sides of envelopes.) All three sets had shown evidence of focusing: mild focusing with white, stronger with blue, and strongest with red.

Each set consisted of ten numbered white/green cards, ten numbered envelopes, and ten covers labeled with letters. To unify the system of identification, numbers were substituted for letters on the covers. From each set the researchers selected eight packets. The choices were random for the white and blue sets, but the two packets on which focusing had been weakest were removed from the red set. In addition to these three old sets (now eight packets each), three new sets of eight had been made in Charlottesville prior to JGP's trip to Prague. The new sets used black, brown, and yellow tape. Each new set, like the old ones, consisted of numbered cards, envelopes, and covers.

Two used sets of jackets were available, made by stapling together two thicknesses of manila file folder sheets, leaving the tops open. The jackets formerly used with the red set were called *A*, those with the blue set were called *B*. A new third set, *C*, was prepared. The jackets were also numbered, presumably on the inside of their flaps.

In the experiments at Charlottesville the focusing effect had been strongest on covers. As JGP now puts it: "The focal point of this phenomenon had, for some reason that we cannot now identify, shifted from the innercard/envelope to the outer cover." This focusing continued, as we saw in the previous chapter, even when the covers were inside jackets.

> But we had no reason to think that the outward migration of the focusing effect had permanently ended in the covers. We were curious, therefore, to see whether any evidence of focusing upon the jackets would show up as their use was continued. If so, we would be faced once again with the necessity of changing conditions so as to be able to distinguish between the sensory and ESP interpretation of the effect on the jackets.

The visiting Dutch researchers had only one day to devote to the test. It used the eight targets from the red set, each inside a *C* jacket. Because PS had shown strong focusing on the red covers, JGP expected this experiment to continue to show such focusing, especially on the two covers (previously labeled a/b and q/r, now 1/2 and 15/16) that had shown the most intense focusing in Charlottesville. To expedite randomizing, the set of brown targets was alternated with the red set. The brown targets were inside *A* jackets. With two sets of packets, one could be randomized while PS was calling the other.

There were a hundred runs with each set, or 1,600 calls altogether. It was the first time in the testing of PS that all parts of the targets were separately randomized, and all recorded along with the calls. PS handled the targets in the usual way, making his call as he picked up a jacket and placed it aside. The randomizing was done after each run behind a "screen," the nature of which is not given. Perhaps it was a briefcase, perhaps a suitcase. (I asked Jacobson, but he could not recall.) JGP recorded the calls, after which he went through the stack to write down the numbers on the cards, envelopes, covers, and jackets. The data were later analyzed by a computer program at the University of Virginia.

There is no need to go into details of the computer analysis; interested readers can consult the paper. As expected, the data showed significant focusing on the red covers, none on their envelopes or cards. Cover 15/16, which had shown high focusing in Charlottesville, again showed high focusing—PS called white 42 times out of 50. Cover 1/2, the other high focusing cover, also rated high again, with 37 green calls out of 50. There was no evidence of any kind of focusing on the brown set.

Continuing with our assumption that PS had now become skilled in asymmetric marking, these results are easily explained. He knew what JGP desired in this test: evidence of strong focusing on red covers to support his theory that there was something on those covers—JGP couldn't figure out what—that PS had learned to identify by ESP. It was not even necessary for PS to put marks on those covers, because in our view they were already there from previous testing. As for the brown set, PS simply ignored it and made random calls. To JGP, who still had not conceived of tactile marks on covers, the fact that his manila jackets were opaque (double thicknesses no less) "ruled out the possibility that the subject could distinguish among the enclosed covers on a sensory basis."

At this point let me pause to go over once more some aspects of asymmetric marking. How could it be, some readers are justified in wondering, that a parapsychologist with the reputation of JGP could fail to notice or even to think of this technique? The answer is that JGP, like most parapsychologists, knew absolutely nothing about methods of deception and the use of misdirection. It is this ignorance that explains how easily Jule Eisenbud was fooled by Ted Serios's "Thoughtography"; and Charles Honorton by Felicia Parise's trick with the animated pill-bottle; and scores of parapsychologists by the simple conjuring of Uri Geller and Nina Kulagina, and the paraphysicists of the nineteenth century by the great physical mediums who levitated tables, floated in the air, and performed other wonders. Scientists untrained in magic are putty in the hands of such charlatans. Only a trained magician knows exactly what to look for and how to set up adequate controls.

Inserting a finger into the open end of the outside covering of a packet, while in the process of picking it up and moving it to one side, takes only an instant. As we saw in Chapter 3, and shall see in Chapter 25, the move can be made in such a way that it is undetectable even to a person observing from behind the psychic, especially if the packet is horizontal while being picked up. Recall also that the move needed to be made only at infrequent intervals to boost a score to significance. If a psychic sees his hands are being closely watched, he can avoid the move. If the attention of observers is not on his hands, he knows that even a clumsy move will not be noticed.

Nowhere in the paper do its authors say whether PS held each jacket vertically or horizontally while he called. I am assuming that JGP continued to insist that the jackets be kept horizontal to prevent peeks. If for some reason he relaxed this control and allowed the jackets to be held vertically, then of course PS could have made use of peeks. It is, let me continue to remind readers, entirely possible that throughout his career PS never made use of either peeks or tactile marks, and that all his successes were genuine manifestations of his peculiar kind of clairvoyance— peculiar because it operated in no way except on the two sides of pieces of cardboard.

In Chapter 3 I did not decide between alternate ways of tactile marking, nor is it possible now to decide, if indeed such marks were used. In some cases, as I pointed out in Chapter 8, there was not even a need for placing such marks because of differences in the ends of tape used for sealing the sides of envelopes. As I said in Chapter 3, indentations, nail marks, and crimps are the simplest ways to put tactile marks on the top edges of cards, envelopes, and covers, but the use of beeswax is almost as easy and should not be ruled out. Crimps are easily removed at the end of a session while still calling, and with further handling even indentations and nail marks soon disappear. I do not know how long spots of wax will remain on targets before evaporating or getting rubbed off in handling. A tiny, totally invisible smear of beeswax that I put on the folded edge of a cardboard cover of my own making is still instantly felt by brushing a fingertip along the edge, and this after a period of several months. Whether it would remain detectable after a period of several years I cannot say.

If many of JGP's original envelopes are preserved among his archives— envelopes on which PS had shown strong focusing when they were inside covers—it might be worthwhile to subject them to very careful examination. There may be chemical tests that would show the past presence of wax. Covers with taped sides should also be carefully examined for chance tactile differences in the ends of tape at the folded edge. I would not blame Mrs. Pratt for refusing me permission to look through her husband's papers; but even if she agreed, I feel it would not be right for me to go through them on a fishing expedition.

The second test, conducted by JGP and Jacobson alone, used the yellow targets hidden inside A jackets, and the black targets in B jackets. Jacobson randomized behind the "screen" (whatever it was), but this time it was decided that randomizing all four parts of each packet would be too time-consuming. The cards remained in their envelopes throughout the experiment. There was no focusing on cards, envelopes, or covers, except for slight side focusing on one envelope in the black set. But there was strong focusing on *jackets*. In other words, the focusing had taken another step outward.

This migration presented no great problem even to JGP because, as he recognized, PS could simply have memorized blemishes on the manila jackets. On one side of jacket 5/6, in the yellow set, he made 38 white calls to 9 green, and on the other side of the same jacket he made 37 white calls to 16 green. On one side of a black jacket he called white 30 times to 7 green calls, and on the other side, 36 white calls to 27 green. As JGP perceived: "In these two instances of unusual effects on the jackets it is not possible . . . to conclude that we are dealing with an ESP phenomenon. But past experience makes it seem worthwhile to keep in mind that these may be examples of ESP focusing. . . ."

In Series 3, eight white/green cards were randomly placed in eight envelopes, which then were sealed. No covers were used. Instead, the envelopes went directly into jackets. We are told nothing about procedures, but it doesn't matter because there was no focusing on colors or envelopes, only focusing on the outside jackets. Thus in this test, as in the previous one, there was no need for the "move." PS did nothing more than concentrate on jackets.

On the fifth day of JGP's visit, he, Jacobson, and PS visited two Czech parapsychologists who participated in a fourth test. (In his monograph on PS, JGP identifies one man as Dr. Z. Rejdak and the other as Rejdak's "friend.") Eight targets from the red set were used, concealed in *C* jackets as before. The location of the experiment is not given. Jacobson randomized behind an undescribed "screen." PS made fifty runs, his calls recorded by JGP. There was slight focusing on covers, strong focusing on jackets, and of course no success on cards, even though PS was still striving to hit on colors.

JGP's lengthy discussion of all four tests contains some interesting remarks. He writes that during the first series, while recording calls, he was closely watched by Blom to make sure he made no "motivational errors." While recording, JGP was surely not watching PS's hands, and neither was Blom, who was watching JGP's hands. The other two men were usually busy randomizing targets. Since no one present imagined the use of a "move," it is hard to suppose that PS's hands were watched at all times while he made his calls and moved the target to one side. Even had they watched, they would have seen nothing suspicious. Only a magician on the scene would have known what to look for in the way PS gripped the targets.

JGP is enormously puzzled by the fact that in the last three tests the focusing effect moved from concealed aspects of the targets to the outsides of certain jackets:

> Thus it seemed that what we were witnessing in these results was an effect that we anticipated might occur—a logical extension of what had apparently taken place previously. This was an outward migration of the locus of focusing from the center of the target packet toward the surface layer or aspect. Previous results, as well as the results of Series I of the present investigations, showed that this migration did not take place immediately when a new layer of shielding material (the jacket) was added. But nevertheless we were prepared to have it occur gradually and to some degree unexpectedly; and this is apparently what happened in some of the series presented in this paper. The most striking instance was the evidence for a side focusing effect on jacket 5/6 of the A set, *beginning with the second series in which these jackets were used in Prague.*

Why, indeed, did PS in the last three series shift his focusing from covers to jackets? My guess is that he was being cautious in the presence of a new researcher, Jacobson, and in the last test, two new Czech observers. Remember that in the first series, when he scored on covers, he was working with covers in the red set, which, from our point of view, had already been marked. In Series 2 and 3, the covers were new, and PS may have considered it too risky to mark them. In the last test, the red covers were used again, but now he was being observed by two strangers, and PS may have decided it best to avoid the move altogether and confine himself to jacket blemishes. We should remember also that JGP had discussed with PS his observation that focusing was, for some unknown reason, migrating outward. Always obliging, PS may have decided to continue the migration. Nothing was easier than recalling blemishes on jackets, and such focusing would be sufficient to keep JGP interested in further testing.

JGP was thoroughly persuaded that PS's focusing on jackets was an ESP effect, not a sensory one. What obviously was needed was a test in which this sensory possibility could be eliminated. That was the purpose of an experiment we will examine in Chapter 23, which took place during PS's second trip to Charlottesville. But before then, JGP and Jacobson continued their testing in Prague, as we shall see in the next chapter.

Chapter 22

Prague, 1967

DATE: September 1967

PLACE: Miss R's apartment in Prague

PAPER: "Prediction of ESP Performance on Selected Focusing Effect Targets." J. G. Pratt and N. Jacobson, in the *Journal of the American Society for Psychical Research,* 63 (January 1969), pp. 38–56.

After the tests of the previous chapter, JGP and Nils Jacobson continued their investigations of focusing with a new series of five tests. Focusing now seemed permanently confined to target exteriors, raising a number of puzzling questions on which they hoped to obtain light; unfortunately the new tests only increased the darkness.

For the first test (Series 6, to continue the numbering) the experimenters "improvised" a horizontal screen to cover half of the table nearest the spot where PS sat. Four "pedestals" about six inches high (in a photograph they look like food or drink cans) supported the four corners of a large inverted tray. On top of the tray they put a large flat piece of cardboard, which extended over the table's edge on PS's side and over the table's edges to the left and right of PS. On top of the cardboard, a briefcase turned on its side kept the structure stable. A photograph and a drawing show the seating arrangement. JGP and Jacobson sat facing each other at the end of the table farthest from the tray and cardboard canopy. PS sat between them on the canopy side.

Here was the plan. Covers 1/2 and 15/16 from the red set, on which there earlier had been strong focusing, were fastened together—sides 1 and

16 on the outside—by a rubber band around their middles. This "sandwich" (as the authors call it) was shown to PS, but he was not allowed to touch it. He was told that both covers were empty.

Using random numbers, the two experimenters randomized the sandwich's orientation before each call by a complicated procedure designed to prevent either man from knowing which side was finally up. First Jacobson lowered the sandwich out of sight of both JGP and PS, then consulted his list of random numbers. If the next digit was even, he left the cover with the same side up. If the digit was odd, he turned the sandwich over. He then slid the target across the table, under the canopy, to JGP who held it below the table while he consulted *his* list of random numbers. If the next digit was even, he left the sandwich as he received it, and turned it over if the digit was odd.

JGP then slid the sandwich under the canopy to PS. It was assumed that PS could not see the target because it was screened by the cardboard that projected backward toward his chest. PS then placed his fingers on the sandwich and called either white or green. "In all the work presented in this paper," we are informed, "the subject only briefly and lightly brought his fingers into contact with a small part of the area of the upper surface of the target object, and the spots touched varied from trial to trial." From this and similar remarks one gathers that the experimenters could at all times see under the canopy and observe PS's right hand while he felt the target.

We are assured that when PS touched the sandwich he could not see it, but this certainly is not obvious from the schematic drawing of the setup. (See Figure 6.) It is not easy to determine the exact angle of vision of someone seated a few feet away. The authors say they sat in PS's chair to make sure the canopy hid his hand, but the cardboard sheet was simply resting on the tray, with a briefcase holding it in place. It could easily have been shifted a few inches away from PS during the testing. Such a shift would not be apparent, and it might be just enough to bring one end of the target into PS's line of vision. If this happened, it would be easy for PS to distinguish the two sides of the sandwich by observing blemishes. However, it is not necessary to suppose this.

It occurred to the experimenters that PS might distinguish the sides of the sandwich by feeling its elastic band. To eliminate this they repeatedly altered the band's position as well as its twists. They also checked the room for mirror reflections. They noticed that the metal rim of a ceiling light gave a "greatly distorted, small image of the side of the table" where the experimenters sat. They covered this with paper to make sure it would not provide PS with information—obtained unconsciously of course. If the pedestals were cans, were they also checked for reflections?*

In randomizing the targets, the experimenters tried to go through the same motions regardless of whether they did or did not reverse the sandwich. However, they admit that "the upper part of the body of each one was visible to the other, and if we had tried it might have been possible for either one to infer with some degree of accuracy whether the other left the target as it was or turned it over. But we consciously kept our eyes diverted to minimize this risk, and each of us is convinced that he did not know what the other did to the target."

I find this disclosure astonishing. Note that although it occurred to both men that PS may have seen a tiny distorted reflection of their behavior in the metal rim of an overhead light, it seems not to have entered their minds that PS might have obtained cues from the movements of their upper arms! Their only concern in this paragraph is that one researcher might have perceived what the other had done! "We are confident, therefore, that we did not make a sensory identification of the target." PS had as clear a view of the two men as they had of each other. If each man, trying to follow the target turning of the other, was able to do so with "some degree of accuracy," surely PS could have done the same thing.

However, there is no need to assume that in this series PS picked up any cues by seeing the target below the cardboard shield, by seeing a reflection anywhere, or by following the arm movements of the two researchers. All he needed for a high score was a tactile mark anywhere on one side of the sandwich. The red-taped covers had been used in earlier testing. From our point of view they *already* had been marked, although there was nothing to prevent PS from putting a fresh mark on one side. It could have been a thumbnail indentation, a slight corner crimp, or a spot of wax.

It could also have been a mark inadvertently created, as I observed in Chapter 8, by the way the sides of the covers were taped. It is difficult to tape sides of cardboard envelopes or covers so that ends of the tape at the folded edge are uniform on both sides. As I said, I own two cardboard envelopes from the yellow set. On both of them the end of one piece of yellow plastic tape is cut on a slight bias, with a corner projecting beyond the cardboard just enough to produce a needle-sharp point that jabs any finger sliding along the folded edge. If there was a difference, less extreme than this perhaps, between the ends of the red tape on the sides of the two covers used in this test, it would provide just the tactile cue that PS needed.

The outcome of the test was the highest success rate PS ever attained

---

*I asked Jacobson by mail if the pedestals were food or drink cans. He could not recall, but he said that as far as he could remember they were checked for reflections.

in formal testing by JGP. Neither side of the sandwich had been identified as green or white, but assuming side 1 was "green," and side 16 "white," PS scored 143 hits out of 200 calls, an extraordinary score of .71+. But there was something even more extraordinary. On the first off-the-record set of "about ten" calls, he made a perfect score. This was followed by a perfect score on the next 11 calls. Thus the first 21 or so calls were all hits. Although calling was continuous, the record sheets divided the calls into sets of eight, which were designated "runs." On two later runs PS also made perfect scores, and he had only one miss on the final run. As the authors correctly observe, there is no way chance could account for such miraculous results.

Although neither experimenter was capable of imagining that PS would put a mark on the sandwich, or consciously feel a mark already there, it did occur to them that maybe his fingers unconsciously detected some slight difference in the surface of the sandwich's two sides and that his calls were unconsciously based on this sensory input. So what did they try next to eliminate this possibility? They put a mitten on PS's right hand!

From our point of view this was a splendid idea. As the authors sensibly write: "This change of conditions further isolated the subject from sensory contact with the target. The mitten did not hamper his knowing by pressure contact that the target was under his fingers, but he could not get any direct cues through the sense of touch." Why they deemed it essential for PS to have pressure contact with the target is not explained. Did they suppose that his clairvoyance could operate only by going through his fingers?

PS was then working until 2:00 P.M. at his regular job as information clerk in Prague's main library, but he was available for testing after that hour. Two hundred calls were planned (twenty-five runs of eight) for the mitten test. From the start, however, it was obvious that PS was failing. There were no perfect runs. After thirty minutes PS interrupted the test for a cup of coffee. Ten minutes after the testing resumed he announced that he had a severe headache and wished to stop the experiment.

No one had any headache medicine, so the three men walked to a drugstore to obtain it. "The investigators did not doubt," they write, "that PS was suffering extreme discomfort from headache at the time." Only 130 calls were completed. No sign of focusing.

From now on this series begins to resemble a Laurel and Hardy comedy, with JGP doing his celebrated imitation of Stan, but without realizing it. The same test was repeated the next day, with the same mitten, except now an envelope containing a green/white card was put inside each cover. Green faced out on one side of the sandwich, white on the other. PS was told about the color cards and asked to call colors as before. The hope was that the cards inside the sandwich would somehow reinforce his ESP on the outsides of the covers.

PS complained that he had had little sleep the night before and that his headache persisted. Nevertheless, he insisted on going through all 200 of the planned trials. Again results were at chance. Indeed, of the 200 calls he had exactly 100 hits. The reader will have noticed that exact equalities between hits and misses appear often in JGP's published data. As we pointed out in Chapter 7, when another 100/100 split occurred, the probability of such a distribution by chance is about .06, or six times in a hundred. A chart showing the results of this second failed test with the mitten is headed: "Results of Series 7 showing an absence of focusing with continuing headache and following loss of sleep."

For Series 8, the next day, jacket 5/6 from the *A* set was used, with the 5/6 card of the white set inside to provide reinforcement for PS's ESP. The 5s faced out on one side, the 6s faced out on the other. Before the test, JGP wrote a prediction. Based on previous focusing on the 5/6 jacket, he predicted that PS would make more white calls than expected on the 5 side, more green calls on the 6 side. The prediction was based on JGP's theory that some occult quality could persist for months on high-scoring targets. Although PS no longer had a headache, and nothing is said about a poor night's sleep, the mitten was abandoned. One cannot help wondering why. If it was not the mitten, but a headache and insomnia, that killed PS's ESP, why was the mitten not used again? It is characteristic of JGP's testing of PS that whenever he thought of controls adequate enough to rule out visual and tactile cues, and the results dropped to chance, the controls were simply abandoned.

PS was now allowed to feel the target directly. The focusing returned, with 134 hits out of 200 calls, another high score of .67. The distribution of color calls fulfilled JGP's prophecy, but it turned out that this was because the prediction was opposite to what it should have been! JGP discovered to his surprise that he had incorrectly remembered the way calls had earlier been distributed on the sides of jacket 5/6. For some strange reason, PS had switched what the authors call his "polarity."

From our perspective this presents no mystery. PS simply felt for a mark on one side of the jacket, calling one color for one side, the other color for the other side. He had a fifty-fifty chance of fulfilling the prediction. As it was, he met the prediction, but only by switching colors from the way he had previously focused on the jacket. As we shall see, a change of polarity was soon observed on another test.

Here is how the authors describe this puzzling state of affairs in the abstract at the top of their paper:

The results showed that the subject continued to show focusing on the same objects as before, though he sometimes showed a reversal of response tendency from that previously observed for two targets selected for comparison. That is to say, he sometimes called white preponderantly for one that he had previously called green; and vice versa. Thus it seems that the tendency to show a focusing effect in relation to a particular object is more persistent than is the direction of the calling tendency by which the favoring of that particular target is revealed.

In plain English, PS found it easier to distinguish between two sides of a target than to repeat on those sides the polarity of his previous calls. A chart showing the results of Series 8 is headed: "Results of Series 8 with jacket 5/6 of the *A* set selected because of strong side focusing but showing a reversal of the previous pattern of response, possibly related to the experimenter's mistaken prediction." This means that maybe PS's ESP picked up the false prediction and fulfilled *it* rather than conform to the mysterious psi qualities supposedly clinging to the jacket.

For Series 9, done in the afternoon of the same day, the red sandwich was again used to see if any weakening of focusing on sides 1 and 16 had occurred because of the failures of Series 6 and 7, when PS was feeling this target with his mitten. After every five runs of eight calls, the covers were reversed to change the sides facing out. JGP made another prediction, this time based on a correct memory of previous focusing. The results showed strong focusing—hardly surprising, because PS was using an un-covered hand—but once again the focusing pattern was opposite to what it had been before and to what JGP had predicted. This instability of polarity continued to mystify the experimenters.

For Series 10, the final one, jacket 5/6 from the *A* set (it had shown strong focusing before) was alternated every five runs with jacket 9/10 from the same set. Jacket 9/10 had shown no prior focusing. Each jacket con-tained a color card "primarily to make it possible for us to tell the subject that he needed only to think about the color on the upper face of the card inside the jacket." The experimenters were still hoping that PS might again perceive card colors, but in the absence of that, they at least hoped he would continue to focus on the 5/6 jacket, and show little or no focusing on the 9/10.

Another effort was made to exclude tactile cues. Because PS had com-plained that the mitten was "awkward and uncomfortable," the experimenters wrapped the ends of his five fingers with paper tape, two runs around each finger. The paper cylinders extended beyond each finger (we are not told how far) and down to the first knuckle. Apparently PS found these cylinders less "awkward and uncomfortable" than a mitten, though most people, I suspect, would have found them more awkward and uncomfortable.

Success! The focusing continued as predicted, with more white calls (68 to 30) on the 5 side, and more green calls (54 to 48) on the 6 side. From our point of view this means that PS simply used the same tactile mark already on the 5/6 jacket. Also as hoped, there was no evidence of focusing on the 9/10 jacket.

The authors make much of the fact that PS had no way of knowing that two different jackets were being alternated in this test. They tried to do the switching of jackets in ways that PS could not pick up from their arm movements, but the main reason they are convinced that PS did not know two jackets were involved is one you would never guess. They asked him, and he said he didn't know!

In view of the paper cylinders of PS's fingertips, how can we explain the focusing on jacket 5/6 and chance results on 9/10? Of course one would have had to be there as an observer to offer good guesses. At this distance from the time and place, I can suggest only possibilities.

We can rule out the possibility that PS removed a paper cylinder, or pushed it down over the first knuckle, because the experimenters could always see his hand as he ran his fingers over the target. We are not told how far the cylinder projected over each fingertip. I suppose it is possible that one cylinder could be pushed down far enough to allow PS to touch the target with the extreme tip of a finger in a way that would not be noticeable to the researchers, but this seems unlikely.

How far back under the canopy could the experimenters see? It is possible they saw only the main part of the target. But not the edge farthest from them. If this were the case, there would be nothing to prevent PS from raising his *left* hand and feeling for a mark on the folded edge of the jacket. This, too, seems unlikely, though not ruled out by anything said in the paper.

A better conjecture is that at this late stage of the game the cardboard sheet covering the tray got moved slightly away from PS, giving him a view of a portion of the target, especially if he leaned back a bit in his chair. It is good to recall that the jackets were made from manila folders stapled along the sides, and that such folders were much larger than the covers being used. When pushed over to PS, they may have extended back to the edge of the table or even beyond. If this occurred, and PS could see a portion of the folder, he may easily have distinguished the two sides by blemishes.

A ridiculously simple way to make sure PS could at no time see the targets would have been to put a cardboard (or better, aluminum) box over his head, closed around the neck and with air holes at the top or back for breathing. No doubt both PS and the experimenters would have considered this too insulting and undignified, and PS would have professed another headache. To screen his vision by such a crude device as a large piece of movable cardboard, attached to a tray only by gravity, makes this one of the most crudely designed experiments in the annals of JGP's career.

It is understandable that during Series 10 the experimenters, weary from long hours of randomizing, observing, and recording, would have paid little attention to the exact position of the cardboard sheet. They tell us that at the start of the series each sat in the subject's chair to make sure he could not see the target while he felt it, but did they make similar checks on the last day? Only an inch or two of displacement of the cardboard may have given PS a clear view of the part of the folder closest to him.

Let's assume that the experimenters made sure the cardboard at all times screened PS's vision from the entire target. Is there another way he could have distinguished the sides of jacket 5/6 by nonparanormal means? There is, and to me it is the most plausible of my conjectures. Jacket 5/6 had not only scored high in Series 8; it had also scored high in earlier tests. From our point of view, that jacket had already been given a tactile mark. There was no need for PS to make another one while his fingers were taped. He simply felt the old mark with the fleshy part of his thumb or the heel of his hand. If the mark were a spot of wax, it would have persisted for months and could easily be felt in this way. If it was an indentation along the closed edge of the folder, the edge facing PS, moving the heel of his right hand along the edge would easily detect the nick.

It is also possible that the sides of the folder could be distinguished by tactile differences placed on the jacket by JGP himself when he made it. It is difficult to staple the sides of cardboard so perfectly that the staples are in exactly the same positions on both sides. We know that the experimenters took care to avoid the obvious difference between the smooth middle of a staple and its bent ends by seeing that staples on opposite sides penetrated in opposite directions, but subtler differences in how the staples felt could have been present. I do not know if folder 5/6 has been preserved. If so, it would be worthwhile to examine it carefully for tactile differences in the stapling.

Why did PS, if one of our scenarios is correct, avoid boosting his score on the 9/10 jacket? There may have been no tactile markings on this folder—he had not focused successfully on it before—and with his fingers taped there would have been no easy way to mark it. Or he may have realized early in the test that two jackets were being alternated, and guessed that the experimenters hoped for high focusing on the marked jacket and low or no focusing on the unmarked one.

In discussing the significance of the five tests, the authors are pleased to report that in all but two there was focusing on targets that had previously been high in focusing. This supported JGP's view that some property on the outsides of targets would remain there for an unknown length of time. They continue to be puzzled by PS's loss of ability to score on colors, and by the fact that in two of the tests he reversed the polarity of his calls. As they put it: "The mere occurrence of a focusing effect on a particular object may be a relatively more stable feature of the subject's ESP responses than the pattern or preference in responses which shows that focusing has taken place. It will be interesting to observe in future work whether this difference in stability of these two aspects of the focusing effect is confirmed." It still has not occurred to JGP that focusing stability could be due to the stability of a tactile mark, or that the instability of polarity could be due to PS not remembering how he had earlier called the sides, or not caring, or not knowing how he was expected to call them.

Nowhere in their discussion do the authors point out that the two failures occurred when PS wore a mitten. They have already convinced themselves it was PS's headache, not the mitten, that caused both failures. The big mystery of course is whether the focusing effect is psychological, somehow tied up with PS's "motivational system," or whether "there is some quality of an unknown kind in the objects themselves which makes them differ in their effectiveness as ESP targets and in the pattern of ESP responses they evoke in the subject." They note that focusing has persisted with certain targets for many months, and they wonder if it will persist longer. They wonder, too, if targets on which PS showed no focusing will at some future time become "effective in this respect."

> These are only a few questions that come to mind for which answers may be sought in future research. Doubtless there are many other questions that could be raised at this time, and many more will be raised as the research is continued (if the subject's ESP success also continues). But we can better decide on the basis of future results both what these will be and the order in which to take them up.

Chapter 23

Charlottesville, 1968

DATE: February 1968

PLACE: University of Virginia, Charlottesville

PAPER: "Further ESP Tests with Pavel Stepanek in Charlottesville Dealing with the Focusing Effect." H. H. J. Keil and J. G. Pratt, in the *Journal of the American Society for Psychical Research,* 63 (July 1969), pp. 253–272.

Stepanek visited the University of Virginia a second time, in February and March 1968, for thirty-nine new tests of focusing that were spread over a period of seven weeks. Most of the tests were conducted by Pratt and Jürgen Keil, a parapsychologist from the University of Tasmania, where he continues to teach. Keil is the editor of *Gaither Pratt,* a book we looked over in Chapter 16. At the time, he was on a six-month sabbatical to work with JGP. In three of the tests Ian Stevenson, JGP's superior at the University of Virginia, participated with Keil and Pratt. These will be discussed in Chapter 25.

By now PS was thoroughly aware that he had lost his ability to score on colors and was doing nothing more than focusing on outside containers. Because he had over the years grown accustomed to calling green or white, this "word association" practice (as JGP called it) was continued even though it no longer related to the colors of hidden cards. As the authors explain, "green" and "white" had become the symbols of a "binary code" that could just as well be thought of as 1 and 0, or x and y.

Two types of outside containers were used in the new tests: shallow cardboard boxes in which targets fitted loosely, and specially constructed jackets. The jackets in turn were of two kinds: manila folders stapled on the sides, as used earlier, and "Jiffy book-mailing bags" with a slot at one end. In most of the tests white/green cards continued to be used for reinforcement even though PS's calls had no connection with them.

In reviewing possible explanations of PS's ability to focus on containers, the authors rule out four nonparanormal hypotheses. The positive results are caused by:

1. Statistical anomalies arising by chance.

2. Unconscious sensory communication of information by the experimenters in the form of body movements, sounds, and so on, that PS picked up unconsciously.

3. A conspiracy of fraud between PS and the experimenter, or at least one experimenter if there were more than one.

4. Focusing on "minute sensory cues of which neither the subject nor the experimenters were necessarily aware." The authors admit that excluding such cues is "more difficult than it would be in other test situations (for example, one where subject and targets are situated in separate rooms)." They offer no theory about why PS's clairvoyance would not work under such conditions—parapsychologists have long claimed that ESP is independent of distance—but are always limited to the "narrow range of conditions" in which he is in close contact, by eyes or fingers, with the targets.

A fifth hypothesis, the basis of our scenarios, is never considered— namely, that PS could be cleverly placing or feeling tactile marks on targets, often combining this with memory of visual blemishes.

Persuaded that all four of their nonparanormal hypotheses are unreasonable—and I fully agree—the authors are faced with providing a reasonable explanation of the outward migration of PS's ESP. Although PS was successful in the new tests only when he "could see and to some extent handle the containers," the authors are convinced that ESP was the basis of his focusing because in some of the tests PS focused on containers that were inside still larger containers. As we shall see, this not only fails to invalidate our point of view, it actually strengthens it. It allows for asymmetric marking in the same manner as always, except the marks are now on the second layer of containers (moving inward) rather than on any part of the packet below the second level. It is just as easy, while holding a packet and calling, to feel a mark inside a jacket as it is to feel a mark on an envelope inside a cover, or a card inside an envelope, when the envelope or cover is the outside container.

All thirty-nine of the tests were made in room 340 of the Staff Quarters Building at the University of Virginia Hospital. As we learned earlier, this was a very small room that had formerly been a bedroom. JGP sat at a table to the right of PS to hand him test objects. For the first time, a "screen" was used that was more adequate than a piece of cardboard held on the lap or a briefcase or suitcase standing upright on a table. The new "screen" was a bookcase five feet long and eight feet high, behind which Keil randomized targets.

Randomizing procedures also were better than before. Random number tables were used, with the experimenters shuffling and cutting a deck of playing cards to determine entry points. Targets were handed around the bookcase through an opening under a plywood panel that projected beyond the side of the bookcase at eye level of the seated experimenters to screen them from each other. In most of the tests PS made 100 calls in runs of four each through a set of four targets. The calls were simultaneously recorded by the two experimenters.

The authors do not describe each test individually. Instead they break them down into classes based on the procedure used. Four of what they call "nonstandard procedures," because they departed from customary practice, produced no significant results:

1. The double-table procedure. A shallow open-ended box was fastened to the table, its open end pointing away from PS. He sat with his hand resting on the box. A second table, five inches high, was placed on the main table to screen the box and PS's hand from his sight. At the other side of the main table JGP pushed targets into the open box. PS could neither see nor touch the targets when he called.

A variation of this dispensed with the box, allowing PS to touch the targets, but with his fingertips "heavily covered" by "several layers of tape." (The mitten had been permanently abandoned.) In another variation, "a piece of corrugated cardboard larger than PS's flat hand" was taped to the bottom of the hand. Again, he could not see the target, though he could touch it through the corrugated cardboard.

From our perspective, these were admirable controls because they prevented PS from obtaining either visual or tactile cues. In all tests using the double table, results were at chance.

2. Procedure with shallow boxes as containers. Instead of putting targets in manila-folder jackets, they were put in shallow, open-ended "stocking boxes" that were fastened to the inside of book-mailing bags. A target could be slid in and out of the box through the bag's slot. PS was allowed to see and touch the boxes, but not to see or touch the targets.

Again, there was no way PS could have boosted his score on the targets by seeing blemishes or feeling marks. Results were at chance.

3. Procedure with the box screen. A cardboard box was used with an open end pointing away from PS. On the side nearest him, a hole was cut through which he could put his left hand. The hand rested on a block of wood inside the box. JGP pushed each target against the block.

PS was allowed to lower his fingers or his palm down onto each target.

"PS consistently obtained significant results on the outside containers, which he could not see but which he could directly touch. However, no significant results were obtained on the targets inside the containers." This offers no problem to our point of view because it would have been easy for PS to make and feel tactile marks that would distinguish opposite sides of each target.

A variation put a book-mailing bag over PS's hand. He was allowed to touch targets, but only "indirectly through the mailing bag." Evidently PS found this more comfortable than a mitten. Nevertheless it was sufficient to cause chance results and the use of a book bag as a glove was never tried again.

We turn now to thirteen tests in which there was significant focusing. Eleven of them used four packets from the red set that had shown strong focusing in earlier tests—two of the covers had been consistently called white, and two had been consistently called green. Each cover contained an envelope and a color card. Because the envelopes and cards remained unchanged throughout all the tests, only the covers functioned as targets for the calls. The covers were put inside jackets from the C set.

The tight controls of the unsuccessful tests were abandoned. PS was allowed his "standard" handling—namely, to pick up a jacket, make a call, and place it aside. This obviously permitted asymmetric marking on the covers as well as memorizing imperfections on jackets, although this may not have been necessary because the covers and jackets had been used in earlier tests. The covers may have maintained earlier markings, and PS may have recalled jacket blemishes.

The experimenters noticed that the red covers, having gone through much earlier use, had acquired bends in their flaps, and different covers were bent in different ways. It occurred to them that PS could be picking up these differences by sensory means. They did not think of PS secretly inserting a finger to feel the bent flaps. Instead, they thought that the bent flaps might "open the jacket flaps in slightly different ways" that would be visible to PS. To eliminate this, after the first test they taped a piece of cardboard around the open end of each cover to keep its flaps rigid and "eliminate differences in the tendencies to stay open." Of course this would not interfere in any way with PS inserting a finger between flaps to feel marks on the top edges of covers.

A second alteration was soon adopted. "Although the covers were made from the same sort of material . . . there is no doubt that by looking at them differences could be noticed." It was conceivable, they continue, that some of these surface differences might produce "identifiable kinds of bulged surfaces on the fairly tight-fitting container." As preposterous as this seems (both to the experimenters then and to me now), cotton balls were inserted into each jacket, on both sides of the cover! The cotton wads produced a space of about 1/8 inch between covers and outside jackets. Again, this precaution has no effect on our point of view.

It next occurred to the experimenters that PS, because he held each jacket, might detect variations in weights. A postal scale showed no differences, but using a more accurate scale, slight variations in cover weights were found. Accordingly, the experimenter increased the weight of two covers "by taping small amounts of material to the lighter ones to make them all equal in weight within a range of 0.1 gram." (I quote from page 18 of JGP's monograph on PS.)

Still later, the investigators had another thought—never, of course, the thought that PS might insert a finger in a jacket while calling. They realized that in handling a jacket PS might occasionally view it "obliquely from the side" and thus "get a glimpse of the edge or a corner of a cover inside a jacket." To prevent this, the sides of the jacket flaps above the top staple on each side were taped together, leaving only the "narrow opening of the jacket." It was "quite inconceivable," they write, "that the subject could obtain a direct view of any part of the cover." It remained entirely conceivable, however, that he could put a finger in the opening, but the authors never conceived of it.

Since jacket numbers were written inside the flaps at the open end, it was possible for PS, while handling jackets, to glimpse these numbers. To prevent this, cardboard was added to the flaps to make them longer. Prior to this, we are told, the top edge of a cover came to within "about one inch" of the top edge of a jacket. We are not told how far the jacket flaps were extended by these cardboard strips. Such an extension would make it more difficult for PS to feel the top of a cover. Perhaps it is significant that the three tests made after the flaps were extended yielded near chance results on covers, with focusing confined to jackets.

There is no need to go into more details about results; interested readers can consult the paper. Nine of the eleven tests showed either object focusing (a tendency to make more than an expected number of same-color calls on a cover or jacket regardless of its sides), or side focusing (more than expected same-color calls on individual sides of covers or jackets), or a mixture of both kinds of focusing. In a footnote, the authors say it is best not to consider the focusing to be of two separate kinds, but to look upon them as different aspects of the same process, which they call "focusing in general." Object and side focusing, they remind us, clearly are not statistically independent.

Computer analysis of the data, summarized by a large chart, shows significant focusing on both jackets and covers. On the covers, side focusing was more significant than object focusing. Cover 15/16, for example, was called white more often than expected, regardless of the sides, but cover 1/2 showed even stronger focusing on each side.

To test focusing on jackets, in Series 22 the cotton balls were left inside jackets, but the jackets contained nothing else. They were put inside book-mailing bags. Focusing effects were found on the jackets. Since PS could see each jacket, this was hardly surprising. In Series 23 the cotton was removed, replaced by covers, and the jackets put in book bags. Again, focusing was found on jackets, but not on covers inside them. (Apparently the book bags were never labeled or checked for focusing.) Again, hardly surprising. The reader will observe that focusing never went beyond the second layer from the outside. From our perspective this reflected the fact that there was no way PS's finger or thumb could go deeper than the second layer.

As the authors correctly perceive, these two series "gave clear-cut results indicating that the association habits built up upon the jackets when they were the outside, exposed container continued to set the pattern for the subject's performance in relation to these same objects when they became the inside, concealed targets." From our point of view, PS simply memorized the outsides of jackets when they were outside containers, and identified them by tactile marks when they were at the second layer inside book bags.

The authors are aware that PS may have memorized the exteriors of packets by observing blemishes, but once having done so, the persistence of focusing when those exteriors became second-layer interiors can only be explained, they argue, by ESP taking over after the visual cues were removed. With this in mind they make an astonishing suggestion. In the early work of Rhine and others, perhaps it was the *looseness* of controls that allowed talented subjects to build up their ESP by first basing it on sensory cues! "The relative lack of spectacular results in the later period of the Duke Laboratory may have been due to better controls from the very start which did not allow sensory cues to assist in the building up of a supporting frame of reference for ESP."

In other words, the sensational results of Rhine's early work, in which controls were mild or lacking, may be accounted for by the fact that this allowed subjects first to learn sensory cues, then go from there to ESP. Good controls from the start may tend to stifle this training process and lead to poor results! This is the most curious explanation for the well-known steady decline of successes in Rhine's laboratory that I have yet come across. It is amusing to find it put forth by a parapsychologist who abandoned every tight control with PS as soon as he discovered it yielded chance results.

Let me summarize. Among the thirty-nine tests there was general focusing, easily explained by our hypotheses, in all the tests in which PS saw or handled packets. In the twenty-six nonstandard procedure tests, where controls prevented seeing or feeling packets directly, results were at chance. "The only other alternative to the ESP hypothesis," the authors conclude, "would be to postulate other unknown sensory cues which we did not take into account and which were not affected by the alterations. However, until such cues can be suggested it seems reasonable to assume that the subject was able to discriminate by ESP."

I agree. The main purpose of this book is to postulate sensory cues which the authors indeed failed to take into account.

Chapter 24

Charlottesville, 1968

DATE: February 1968
PLACE: University of Virginia, Charlottesville
PAPER: "The Focusing Effect as Patterned Behavior Based on Habitual Object-Word Associations: A Working Hypothesis with Supporting Evidence." J. G. Pratt and H. H. J. Keil, in the *Journal of the American Society for Psychical Research,* 63 (October 1969), pp. 314–337.

Parapsychologists and skeptics alike will surely agree with this paper's opening statement: "Perhaps the central mystery of ESP is that of how the subject makes contact with a remote or concealed target. This mystery seems particularly baffling in clairvoyance when the target is an 'inert' physical object."

The paper analyzes twenty tests, fifteen selected from the thirty-nine that are the subject-matter of the previous chapter, and five similar tests made three months later when the authors were in Prague for a three-month visit. The focus is on manila jackets when they served first as outside containers, later as objects inside book bags. The purpose of the analysis is to support the hypothesis, suggested at the end of the previous chapter, that PS's clairvoyance on second-level containers can be explained as a learning process. First he learns to recognize the sides of outermost containers by unconsciously observing blemishes, then in his unconscious mind the sides become linked to green and white calls by a process similar to that of learning the meaning of words by associating them with objects. Once an association has been firmly established, ESP slowly takes it over, allowing PS to identify memorized sides when they are hidden within still larger containers. This is put forth as a tentative, working conjecture to compete with Ryzl's theory of mental impregnation and W. G. Roll's theory of psi fields.

The twenty tests analyzed in the paper are mostly those that involved what the authors call the "standard procedure," which permits PS to pick up each packet, call, and put it aside. The packets usually consisted of four covers, each with a white/green card inside, and concealed in jackets made from manila folders stapled along the sides.

> Although the jackets are similar in appearance it is possible even on casual inspection to notice differences among them. Obviously PS did not deliberately try to pattern his responses to these visible cues; otherwise he could have achieved complete accuracy at least with some of them. His task was after all to respond to the inside targets. Nevertheless his responses were gradually and presumably without his awareness influenced by the outside containers.

It is difficult to exaggerate the naivete of these remarks. If our conjectures about PS are right, he was a highly intelligent, clever person with an excellent memory—after all, his job was information clerk at a library. To make perfect scores on both sides of a jacket would have given away the game, quite apart from the fact that he was supposed to be trying to hit on inside covers.

Computer analysis of the twenty tests is complicated; readers who are interested in details can consult the paper. Here is how JGP summarized the results in his monograph on PS:

> During the conditions of sensory exposure to the jackets, PS gradually developed strong patterning of his calls on these objects, while the focusing effect on the concealed covers was continuing at a high level of statistical significance but gradually getting weaker. Eventually we concealed the jackets inside Jiffy book-mailing envelopes as outside containers for them. With the jackets, as with the covers previously, the significant patterning of calls continued when those objects were concealed in large containers. In the research report presenting these results, Keil and I discussed at greater length than in our preceding report the "habitual object-word associations" hypothesis of the focusing effect.

How could PS recognize the sides of jackets when they were inside Jiffy bags? The posssibility of inserting a finger or thumb to feel a mark on the jacket's top edge has still not entered JGP's mind. The best he can think of is that when cotton balls were put inside bags, PS somehow "recognized differences in the distribution of the cotton balls." The authors spend much time explaining why they consider this an unreasonable possibility, and of course I agree.

Because none of the twenty experiments presents anything not completely explained by our point of view, there is no need to go into details about how the authors analyze the results. However, one test (Series 24), not described in the previous paper and not part of the twenty, deserves mention. Two covers were put in jackets that in turn went into bookbags. Two other covers without jackets went into two other book bags. Because the covers without jackets were lighter than the other two, the weight was equalized by adding "a border of stiff wire around the covers and taping this in place." A hundred runs were planned, but during the first fifty trials PS repeatedly called the bags holding jackets green, and those without jackets white.

> The covers with the wire borders attached were narrower and thinner than the jackets with their contents, and there was a noticeable difference in the outside appearance of the book bags. Apparently PS, in carrying out the task assigned in this test, became aware (perhaps unconsciously) of this difference and quickly formed the habit of responding on this basis. This observation is presented here as further evidence that PS forms habitual response patterns on a sensory basis when cues are available.

Can you imagine a more preposterous experimental design? For the second half of the experiment a ten-inch-long box, wider and thicker than a jacket, was forced into each book bag. Each box contained loosely fitting material. Fifty more runs were made. Lo and behold PS responded differently to the bags! He called one bag white 35 times out of 50, another one green 39 times out of 50, and responded neutrally to the other two. Another remark of incredible naivete follows: "The results . . . suggest that the book bags had differences in appearance which the subject learned to recognize and on the basis of which he developed strong response habits." The authors naturally regard these habits as completely unconscious, otherwise why would PS not have scored perfectly on all four bags?

The experimenters report a test with an unnamed woman who had no previous experience with ESP testing. Four red-set covers holding envelopes and cards were randomly put in four jackets. Her task was to guess the colors on the cards. The first 100 calls showed nothing above chance on jackets, covers, and cards, but during a second run of 100 calls she began calling a certain jacket side white 43 times out of 50, and in a third series of 100 runs she called the same side white 36 times out of 47. Would this habit continue when the jackets were hidden in book bags?

"Unfortunately, the white-calling tendency for side 3 completely disappeared and all the results were within the range of chance variation."

The authors conclude that the woman unconsciously developed a response habit to one side of the exposed jacket. Because she lacked PS's ability, the habit "failed in her case to serve as a vehicle for ESP performance when the jackets were hidden from her senses." From our perspective the woman lacked PS's talent, perfected over many years, for secretly making and feeling tactile marks on second-level parts of packets. The authors suggest that PS's talent to transfer sensory cues to ESP cues may be relatively rare, but the fact that it may occur in other individuals "is an inviting avenue for further exploration."

The authors now make a startling speculation. Is it possible that PS's ability to transfer from sensory cues to ESP cues may depend on the fact that outside differences on packets are not obvious? Put another way, if the differences are hard to see, perhaps this makes it easier for a psychic to make the shift from unconsciously perceived sensory cues to ESP perceived cues. "It may well be," they write, "that the ability of PS to react without becoming aware of what he has been doing is essential for the kind of ESP performance he has been showing."

Did the authors ever think of *asking* PS if he was aware of imperfections on outside containers? Yes, but they "deliberately avoided [it] . . . for fear he might become self-conscious about the test and no longer give significant results." I find this one of the funniest sentences in a paper that swarms with funny ones.

On their last three pages the authors ask no less than fifteen questions about focusing that they hope further research with PS and others might answer. Glaringly absent from this list are questions they should have asked, but didn't. Here is the most obvious one. How well would PS do on second-layer parts of targets if, while holding and calling packets in a standard test procedure, he was asked to hold each packet by the *bottom* corners, opposite the open ends? During the ten years PS was tested, there is no evidence that any researcher ever thought to ask this simple question.

Chapter 25

Charlottesville, 1968

DATE: February-March, 1968
PLACE: University of Virginia, Charlottesville
PAPER: "Three-Experimenter ESP Tests of Pavel Stepanek During his 1968 Visit to Charlottesville." J. G. Pratt, H. H. J. Keil, and Ian Stevenson, in the *Journal of the American Society for Psychical Research,* 64 (January 1970), pp. 18–39.

This is the third and last paper on experiments with PS during his second visit to Charlottesville. It concerns three tests by JGP and Jürgen Keil. Ian Stevenson, head of the parapsychology division of the psychiatric department of the University of Virginia, joined them as advisor and observer.

In their introduction the authors summarize earlier work with PS, calling him "the most outstanding example among gifted experimental ESP subjects who have been able to demonstrate their abilities for investigators while they were still new acquaintances." Only two researchers, they assert, failed to get significant results: Stevenson, in an unsuccessful series of 1,600 trials in Prague (see Chapter 9), and K. R. Rao, whose tests have never been published (see Chapter 13). The authors fail to mention John Beloff's failure (Chapter 13), apparently because he obtained psi missing in a second test, during which former controls were abandoned and Beloff reverted back to the "standard procedure."

"PS remarked several times that he was sorry that he had disappointed Dr. Stevenson and Dr. Rao through his poor results," the authors write, "and that he would like to show them a successful demonstration of his

ESP ability." The opportunity came during his second visit to Charlottes-ville. The three experiments in which Stevenson participated as an observer are identified as Series 18, 23, and 24 of the thirty-nine tests that were the topics of the two previous papers. All three were mentioned briefly in those papers, but are now described in more detail.

Series 18 used the standard procedure, with PS holding each packet while he called, then laying it aside. The packets were four jackets, each containing a cover from the red set (covers 1/2, 7/8, 13/14, and 15/16). Wads of cotton were inserted between covers and jackets for reasons given in Chapter 23, and the covers were made equal in weight by adding pieces of cardboard to the lighter ones. Keil did his usual job of randomizing behind the bookcase and passing the packets around the bookcase to JGP, who sat to the right of PS at a table alongside the bookcase.

PS held each packet while he called. The reader may have noticed that JGP habitually sat either in front of or to the right of PS. This was an advantage to PS. If (as we conjecture) he occasionally made his "move" to feel a tactile mark, it would be best concealed by the back of his right hand if an observer was on the right. We are told that the cover inside each jacket came to within 1/2 inch of the jacket's opening.

The experimenters were concerned (unduly from our point of view) over the possibility that PS might tilt a jacket just enough to glimpse its inside covers through the open end. To make sure this did not occur, Stevenson sat behind PS throughout the experiment, moving his chair occasionally so he could observe PS's hands from different angles. He saw no evidence that PS attempted to "palpate or otherwise study them [the jackets] with his tactile sense."

We were told in the first paper on the thirty-nine tests (Chapter 23) that the packets were always handed to PS with the open end facing away from him. The standard procedure was for PS to keep a packet hori-zontal while he looked down on it and made a call. Apparently he did not always keep it horizontal. Of the 400 calls in this experiment, Steven-son reported thirteen occasions on which PS tipped a packet. On eleven occasions Stevenson "was busy making notes or was prevented for some other reason from making an adequate observation." Thus there were twen-ty-four trials among the 400 when Stevenson "was not able to say that the subject could not have glimpsed the inner target."

This left 376 trials on which glimpses presumably could not have oc-curred.* A chart of the calls shows significant focusing on side 1 (32 green

---

*I say "presumably" because if in this experiment PS held the jackets vertically while he called, and well below his eyes, a slight bending back of the flap nearest him by the tips of either forefingers or thumbs (as explained in Chapter 3) would not be noticeable by anyone sitting behind him. This might explain why PS occasionally tipped a jacket back-

calls to 9 white), on side 7 (32 green calls to 14 white), and on side 16 (36 white calls to 13 green).

From our perspective, these results indicate that PS continued to make his move often enough to produce the scores. If so, how could it be that Stevenson, watching from behind, did not observe the move? I have several points to make in this connection. First, Stevenson was not watching for a finger move (such a thought had not occurred to anyone), but for a tilting of a jacket and a possible glimpse inside. Second, the move is easily made in such a way that it is invisible even to someone watching from behind. We must remember that (if our conjectures are correct) PS had many years to practice such a move.

The reader is referred back to Chapter 3, where a photograph shows how the move can be made so that it cannot be seen by someone behind the subject. The jackets used in Series 18 were the same as those used in the experiment covered in Chapter 19. They were $7\frac{1}{2}'' \times 10''$, with the manila sheets stapled along the sides and the bottom at two-inch intervals. On the sides (we were told in the earlier paper) the staples extended "for approximately half the length." As we saw in Chapter 3, this would allow a finger to go between the flaps while the hands held the container by the sides. Nothing looks suspicious from behind even when the packet is held vertically, and there is even less to see when it is horizontal. If you will staple the sides of a manila folder, leaving flaps that extend halfway down the sides, you will find that your index finger can enter the jacket invisibly, sweep quickly over the folded edge of a cover that is a half-inch below the top of the jacket, then come out again as the jacket is laid aside. Watching from the rear, Stevenson could say with confidence that he saw no evidence of PS "palpating" the jacket or exploring its surface.

Surely it is not necessary to convince the reader that scientists, no matter how competent in their specialty or how high their I.Q., are among the easiest people in the world to flimflam by the simplest of techniques. This has been proved over and over again during the past hundred years of psi research, but never more hilariously than a few years ago when two young magicians completely bamboozled a paraphysicist into believing they were powerful psychics. (For details see James Randi's book *Flim-Flam!* and the first chapter of my *New Age*.)

Stevenson is a parapsychologist incapable of believing that Ted Serios used deception in projecting photographs he had seen in the *National Geo-*

---

ward—it would give him a slightly better view of cover labels through a very narrow gap between flaps. My best guess, which is sheer unfounded speculation, is that PS focused by tactile marking rather than peeks. On the other hand, nothing in the published paper rules out the possibility that PS could have used a simple peek move, occasionally tipping a jacket a trifle too far and so catching Stevenson's attention.

graphic and elsewhere onto Polaroid film by staring into a Polaroid camera lens through the rolled-up piece of black paper he called his "gismo." It is a pity that the only investigator ever to watch PS make his calls from behind was Stevenson, and not a knowledgeable magician who would know what to look for.

What precisely *would* the magician look for? At this point let me call attention to an extremely important refinement on the way PS could have made his move, assuming our conjectures are correct. I have not stressed this before because it was unnecessary, but now is an appropriate time. The refinement makes use of what magicians call "misdirection."

In calling targets PS's actions have three phases: (1) accepting a packet handed to him, or picking it up from a stack, (2) holding the packet in front of him while making a call, and (3) placing the packet to one side. When is the best time to make the move? As any knowledgeable magician can tell you, it is *not* while holding the packet for a call, but *while it is being taken from an experimenter or from the top of a stack.*

One scenario goes like this. PS takes the target in his right hand, holding it by the right side near the top, and carries it to a position for viewing. While the hand is in motion, his finger makes the move. The motion of the hand, as it carries the target to a spot in front of him, hides the movement of his finger that might otherwise be noticeable. Another scenario: PS picks up the target in both hands, as shown in the photograph in Chapter 3, making the move while the hands and target are in motion. Covering a finger move by a motion of the hand is one of the oldest of magic techniques.

Once the target is in position for calling—horizontal, vertical, or in-between—PS alters his grip, taking the packet in both hands at the side edges, many inches below the opening. This is how he holds it during the few seconds it takes to make his call. Who but a magician would watch his fingers while he picks up a packet? It is *while he is calling* that his hands are closely watched. Because the hands are at the side edges of the packet, well below its flaps, the thought of a finger entering the opening would never occur to a nonmagician.

Although no paper on PS gives a precise description of how he held a target while taking, calling, and putting it aside, it is often mentioned that he held the packets by their "edges" and made no effort to move his fingers over a target's surfaces. This is how Stevenson, Pratt, and all other observers remember the calling process. Picking up a target, like putting it aside, would seem totally irrelevant to any method of obtaining tactile information about an inside part of the packet. Observers would retain accurate memories of PS holding targets by the sides when he called, his fingers far from the opening. If PS adopted this misdirection to cover his move—and there is no reason why over the years he would not have thought of it—it would go a long way toward explaining why it never entered an experimenter's head that PS could possibly touch the second-layer component of any outside container.

Having an observer stand behind PS while he called was such an excellent idea, even though the observer knew nothing about magic, that it is astonishing it had not been done before. One suspects it was done now because of a growing suspicion that somehow PS was obtaining sensory information from the second-layer targets. Of course a much simpler safeguard, which no one thought of, is the one cited at the close of the last chapter—insisting that PS always hold targets at the corners of the end *opposite* the opening, not just while he called, but at all times. If our conjectures are right, this would have permanently eliminated second-layer focusing by either peeks or tactile marking. There would have been no conceivable reason why this simple proviso would have affected PS's ESP, and it is a strong count against the competence of JGP and others that not once did they think of applying it.

For Series 23 the seating arrangement of the experimenters was changed. PS and JGP sat facing each other at the table by the bookcase. A desk was placed opposite the table where Keil sat behind the bookcase, and a plywood screen between his desk and Keil's table prevented him from seeing Keil while he randomized. He could see the table where JGP sat with his back to him, and PS sat facing him on the other side.

The packets in this test had four layers: a green/white card at the center, an envelope around the card, a manila-folder jacket around the envelope, and a Jiffy bag around the jacket. It was like a set of nested Chinese boxes. As in other four-layer packets, the cards and envelopes remained sealed throughout the experiment, so only the jackets served as the (second-layer) targets. The bags were always presented front side up, which explains why focusing on the bags was meaningless. The randomizing procedure, described in great detail, was certainly adequate.

The jackets bore the same numbers as the envelopes inside, and which had been used in the previous test: 1/2, 3/4, 7/8, and 13/14. Focusing on the jackets was significant, and similar to earlier patterns on the same jackets. Only jacket 7/8 showed strong focusing. PS called side 7 green 41 times out of 53. Side 8 was called green 39 times out of 47. The authors claim a slight focusing on envelope sides, but the chart shows these calls within chance. In estimating probabilities, by the way, it is good to remember that because green and white have no relation to the colors of interior cards, a deviation from an even distribution of calls could go either way and still be counted as side-focusing. This of course doubles the probability of a given deviation.

The Jiffy bags presumably were of the sort that have one open end and no flaps. For PS to make the move, therefore, it would be necessary to hold the bag at a top corner as shown in Figure 7. Observe that there is nothing suspicious about the hand even when observed from the subject's side, and from the other side there is likewise no indication that a finger has gone into the opening. PS could pick up the bag with his right hand, holding it as shown, and make the move while carrying the bag to a position for viewing, at which time he would shift his grip to holding the bag by the two sides, below the opening. Such would be the way he held the bag while calling, and of course it would be the grip that experimenters would recall.

The next test was designed in the hope of learning why PS had done so well on second-layer jackets and so poorly on their inside envelopes. Was it "because he had to penetrate through only one screening layer to make contact with them [jackets]? Or did the subject show a stronger ESP performance upon jackets because these objects were more effective as ESP targets at the time of that experiment than were the covers?"

From our point of view it was precisely because PS had to "penetrate" through only one layer that he focused on the jackets, but we have a different understanding of how the penetration occurred. To the authors, this was "the most rigorously-controlled experiment that Stepanek had ever been asked to participate in."

Series 24 was the test mentioned briefly in Chapter 23, in which two covers were concealed in Jiffy bags and two other covers were inside both jackets and Jiffy bags. The bags with covers alone were made equal in weight to the other two bags by taping a border of stiff wire to the three closed edges. The seating arrangement and procedures were the same as in Series 23.

As we learned earlier, it took only a few runs for the experimenters to realize that PS was repeating green on the bags containing both covers and jackets, and white on the bags with just the covers. When they inspected the bags "it became apparent that it was easily possible to tell which of the two bookbags contained the jackets. The jackets (with the covers enclosed) were wider and thicker than the covers with the added wire border. They therefore made a difference in the appearance of the book bags as well as a difference in 'feel' that could be detected when picking up the Jiffy bags by their edges. It proved to be easy to tell the difference by either sight or touch."

It is hard to imagine that such glaring differences would not have been detected by the experimenters until the test was well under way. Surely it testifies to the carelessness with which they designed experiments. Did they ask PS if he noticed these obvious differences? "We did not ask PS about the basis of choices because we have avoided discussing questions about the results with him that might make him self-conscious and might, as a consequence, interfere with his performance in further ESP tests." It is inconceivable that PS would not have noticed the differences. Why did he not mention them? Did he overestimate the incompetence of his testers, and think perhaps they would not notice the differences? Or was he just trying to strengthen the impression that when he called he paid not the slightest attention to the look or feel of outside containers?

For the first fifty trials PS called the two bags with jackets and covers green 85 times out of 100, and the other two bags white 74 times. Since he obviously was responding to the bags, the authors write, he had no opportunity to "demonstrate ESP in relation to the hidden targets. It came as no surprise, therefore, when subsequent analysis of the runs as a group revealed no evidence for ESP."

As reported in Chapter 23, the packets were now modified to eliminate their "gross differences in thickness and width." Four Jiffy bags of much larger size were used. Inside each was taped a shallow cardboard box open at one end. In two of the boxes were put the wide jackets. In the other two were put just the covers. Although the bags were "larger, heavier, and thicker than before" PS again gave no indication that he noticed any change!

From our point of view the results were to be expected. There was no evidence of ESP on covers or jackets (both inaccessible to the move), although there was focusing on two of the four book bags. One was called white 35 times out of 50, the other called green 39 times out of 50. Calls were at chance on the other two bags. "We presume," the authors write in the greatest understatement of the paper, "that the patterned responses to the two book bags had a sensory basis."

What about the failure to show focusing on the loose material inside the four boxes? "We can offer no explanation at this time," the authors confess, "for the failure of the subject to respond to the targets hidden inside book bags that had shallow cardboard boxes embedded in them." Their tentative conclusion is that this failure was not due to absence of sensory cues, but "to purely psychological factors even though we cannot now say what they were."

The authors add that they did their best to avoid psychologically influencing PS by not telling him that the large bags contained shallow boxes. They hoped he would not associate the thicker bags with boxes and find the boxes inhibiting his ESP as they had done in all earlier tests in which boxes were used. "But chance results were obtained, and we can only say that this hope was not justified." They suggest that even though PS did not know about the boxes, he may have sensed their presence by ESP, and this inhibited the operation of ESP on the contents of the boxes!

On the other hand, the authors realize that the failure of the test may have had nothing to do with boxes, their use merely coinciding with days when PS's "ESP ability failed to function for entirely different reasons." The situation, they write, "merits careful study. . . . Further trials with the boxes are needed before we could be completely confident that his reaction to the boxes involves a permanently negative factor." So far as I know, no more trials with boxes were undertaken. From our point of view the boxes were indeed a permanently negative factor.

Because two of the three experiments showed significant focusing, the authors conclude that PS had demonstrated ESP in the presence of a third experimenter "even though this was a person with whom he had previously failed." They regard the results of Series 19 and 23 as the "strongest evidence for ESP available from the 1967 and 1968 visits of PS to the University of Virginia. In the opinion of the writers the level of safeguarding conditions reached excludes any interpretation of the results on a sensory basis."

The authors close by repeating their opinion that PS first forms habits of associating the words *green* and *white* with the outsides of containers, though this is done unconsciously. The associations are slowly taken over by ESP when those containers go inside larger containers. They find this view supported by the quickness with which PS associated white and green with the sensory differences between the width and thickness of the Jiffy bags in the first half of failed Series 24. They urge further research, especially with other subjects, to confirm or deny their hypothesis, and they hope other workers will take up the challenge.

In his monograph on PS, Pratt cites this study as one of two that he considers the most conclusive in proving that PS had genuine clairvoyant powers. (The other instance was the Blom-Pratt work discussed here in Chapter 11.) "Except for the committed skeptic who is unable to grant the reality of ESP on any basis," JGP writes, "I do not see how any careful readers of the reports could study the evidence and fail to concur with the investigators that PS has repeatedly demonstrated an ESP ability."

Chapter 26

Charlottesville, 1968

DATE: May 1967-February 1968
PLACE: University of Virginia, Charlottesville
PAPER: "Identification of Concealed Randomized Objects Through Acquired Response Habits of Stimulus and Word Association." J. G. Pratt, Ian Stevenson, W. G. Roll, J. G. Blom, G. L. Meinsma, H. H. J. Keil, and N. Jacobson, in *Nature,* 220 (October 5, 1968), pp. 89–91.

This article in *Nature* is a summary of how PS responded to a single target in eighteen tests, sixteen made during two visits to the University of Virginia in 1967 and 1968 and two made in Prague in 1967. JGP was the sole or principal investigator in all eighteen. The numbers 1 to 18 assigned to these tests do not correspond to numberings given in the preceding papers.

The *Nature* paper focuses on cover 15/16 from the red set, chosen because it was the red cover on which PS had shown the strongest focusing. As we have seen in earlier chapters, this cover was first used with nine others. Then the number of covers in a test dropped to eight, and in the last eleven tests to four.

"In 1965," the authors write, "the research with Stepanek was interrupted when it was found that his response of 'green' or 'white' no longer correlated with the randomized sequences of concealed targets. Later it was discovered that he was associating his responses with the opaque covers in which the cards were hidden. . . . It seemed that the subject . . . had shifted his attention away from the cards and had formed habits associating the word 'white' or 'green' with particular covers."

From our perspective, this migration of ESP from color cards at third or even fourth levels in packets to containers on the second level is easy to understand by postulating what we are now calling "the move." Whenever PS handled the packets, and an opening at the top allowed the secret insertion of a finger, he succeeded in focusing on second-layer containers. When this move was made impossible, he failed to score on second-layer containers.

In Series 1, when the covers were outside targets, PS called 15/16 white 86 times out of 100. "This consistency of choice showed that he somehow recognized this cover as an object regardless of which side was presented upward." The authors discount PS's accomplishing this by recognizing blemishes on the grounds that PS never turned a cover over, so how could he associate the two sides? They fail to mention that covers of the red set had been used in earlier experiments in Prague, and PS was thoroughly familiar with all their sides.

Before Series 2, the contents of cover 15/16 were secretly exchanged with the contents of another cover on which green had been the predominant choice. "The response preferences followed the covers rather than the contents." Why this mystified the researchers is beyond understanding. PS had no knowledge of, or access to, the contents of the two covers, so naturally he continued to call the covers as he had done before.

Focusing on the outsides of 15/16 continued in Series 3, 4, and 5, when the cover was inside manila jackets open at the top. In Series 6 all four parts of the targets (cards, envelopes, covers, and jackets) were separately randomized before each run. "The associative tendency was found to be localized entirely in the covers." The covers were, of course, at the second level, where they were readily accessible to the move. Series 7 was a repetition of Series 6. Both tests (6 and 7) took place in Prague (see Chapter 21) in the presence of two Czech citizens, here identified (though not named) as a psychologist and a government official.

Series 8 was the first to reduce the number of targets to four, and to use jackets with double-thick sides cut from manila folders. Series 9 and 10 had cardboard strips taped to the flaps of covers to keep them from curling outward. PS continued to show focusing on 15/16.

Before Series 11, cotton balls were introduced to keep the sides of covers from touching the jackets. In Series 12 the covers were made equal in weight. White preference for 15/16 continued as before. In Series 13 Stevenson did his observing from behind (Chapter 25). "No evidence was found suggesting that the performance depended in any way on glimpsing an edge or corner of the enclosed covers." As we have seen, Stevenson's observations did not rule out use of the move.

For Series 14 through 18 we are told: "For more objective safeguarding . . . the jacket sides were stapled together throughout their entire length so that short flaps left previously at the open end for convenience of access were fastened down." This would have prevented any glimpse move, and also made the tactile move more difficult. On Series 14, PS's calls of white on 15/16 dropped to 44, a negative deviation of 6, well within chance limits. On Series 15, PS made 67 white calls out of 100. The positive deviation could have been luck, or PS could have managed the tactile move. It is also possible that, because of the increased difficulty in removing and reinserting covers, there was no randomizing of covers inside the jackets. If PS knew the results of Series 14, in which his score on 15/16 was negative, it would have been easy to score positively on the next test simply by observing blemishes on the jacket that held it. Perhaps the covers were randomized in jackets after Series 15. This would explain his score dropping back to chance on Series 16, 17, and 18. It is worth noting that after the failure of four out of the five tests using jackets stapled all the way to the end, this practice of stapling to the end was abandoned.

In this series it is useful to know how PS distributed his calls on all four targets. A chart shows that on 15/16 he made 67 white calls, and his white calls on the other three targets were 133. The sum of 67 and 133 is 200, which means that in this experiment he divided his calls an even 200/200. We have noticed many times before how often these perfect splits turn up in JGP's data. The probability of a 200/200 split is about 1/25, or 4 times out of 100. Put another way, if you toss 400 coins in the air 100 times, you can expect a deviation from a 200/200 split of heads and tails 96 times. Add to this PS's tendency on previous tests to make far more green calls than white, and the 200/200 split becomes even more remarkable. Either this is another strange anomaly, or JGP's data are not trustworthy.

Whatever the explanation, calls dropped to chance in Series 16, 17, and 18. The authors blame the last two failures on psychological disturbances. Photographers were present for Series 17, making a motion picture film. Series 18 occurred in the evening just before PS left to return by ship to Prague.

The authors regard PS's ability to focus on second-layer containers as evidence for JGP's hypothesis that PS first uses unconscious sensory cues to form an association between the words green and white and the outsides of containers, then he continues to focus on them by ESP after they are hidden inside larger containers. They urge research along these lines with other subjects. A brief comment by an unidentified referee points out that in all these tests PS was allowed to handle targets. This suggests tactile cues of some sort, but he admits that the controls seem to rule out "any known sensory mechanism."

Psychologist Mark Hansel wrote a critique of the article by Pratt and others for *Nature* (21, March 22, 1969, pp. 1171–1172). Hansel is the author of *ESP—A Scientific Evaluation,* first published by Scribner's in 1966 and later reissued by Prometheus Books. He too points out that no tests were made in which targets were screened from both PS's sight and his hands.

Hansel calls attention to the fact that focusing on 15/16 improved when the number of targets dropped to four. If ESP was responsible for his successes, it is hard to see why it would be affected by the number of targets, but if PS was recognizing 15/16 by tactile cues, it would be easier to distinguish it from just three other covers than from seven or nine.

Hansel is puzzled by the fact that the investigators "at no time asked themselves whether Stepanek's ESP powers depended on his handling the materials. No experiment is reported, however, in which he was kept out of contact with the jackets. Did such an experiment ever take place, or did Stepanek refuse to perform in such conditions?" Again, rather than use jackets with open ends "it would have been a simple matter to have placed the covers inside boxes with lids that could be easily removed."

Hansel wrote this before the publication of the previous paper in which just such box experiments were reported. As we have seen, all were failures. The failures were blamed on the fact that boxes are somehow inhibiting to PS, though why they should be is a total mystery. Hansel closed by pointing out that Pratt was the major designer of all the tests. "At no time was a complete change of personnel attempted even in the puerile conditions in which Stepanek was being tested."

Hansel also mentions briefly the possibility that in earlier tests a warping of test materials might provide cues, and he even suggests the possibility of olfactory cues. He did not, of course, think of the possibility of the move—a possibility more likely to occur to a magician than a psychologist. Once the move is understood, no other kind of cues other than visual are needed to explain all the results so far.

I do not believe that warping ever played a role in PS's scoring, and olfactory cues are even less likely to have been involved. They raise, however, a whimsical possibility. I suppose it is conceivable that part of a target could be secretly marked with an aromatic substance, but there is no indication that PS ever brought a target up to his nose. I know of no use of olfactory cues in mental magic, but magicians should take note. It suggests some intriguing possibilities, especially in psychic feats involving mind-reading dogs.

Before proceeding to the next experiment with PS, a paper by Rex G. Stanford and J. G. Pratt is worth mentioning. Titled "Extrasensory

Elicitation of Sensorially Acquired Response Patterns?" it appeared in the *Journal of the American Society for Psychical Research,* 64, 1970, pp. 296–302. The paper is no more than a fuller analysis of data for the first seven tests in which eight or more targets were used. The authors maintain that this data confirms the view, so strongly held by JGP, that PS first associates colors with the sides of an outside container, then uses ESP to continue that association after the containers are hidden in larger ones. Here is their paper's final conclusion:

> With the covers exposed, the subject would surely have used visual cues or, conceivably, tactal ones. To suppose that he then discovered other sensory cues by which he continued to identify the object sides when the covers were concealed, *and did so with a distribution of responses among the hidden targets remarkably similar to the one shown when they were exposed,* would represent an unprecedented sensory achievement. But the results taken as an ESP performance (as we feel is most parsimonious) are also unprecedented. Either way, therefore, the findings present a challenge that can scarcely fail to make further research along these lines highly rewarding.

PS's continuation of calling patterns on covers after they become second-level containers may be unprecedented in the sense that such experiments had not been done before in which such a transfer seemed to occur, but certainly not difficult to explain on the basis of our nonparanormal conjectures.

A more general discussion of this alleged transfer from sensory associations to ESP is "A Wider Conceptual Framework for the Stepanek Focusing Effect," by Jürgen Keil, in the *Journal of the American Society for Psychical Research,* 65, 1971, pp. 72–82. Because neither this paper nor the one by JGP and Stanford concern any new experiments with PS, we will move on to the next chapter.

Chapter 27

Prague, 1970

DATE: September 1970

PLACE: Miss R's apartment in Prague

PAPER: "Extrasensory Perception or Extraordinary Sensory Perception? A Recent Series of Experiments with Pavel Stepanek." J. G. Pratt and Champe Ransom, in the *Journal of the American Society for Psychical Research,* 66 (1972), pp. 63–85.

As the authors point out in their introduction, research with PS was highly productive from May 1967 to March 1968, resulting in papers that provide the content of our last nine chapters. However, from mid-1968 to mid-1970, a period of about two years, his performance dropped to chance. This cannot be attributed to the fact that novel procedures were used, because standard procedures were also used and PS "also failed at those times. Eventually, it will be important to give a more detailed report on all the tests attempted during this period, but we think this can better be done later as part of a comprehensive survey. . . ." Unfortunately, such a survey was never published.

Since February 1968, tests with PS were consecutively numbered. We are told that the last reported experiment was Series 43. This must be a mistake, because in Chapter 24 five new tests were added to the 39 previous ones, which would make the last one Series 44. In any case, the tests reported in the paper for this chapter are Series 137 through 145. As we are informed, this leaves a gap of more than ninety tests, all supervised by JGP, none of which have been reported.

This is an astonishing number of unpublished failures. The only additional information about them is provided by JGP in his monograph on PS, where he discloses that PS visited Charlottesville for a third time in early 1969. After that, all experiments with him were made in Prague. He continued to show calling patterns on outside containers, but the authors admit that this was "only the demonstration of a focusing effect based on sensory cues." PS completely lost his ability to transfer this sensory association to focusing on the same containers when they were inside larger ones. I quote from page 21 of the monograph:

> This change in PS's performance, which has been apparent in most of his work for the last four years, clearly shows that there has been some change in the research situation insofar as the subject's demonstration of ESP is concerned. We do not know at this time how to explain this change. At one extreme it is possible that the main factors producing it may be traceable to the investigators who could have allowed their confidence in continued success to lead them to introduce novel test features into the research that inhibited PS. At the other extreme is the possibility that PS has finally lost his ability to demonstrate his ESP capacities, as earlier outstanding quantitative test subjects have all done before they had worked successfully as long as PS. In between these extremes are other possible explanations. Two that appear to me to be worthwhile considering are: (a) PS has continued all along to demonstrate ESP but—as has happened frequently before—in a different way, one that the investigators were not expecting and that they have not yet learned to recognize; (b) PS has been going through a long period of relatively unreliable ESP performance due to unknown adverse psychological factors, but this is a temporary phase and he will return to his former level of success when he becomes "ready" for it.

I find it scandalous that these more than ninety experiments have never been published. It is not just that reports of failures deserve reporting, but something much more important. If a top psychic, who has been successful for many years, loses his powers, it is of enormous value to know what kinds of controls the failed tests imposed, because they may cast light on nonparanormal techniques the psychic could have used in earlier successful testing.

Why did PS's psi ability desert him for two years? From our perspective there are several possibilities. One is that he simply got tired of the whole thing, and decided to stop showing results. Another is that he may have developed some sort of antagonism toward JGP; disappointed because he expected that working with JGP would have brought him more money and fame than it actually did. A third possibility, granting our conjectures of course (which may be totally wrong), is that his conscience began to trouble him. After all, PS is supposed to be a devout Roman Catholic; the use of a tactile move to boost scores may have begun to strike him as something God might not approve.

My own opinion at this point is that JGP had slowly come to realize that PS could succeed in focusing only when he was able to handle packets. To eliminate all sensory cues, he began to develop procedures that made it impossible or extremely difficult for PS to use his move even though JGP never guessed what the move was. If this theory is correct, it would be of great value to know precisely what conditions prevailed in the missing ninety tests. Whether these details are buried among JGP's papers at the University of Virginia, I do not know. He adds in his monograph that a few significant results were obtained with PS after mid-1968, some published, others not. One of the published papers is this chapter's topic.

In September 1970, in Miss R's small apartment in Prague, JGP and Champe Ransom performed a series of nine experiments with PS. Ransom was then a colleague of JGP in Stevenson's parapsychology laboratory. Trained in law—he has a doctor of jurisprudence degree—Ransom is now the owner of a chimney-sweeping service in Earlysville, Virginia. He has authorized me to say that his overall experience at the University of Virginia's Division of Parapsychology has turned him from a believer in psi into a skeptic.

All but the last of the nine experiments conducted by JGP and Ransom used all or half of the sixty small Jiffy bags, each holding a green/white card. The bags were closed at their open ends with a paperclip that also held in place on the bag's back a sheet on which calls were recorded. The clips remained in place throughout each session.

The first experiment, Series 137, was broken into six sessions, each consisting of fifteen runs through the sixty bags. Because the bags had obvious fronts and backs, they were always presented to PS with their front side up. A majority vote was applied to determine the final color to be attached to each target, then these majority-vote colors were checked against the top colors of the hidden cards.

The cards were randomized in the bags before the start of each session, and the bags were not opened until the session ended. After each run, PS "retired to a corner of the room and kept his back turned during the recording" of his calls, as well as during the randomizing of the unopened bags. This was done by repeatedly tossing the bags in a "helter-skelter manner" on a couch, then picking them up again at random. After this, PS was called back to the experimental table and the next run began.

The purpose of all six sessions was to induce PS to score, as he had once done, on the actual colors. The bags were not numbered. Because a large number of bags were used, the experimenters "reasoned that the subject would have more difficulty recognizing individual envelopes [throughout the paper the authors use the term "envelopes" for the Jiffy bags] on the basis of sensory cues. . . ." PS was not allowed to touch the bags. JGP simply held them up to him while he made his calls.

The situation should strike any competent parapsychologist as one of high comedy. Scores on the colors were at chance, but PS showed his usual focusing on the outside containers—that is, on the Jiffy bags. Now comes one of those incredibly naive remarks that so frequently turn up in JGP's writings: "The experimenters examined the envelopes [bags] on which PS had shown the most striking 'white' and 'green' response tendencies. We were not able to discover the basis of his preferences."

The same results were obtained on the next three sessions. The authors are impressed by the fact that PS's focusing on bags tended to be consistent—that is, following essentially the same pattern—over all four sessions. "At the same time, his failure to respond to the hidden colors continued."

Now used book bags, much more than cardboard envelopes, covers, or jackets, develop all sorts of imperfections in the way of wrinkles, creases, bent corners, dirt smudges, indentation marks, and so on, that make a bag easy to memorize. Because PS was not allowed to handle the bags, the best he could do, and it would be ridiculously easy, would be to focus on the outsides of bags. Suspecting that PS was doing exactly that, unconsciously of course, the experimenters had an inspired thought. Why not darken the room and see what happens? They put two blankets over the only window that let in daylight. This made the room so dark that PS had to grope his way to the table. Deprived now even of visual cues, it is easy to guess the outcome. PS failed completely to show any focusing on the bags. "The darkened room had disrupted his calling habits on the envelopes [bags], but this did not bring success at identifying the hidden colors. Only twenty-nine of the cards were 'hits' on the majority vote principle."

In other words, for the fifth session, during which PS could neither see nor feel the targets, his clairvoyant powers totally vanished. One of the great mysteries of the past is why the great Spiritualist mediums needed darkness for their miracles. Here we have an opposite mystery. Why would PS's psi powers need light? In view of recent experiments in clairvoyance, in which subjects are deprived of all sensory input, one would expect clairvoyance to work better in darkness.

Daylight was restored to the room for the sixth and final session with the sixty bags. Focusing on the bags returned "as strongly as ever," but the majority-vote hits on colors remained at chance—28 hits out of 60. The experimenters were now firmly persuaded that PS had developed "strong sensory habits" in relation to the bags—habits that made it necessary to see them. The experiment was discontinued.

Although PS's focusing maintained a consistent pattern throughout the five tests during which he could see the bags, there was a curious change in the nature of his patterns. Instead of showing strong focusing on just a few bags, the pattern suggested that he was somehow dividing the bags into two classes, tending to call one set of bags white more often than chance would permit, and the other set green more often than chance.

When JGP got back to Charlottesville, he made the following interesting experiment with the sixty bags. He wanted to see if he could sort them into two groups based on whether they were more or less wrinkled. "The sorting was done rapidly, without effort and without deliberation." The result was a total surprise. He found he had consistently divided the bags into two sets, but not on the intended basis. "He had put the thirty envelopes [bags] that had been used in *every series* in Prague predominantly into one group, and those that had been used only in the first part of the research into another group. Instead of using the amount of wrinkling, as intended, the experimenter had unconsciously fallen into the habit of sorting on the basis of the difference in appearance caused by the amount of previous handling. This demonstration showed not only that consistent sorting of the envelopes [bags] could be achieved without recognizing individual ones but also that the person doing the sorting might not know how he was doing it."

The authors cite other visual cues by which the bags could be sorted into two groups, such as a bag looking lighter or darker than the average, or its top end bent in one direction or the other. "Since any such criterion would be a matter of degree, all that the subject needed to do to obtain results like those he showed was to settle upon one general aspect and then judge each object as it came along as showing more or less of the selected characteristic. . . ."

Although it was clear that PS was sorting the bags on some such basis, the experimenters report that when they asked him if he was concentrating on the outside containers, he said he was not, "but was thinking only of the color facing him on the card inside." However, Ransom has informed me that he doubts whether JGP believed PS, and adds in a letter that he (Ransom) certainly did not.

If JGP could sort the bags unconsciously into two sets, it surely would be possible for PS to do the same thing consciously. And if the sorting was done on the same visual basis for all five sessions that showed focusing, it would explain the persistence of the focusing patterns from session to session.

Another and even easier basis for binary sorting occurs to me while I type. Paper clips have two sides, a large one and a small one. We know how careful JGP had always been in stapling covers and jackets to make both sides of the target look the same. Was he equally careful to make sure that all sixty paper clips were turned the same way? If so, it would have been worth mentioning. The fact it is not mentioned suggests that neither JGP nor Ransom thought of it. If the clips were randomly put on the bags, it would be easy for PS to focus white calls on clips with the large side on top and green calls on clips turned the other way.

After each session the cards were removed, their colors checked against calls, then randomized and reinserted in the bags. It is possible that the paper clip for each bag was simply moved to one side to allow a card to be removed, then the clip was later moved back to center when the bag obtained a card again. If this was the practice, the clips would preserve their orientations. This would explain the consistency of PS's calls from session to session, except for the one made in the dark, which showed no focusing. If the clips were completely removed, and later returned with random orientations, the consistency of PS's binary division of targets would have to be based on visual cues of some other sort.

For Series 138 the experimenters decided to keep light in the room but to screen the bags from PS's vision in another way. It was also decided to cut the number of bags in half. Fifteen bags on which PS had most consistently called green in the previous series were selected, and fifteen on which he had most consistently called white. A color card went into each bag, its up side the same color as the calling preference previously shown on that bag. All this was explained to PS. His task was to do his best to show the same color preferences on the bags as he had done before.

To hide the bags, a "rigid asbestos fire screen" was placed horizontally above the table, supported by three stacks of smaller Jiffy bags, each stack about eight inches high. A gray cotton blanket was spread over the entire "second tabletop." Target bags were randomized between each run of thirty calls, and there were fifteen runs in all. Each bag was placed under the screen and pushed toward PS until it touched the blanket hanging down over his side of the table. Thus when he made his call he could neither see nor touch the bag.

It was indeed an admirable experiment, simple, elegant, and designed to remove all visual and tactile cues while in a room that remained light. "Analysis of the results . . . revealed that PS . . . showed no tendency to respond consistently to any of the hidden targets. The variations in his responses were no greater than could reasonably be attributed to random factors."

The next seven experiments were so bizarre, and described with such paucity of information, that it is almost impossible to evaluate them. For

Series 139 the experimenters decided to keep the targets out of sight but allow PS to feel them through the cotton blanket used in the last experiment. This was done by pushing the blanket that hung down on PS's side into the opening between the screen and the table top. This formed a pocket into which PS could insert a hand and feel the Jiffy bag through the cloth. The number of runs was increased from fifteen to twenty-one, making 630 calls in all.

The results were encouraging, but all we are told about them is that "the degree of variation found in the calling patterns . . . would be expected only about one time in twenty on a chance basis." A chi-square* figure of 46.84 is given, but we are not told how the calls were distributed on the thirty bags. Without this information, it is impossible to know just what the chi-square value means. Apparently it means that PS was showing focusing similar to the kind of focusing he showed in previous sessions, but of a weaker sort.

Series 140 used the same set-up, except a second blanket was added to form a pocket of double thickness. The top blanket was "taped to the end of the table" to keep the pocket from sliding forward when PS put his hand into it. All we learn about the results is that "PS showed stronger evidence of responding to particular envelopes [bags] in a consistent manner than was found when his hand was separated from the envelopes [bags] by the thickness of only one blanket." The results get a chi-square of 50.98.

To further thicken the material through which PS felt each bag, a large Jiffy bag (nine by fourteen inches) was placed under the two blankets. The side toward PS was taped to the table to form a hinge so that a target could be pushed under the bag until it touched the hinge. PS therefore felt each target by putting his hand into the pocket and feeling it through two blankets and a Jiffy bag. All we are told about the results of Series 141 is the following sentence: "Again, the distribution of calls among the fifteen envelopes [bags] was more widely scattered than could be reasonably attributed to chance variation." The chi-square is 73.42. Note the word "fifteen" in the sentence. This is an error that is surely not the fault of a printer. There were thirty targets in the test, and twenty-one runs. Note that in spite of the increasing amount of material through which PS is feeling targets, his focusing is getting stronger.

Series 142 duplicated the previous one except that now both blankets were taped to the table. "It seemed worth while to make certain that the

---

*The chi-square test is the simplest, most versatile, most popular of all techniques for calculating the significance to which an observed distribution differs from chance. Like most parapsychologists, JGP frequently invokes chi-square results to emphasize the importance of data. For our humble purposes, the percentage of target hits in a set of trials is usually all we need consider.

underneath blanket remained in place by taping down the ends of both of them. We had no indication that it had not remained in place previously, but took this precaution to make certain that it would do so." The results once again showed significant calling patterns. In fact the target focusing was so pronounced that it would be expected, we are informed, on a chance basis "only one time in more than ten thousand such series." However, the chi-square fell to 66.84. As to what the calling pattern was, not even a hint is provided.

Before going on to the next three experiments, we must pause to ask what possible techniques PS could have used to divide the thirty bags into two groups and focus his calls in such a way that one group got more than chance white calls, and the other group got more than chance green calls. (The actual colors of the hidden cards continued to be at chance.) Of course one would have had to be there to make good conjectures. At this distance I will suggest some possibilities that are not ruled out by any information in the brief descriptions of these tests. The point is not that PS used any of the conjectured techniques, but that the experiments were so lacking in controls that he *could* have used any of them.

1. Did PS see the bags as they were being transferred from the couch to the table?

We are told that after each run Ransom took the targets to the entrance hall of Miss R's apartment, closed the door, randomized the bags, and then brought them back to JGP in an "opaque carrying bag." JGP placed the bag on "the end of the couch at his right side under the blanket."

There is no picture of the experimental set-up, making it hard to know just what "under the blanket" means. We are told that the blanket hung down over the table on the side where PS sat. Does "under the blanket" mean that the blanket also hung over the end of a couch on which JGP sat? Or does it mean that the carrying bag was placed on the couch, alongside the blanket, but hidden by the blanket from PS's gaze? In any case, we are told that JGP picked up each target and placed it under the horizontal screen that was eight inches above the table top and pushed it forward until it reached the far edge of the table where it was hidden from PS's gaze by the blanket that hung down on his side.

The question is: Could PS see the target while JGP was taking it from the carrying bag and moving it to the table? As I have said before, it is difficult to gauge accurately the line of vision of someone seated a foot or so away. If PS could glimpse the target before it went under the screen, then of course he would have no difficulty distinguishing between heavily worn bags and those relatively unused,* the same way JGP divided them when he made his experiment on himself. There are, of course, other ways he could have divided them: those with a bent corner, those with the most wrinkles, and so on. If the paper clips were put on in two different ways, a division based on the clips would be the easiest way of all.

A chart showing correlations of calling patterns between tests discloses that the focusing took different forms from series to series in the first four tests (Series 138 through 141). This suggests that if PS was glimpsing the targets in 139, 140, and 141 (138 showed no focusing) he divided them differently each time. If the paperclips were the basis of his division, it could reflect the fact that after each run the clips were removed for checking the colors of the cards, then replaced in a random way that differed from the previous one. Or it could reflect the fact that as conditions changed in the experimental set-up, PS shifted his tactics.

2. Did PS feel the paperclips through the blankets?

Small paper clips easily slide off book bags, so we can assume that large-size clips were used. It is very easy to feel the difference between the two sides of clips when the bag is under a cotton blanket. I found it just as easy to feel the clips through two thicknesses of thin cotton blankets, and even through thicker blankets. One has only to move the hand forward until the finger tips touch the end of the bump to determine if the bump is near or far from the far end of the bag. Unless care was taken before each series to see that all the clips were "one way," feeling the ends of the clips would be an easy way to divide the bags into two sets.

3. Did PS secretly raise the blanket on his side enough to glimpse the edge of a bag or to feel the edge with his thumb?

In series 139, the blanket on PS's side was not taped to the edge of the table. Nothing we are told rules out the possibility that PS used his other hand to go under the blanket and feel the edge of the bag nearest him. It would not even be necessary for PS to put tactile marks on bags, though of course it would be easy to do so. Book bags, after handling, develop a variety of differences along the edges. Corners get bent slightly. Creases form at different spots along the edge. The bags were always presented to PS with the address side up, and presumably with the open end away from him. Dividing the bags into those with a bent corner and those with no bent corners would be one way of distinguishing "green" from "white."

---

*Ransom drew for me a sketch of the set-up, showing PS at one end of the table, and the couch at the opposite end, facing the table. JGP sat at PS's left, and Ransom sat on the right. Ransom said he could not recall how close the couch was to the table or the exact placement of the blanket, and therefore was unable to say that it was impossible for PS to have seen each bag as it was taken from the couch to be placed beneath the blanket.

Another way of gaining tactile access to the edges of bags would be to raise the blanket with the thumb while the fingers were placed on top of the bag. As the fingers pressed down on the cloth, the thumb could slide over the edge of the target. This would eliminate any movement of the other arm. If you will take the trouble to spread a blanket over a table, letting it hang down in front of you, you will find it easy to accomplish this maneuver in a way that is invisible to anyone seated on your left or right side.* This maneuver also allows a peek at the edge of the target. If targets were presented to PS with paper clip ends toward him, seeing the clips would be enough to divide the bags into two sets. If the bags were presented the other way, a glimpse of the closed edges of the bags would provide enough visual clues for a division based on creases.

We are told that when the second blanket was added (Series 140) the top blanket was taped to the table's edge. Would this not prevent PS from raising the blanket with his left hand or his right thumb? The answer depends on how the blankets were taped. Recall that the taping was not done to prevent PS from raising the blanket—such a thought would never have entered JGP's mind. It was done, we are told, solely to keep the blankets from sliding forward when PS pushed his hand into the pocket. Now a very inefficient way to tape the top blanket to the table edge would be to run a long length of tape along the entire edge. Unless the tape were extremely wide, it would hardly hold the blanket down. The best way to tape the blanket would be to take two strips of tape, say about ten inches long, and tape the blanket on the left and right sides. This would leave a large untaped space in the middle of the table, along the edge directly in front of PS. It would be easy to lift up the center of the blanket, either with the thumb or with the other hand, to obtain a glimpse of the end of the bag or to feel the edge with the thumb. Taping the ends of both blankets to the table, as in Series 142, would leave the situation unchanged.

Because the way in which the blankets were taped down to prevent

---

*Ransom is of the opinion that PS could not have raised the blanket enough to glimpse the edge of a bag. He says he was sitting so close to him that he would have noticed such a move. I suppose the question hinges on how low the blanket hung. If only slightly below the table edge, a thumb movement could be made in a flash, without any movement of the hand, and would be undetectable except to someone looking over one's shoulder. However, I myself feel that this maneuver is a less likely explanation of the results than PS's simply glimpsing each bag as JGP moved it from couch to table.

Ransom made an interesting suggestion. Since JGP both saw and felt each bag before presenting it to PS, could he have (consciously or unconsciously) divided the bags into two sets and in some way conveyed this division to PS by a subtle facial expression? He adds his belief that if the raw data have been preserved in JGP's files, the statistical calculations of all of JGP's experiments with PS should be checked carefully by an expert statistician—especially the raw data for the tests covered in this chapter.

sliding is important to know, I wrote to Ransom to ask if he could recall how the taping was done. He replied in a letter of January 29, 1988, that he could not remember. He added that he and his wife had visited Pavel frequently during a two-week stay in Prague in the summer of 1987. PS said no one seemed interested in testing him any more, and even if they did, he had no desire to cooperate. He told Ransom that that part of his life "was over."

As we shall see in the next chapter, Jürgen Keil joined JGP for further testing of PS in Prague, using the same experimental set-up, with both blankets taped to the table, that was used in JGP's collaboration with Ransom. I wrote to Keil to see if he might remember how the blankets were taped. In his reply of December 15, 1987, he told me that he too could not recall. It is to be regretted that no photograph of the table was made to show how the taping was done or that no drawing of the set-up was included in either of the two papers.

In Series 141 a large Jiffy bag was taped to the table to form a hinge on PS's side. The targets were pushed under this hinged bag so that PS had to feel the targets through two thicknesses of blanket and the thickness of the bag. It is not possible to distinguish the two sides of a paper clip through three such barriers. Was there a way PS could glimpse or feel the edges of targets after the hinged bag was added?

Again, it depends on how the bag was hinged. The bag was nine by fourteen inches. We are not told which side of the bag formed the hinge, but since the bag was designed to completely cover each target, hinging the long side would seem preferable. Once more, a horizontal piece of tape along the fourteen inches would not be as secure as two pieces of tape at the left and right sides, perhaps with a third piece in the center. This would leave a large open gap, or two smaller gaps, along the hinged side. When a target was pushed under the hinged bag, its edge would go flush with the hinges and would be open to both sight and touch on the side where PS sat. In brief, it would offer no problem to his seeing or feeling (or both) the edge of the target after he raised the blankets with his thumb or with his free hand.

We turn now to Series 143, which used the same set-up as before. By now the authors were firmly convinced that PS was "consistently sorting the thirty target envelopes [bags]—within each series, at least—into 'white' and 'green' groups." It occurred to them that perhaps JGP was unconsciously doing this sorting in his mind and conveying to PS the difference between the two sets by the manner in which he presented each target.

To test this hypothesis, on about half the trials Ransom gave JGP a secret signal by pressing his foot on JGP's toe under the table. When JGP felt his toe pressed, he pushed the target toward PS more rapidly and with greater force than usual. After a few trials, PS noticed the difference and remarked that JGP was "pushing" some of the targets. However, the experimenters continued the signaling and pushing until they realized that PS was not basing his calls in any way on the pushes, so they stopped the practice.

The results, we are told, continue to show a "significant level of patterning," though we are not told what the pattern was. Its chi-square dropped slightly to 51.50.

Readers will recall that Mark Hansel, in his letter to *Nature* (Chapter 26), mentioned the possibility of olfactory cues. Although the experimenters considered this highly improbable (as do I), Series 144, the last of their screen-and-blanket tests, was designed to rule out odor cues.

Before going to Prague, Ransom had made tests with Saran Wrap that proved it would "lock in" smells. He wrapped some mothballs in the plastic sheets and found that his dog showed no reaction to them, but strongly avoided them when wrapped in other kinds of plastic. Before Series 144 the experimenters selected ten bags from the thirty, with their attached paper clips and record sheets, and wrapped them twice around with Saran Wrap. An additional record sheet was attached to the outside, presumably with tape. The other twenty bags were not covered. Among the wrapped ten, five were targets on which PS had shown strong calling preferences in the previous three tests, and five had been called neutrally.

> Highly significant patterning was found in this series. The targets wrapped in Saran Wrap contributed to these results in the same manner and to same degree as in earlier series. Even the five wrapped neutral targets maintained their position of neutrality, and there was a high positive correlation of the responses to these ten objects before and after wrapping.

During the experiment Ransom informed JGP privately that he could tell from the sound when a wrapped target was presented to PS. "At the end of the series, however, PS, when asked, said he had not been aware of anything unusual about some of the targets, and we have no reason to doubt him." Even if PS had noticed the difference in sound, consciously or unconsciously, the authors add, it was "a matter of no practical importance."

No complete data are given on how calls were distributed on the thirty bags (only the chi-square of 59.86), but we are told how the white calls on the ten Saran Wrap targets compared with the same ten targets in the previous test when they were not wrapped. Four of the targets on which white calls were above average in Series 143 also exceeded the average in Series 144, and three that had white calls below average in Series

143 continued to be below average in 144. In other words, only three targets had calls switched from above to below average, or vice versa. This is taken to show that PS continued the same pattern of focusing that he showed on these targets in the previous test. From our perspective it simply means that whatever method PS used for dividing targets in Series 143, he continued to use for 144. Saran Wrap is transparent. If PS was glimpsing targets before JGP put them under the screen, or glimpsing edges by raising the blankets, he could still do so. If he was feeling for marks on edges, with his thumb or the fingers of his other hand, the wrapping would offer little difficulty. A bent corner is as easily felt through Saran Wrap as it is directly.

The last test, Series 145, used the same screen and two-blanket set-up, with the hinged Jiffy bag, but now the targets consisted entirely of twenty-nine white index cards, four by six inches. This unusual number arose from the fact that that was the maximum number of cards available. They were presented to PS in forty runs, in an experiment that took place on the visitors' last two days in Prague. At the start, the cards were identical, and PS was told this. As he made his calls of white or green, feeling each blank card through the two blankets and the hinged Jiffy bag, JGP divided the cards into two piles under the screen. Tally marks were put on the backs of the cards to indicate the color assigned them during that run. Before each run JGP and Ransom collaborated on hand shuffling and cutting the cards in such a way that neither had any sensory information about their order.

> The results did not look impressive at first glance. When formal evaluations were later made at the University of Virginia we found that the chi-square evaluation of the distribution of responses for the twenty-nine cards was not significant, but there was a suggestive correlation between the frequency of white calls for the individual cards within each half of the series.

Without being given the distribution of calls it is of course impossible to know how "suggestive" the correlation was. Even the chi-square value is not given, so I think it is safe to assume that any correlation was accidental. It is clear from the set-up that PS would have no way of boosting his score except possibly by placing edge marks on some of the cards and feeling the edge. But on identical white cards such marks would be noticeable, and besides, it would be difficult to feel the edges of cards placed flat on a table and under a Jiffy bag. Also, the shuffling would not be likely to preserve the way the cards were turned end for end when presented.

Although we are never given actual distributions of calls, a table shows the correlations from test to test of white calls on the thirty envelopes used in Series 137 through 144. These intercorrelations were significant in the early tests, when the bags were visible to PS. In the tests using the screen and blankets, there were no correlations with the previous ones, or between Series 138 through 141. However, in the last three series (142 through 144) correlations turned up. From our point of view this means that whatever method PS used to bifurcate the thirty envelopes, he used the same means throughout the three tests.

In both this paper and in his monograph on PS, JGP expresses puzzlement over the fact that the same focusing patterns persisted in the tests where PS was allowed to see the bags, but when the bags were concealed under the screen and covers the focusing pattern completely changed. From our perspective, this means that PS changed his techniques whenever conditions changed, but maintained the same technique from test to test when conditions were the same. From JGP's point of view, this switching of focusing patterns contradicted his long-held theory that PS first learned to associate calls with sensory aspects of targets and then, when the targets were concealed, continued the same patterns of focusing by ESP. The changes of focusing patterns in the tests described in this paper "made us wonder whether the hypothesis advanced earlier regarding associative habits formed for individual objects could easily account for the results. . . ." (I quote from page 22 of JGP's monograph on PS.)

"It is also a mystery," the authors write in their paper, "why the focusing effect of PS should have shifted from day to day during that period of the research, but we are at least familiar with many other examples of such unexplained periodic changes in ESP performance in other subjects." They also confess once more their failure to comprehend why PS for several years failed to score on concealed white/green cards, but showed consistent responses to outside containers—responses that persisted when they became second-level concealed containers. "These facts suggest that his attention becomes trapped by sensory features of the test situation instead of immediately focusing upon the concealed targets upon which he is consciously attempting to direct it."

The authors speculate on whether this migration of ESP from original targets to containers may help "clear up the longstanding mystery of why almost all successful psi test subjects have 'lost their abilities.' " The idea here is that they may not have *really* lost their psi powers, but merely shifted them to some other aspect of the targets—aspects that investigators failed to identify.

As for hitting on actual colors, PS failed on all the tests covered in this chapter. In Series 139–144, in which focusing was strong, he scored an overall total of 1,869 hits, a negative deviation of 21 from an expected 1,890. As the authors admit, "The deviation is not statistically significant"— not even enough to qualify as psi missing.

> The objective of identifying the hidden cards by ESP was clearly presented to PS and he seemed both to understand and to accept it. When it became evident that he was responding to the envelopes instead of the cards they contained, we asked him if he was concentrating upon the outside containers. He said he was not, but was thinking only of the color facing him on the card inside. The indications, therefore, are that he was not conscious of the fact that he was responding consistently to the envelopes [bags].

We are nearing the end of our story. Only one more experiment remains to be examined.

Chapter 28

Prague, 1971

DATE: February 1971
PLACE: Miss R's apartment in Prague
PAPER: "Further Consideration of the Stepanek Focusing Effect
in the Light of Recent Research Findings." J. G. Pratt
and H. H. J. Keil, in the *Journal of the American Society for Psychical Research,* 66 (October 1972), pp.
345–356.

In February 1971, four months after the experiments by JGP and Champe
Ransom covered in the previous chapter, JGP made another trip to Prague,
where he and Jürgen Keil, of the University of Tasmania, conducted twenty-
two more tests with PS.

The experimental set-up was essentially the same as before. A board
was supported horizontally about ten inches above the table. It was covered
with two cotton blankets that were taped to the edge of the table on PS's
side, and hung down below the table top on the other sides. As before,
a pocket was formed between the table and the horizontal screen into which
PS could put a hand to feel the targets. Below the blanket was the same
large Jiffy bag taped to PS's edge of the table to form a hinge.* The only
difference between this set-up and the previous one was that a plywood
board was inserted into the hinged bag, apparently to further increase the
thickness of the material through which PS was allowed to feel targets.
In other words, he now felt a target through two blankets, a Jiffy bag,

---

*I asked Keil by mail if he could recall how the Jiffy bag was taped to the table.
He said he could not.

and a plywood board inside the bag.

The targets were the same thirty Jiffy bags used in the previous tests, and with which PS was of course now thoroughly familiar. The testing procedure was also the same. Before each run, Keil randomized the thirty Jiffy bags in the entrance hall, then brought them to JGP in a "closed opaque case." JGP placed them "under the blanket," cut the stack, and "during the run lifted the targets from the bag [case] one by one and slipped them into position under the screen in front of the subject." Again we are told nothing about checks on PS's angle of vision, leaving open (as before) the possiblity that as JGP moved each bag from the stack to under the screen, PS may have been able to glimpse it.

Series 146 (continuing the numbering) consisted of twenty-five runs. We are not told how the calls were distributed; only that the focusing effect was significant (chi-square 54.76), that it continued essentially the same patterns as in Series 141 through 144. From our perspective this means that PS was continuing to bifurcate targets on the same basis as he had done four months earlier with the same thirty bags when he was tested by JGP and Ransom.

Series 147, made the next day, repeated Series 146. For some reason, it was a failure. No focusing was found. We are told nothing about the procedure. From our point of view either PS decided to stop scoring, or some change was introduced, seeming too trivial to the authors to be worth mentioning, that prevented PS from using whatever technique was the basis for his binary division of targets. Did Keil make sure that the bags were hidden while being transferred to the table? Were the two blankets taped more firmly to the table so that PS could not raise them in the middle? Again, one would have had to be there to answer such questions.

Whatever the reason for PS's failure on Series 147, it marked the end of his career. We are told that working conditions were now changed by the experimenters to allow PS "some degree of sensory exposure to the objects in the hope that calling preferences shown under these conditions would become sufficiently strong through practice to transfer to completely screened conditions. Our thinking about the focusing effect at that time was still channeled along the lines of associative habits linked with specific objects."

The number of targets was reduced to four: two bags with the strongest white-calling tendencies in earlier tests, and two with the strongest green-calling tendencies. Two experiments with "maximum screening conditions" (Series 148 and 149) yielded chance results. "A further test with two 'contrasting' objects presented with a single blanket between the subject's hand and the object yielded highly significant results in the expected direction. A repetition of this series, however, showed only random responses to the same two objects."

In an effort to revive PS's focusing on concealed targets, the experimenters next allowed PS to put his hand under a blanket so he could touch targets directly. He at once began to show focusing patterns, "but when we advanced to tests with complete screening the habits formed with the sensory exposure invariably failed to transfer to ESP conditions."

The experiments continued through Series 167. Although focusing effects appeared whenever conditions allowed PS a close sensory contact with targets, he completely lost his ability to transfer the focusing to those same targets when they were screened from his eyes and hands. For this reason, the authors considered only the first series (146) a success.

Most of the paper is taken up with a discussion of the strange shift in PS's focusing from specific targets to what clearly was a division of the targets into two sets, his white calls predominating on one set, his green calls on the other. The authors call the former an "associative habit" and the latter a "judgmental sorting." They attribute the change to the increase in the number of targets. The idea here is that when there are just a few targets, it is easy for PS to associate calls with individual targets, but when there is a large number of targets, this association is difficult to preserve. Accordingly, his ESP switched to "judgmental sorting of the targets in relation to some arbitrarily-chosen characteristic into 'either-or' categories."

> We are not at this time suggesting that the earlier conceptualization of the nature of the focusing effect (habits based upon *identification of individual objects*) is wrong and should be given up. Indeed, it may be correct for tests in which only a small number of objects are used, while consistent response tendencies on the judgmental sorting basis may occur when many objects are used. Our purpose at this time is merely to introduce the second possible interpretation and to keep both points of view in the research perspective until the matter can be decided experimentally.

The new interpretation, the authors emphasize, would also explain why some targets would show a higher concentration than others for the same color call. "The judgment would be easiest to make for those envelopes exhibiting the selected quality to the most extreme degree, and they would accordingly be called in the same way in the largest proportion of runs. Thus, highly consistent responses for particular envelopes could occur even though PS did not learn to recognize those envelopes as individual objects." For example, if PS was bifurcating on the basis of how wrinkled a book bag seemed, the most wrinkled bags would get the greatest concentration of the same color call, and the least wrinkled would get a similar concentration of the opposite call. The two color calls would tend to be more evenly distributed on bags midway between heavy and light wrinkling.

As far as I have been able to determine, the only subsequent testing of PS was by JGP in January 1972, almost a year later. He published nothing on this work, which presumably was done in Prague, but there are two paragraphs about it in his monograph on PS (p. 23). The number of targets was increased to one hundred. They were not book bags but cardboard envelopes of the usual kind, each holding a green/white card.

Four tests were made, each of eleven runs through the hundred envelopes. On the first two tests, when the same sides of the envelopes were "presented" (I assume visually) to PS, focusing appeared, but it vanished on the next two series when both sides of the envelopes were "presented." We are told nothing about testing procedures, but here is how JGP summarizes the results.

> The responses to the exposed envelopes were presumably entirely sensory. This assumption seems more likely to be correct because of the fact that the responses showed no consistent relation to the cards hidden inside the envelopes. Thus the results show once again that PS now develops consistent patterning of his responses in relation to the outside containers without revealing any tendency for his preferences to coincide with the positioning of the W/G card concealed inside. If it continues to be true, as has been observed in tests made over the last three years, that response patterns built up on objects when they are exposed do not continue when those objects are used as concealed ESP targets, I will have to concede, however reluctantly, that the focusing effect has settled into a form, at least for the time being, that is indistinguishable from sensory perception.

One senses JGP's extreme disappointment in this passage. The monograph was published in 1973. Pratt died six years later. I do not know if he and Stepanek saw each other during the intervening years, or whether any other parapsychologist contacted Stepanek for further testing.

Chapter 29

Conclusion

It is time now to summarize what we have learned, and to make some general comments about Pavel Stepanek and his ultimate place in the history of parapsychology.

His claim to fame is not that he produced psychic wonders comparable to Uri Geller's metal bending, Ted Serios's Polaroid camera pictures, or Nina Kulagina's ability to move and levitate small objects. Even these modern PK miracles pale in comparison with the stupendous feats of the nineteenth and early twentieth-century physical mediums. Stepanek's ESP successes, except for the sensational perfect score discussed in Chapter 4, do not come close to such miracles as Hubert Pearce's naming of twenty-five ESP cards in a row, in the presence, alas, only of J. B. Rhine. Stepanek's chief claim to fame is that his powers of clairvoyance produced moderate positive deviations from chance over a period of about a decade.

As JGP never tired of saying, most successful ESP subjects enjoy a burst of success, then their powers mysteriously evaporate and we never hear of them again. Whatever happened, for example, to Felicia Parise, who moved a plastic pill-bottle across her kitchen counter in the presence of Charles Honorton? As far as we know, she never did this again. What happened to the woman who, while asleep and monitored by Charles Tart, left her body and correctly guessed a five-digit number Tart had hidden on a high shelf above her bed? Because this amazing result is not as well known as the others I mentioned, let me digress a moment to describe it.

The subject was a "psychologically disturbed" young woman, identified only as Miss Z, who frequently at night had OBE's (out-of-body experiences). To test the belief that during an OBE one's astral body (soul) actually separates from the body and floats around in some sort of hyperspace, Tart arranged for the woman to sleep in his laboratory with electrodes attached to her scalp to record brain waves. Tart monitored the equipment in the next room, behind an observation window. Each night before Miss Z went to sleep, Tart selected a random five-digit number and wrote it on a sheet of paper that he placed face up on a shelf above Miss Z's bed.

For three nights Miss Z was unable to identify the number. On the fourth night, Tart fell asleep at about 6:00 A.M. He was awakened by Miss Z shouting, "Charlie, I've got it!" She correctly identified the number as 25132. The probability of guessing a five-digit number by chance is $1/10^5 = 1/100,000$.

Reading Tart's first account of this,* I was enormously impressed by its lack of controls. Tart tells us that he used a black marking pen to write 25132 in numerals about two inches high on a "small piece of paper." When he later described the experiment in Edgar Mitchell's big anthology, *Psychic Explorations* (Putnam, 1974), he said he wrote the number on a "large white card." He put the sheet or card into a folder, entered the sleeping room, and placed the card on the shelf. "This now provided a target," he writes, "that would be clearly visible to anyone whose eyes were located approximately six and a half feet off the floor or higher. . . ."

As I have said elsewhere in this volume, it is difficult to gauge accurately the angles of vision of someone several feet away. An old ESP card trick is based on the ease with which indices of playing cards can be seen from a steep slant, but to spectators in front it seems impossible the indices would be visible. Did Miss Z catch a glimpse of the number from her bed while Tart was reaching up high to slide the sheet onto the shelf? It is not easy to do this without tipping the sheet a bit. An even simpler possibility is that while Tart was snoring behind the window, Miss Z simply stood up in bed, without detaching the electrodes, and peeked. And there are several other possibilities, not one of them ruled out by a report that contains almost no information on crucial details.

After Tart's paper appeared, parapsychologists attacked it mainly for insisting that it confirmed the view that during OBEs a soul could actually leave a body and see things it could not otherwise see. One might have supposed that Tart would have preferred explaining the result by ESP. I am surprised no one suggested that Miss Z could have used PK to influence Tart's selection of the number or to translocate the sheet from the

*"A Psychophysiological Study of Out-of-the-Body Experiences in a Selected Subject," by Charles Tart, in the *Journal of the American Society for Psychical Research,* 62, January 1968, pp. 5-27. The paper immediately precedes the paper on PS by Blom and Pratt that is the topic of our Chapter 11. Tart's paper includes impressive diagrams of Miss Z's brain-wave patterns and a bibliography of sixty-five references. Tart wrote the introduction to Robert Monroe's *Journeys Out of the Body* (Doubleday, 1971).

shelf to her bed, then back up again.

Barry Singer, writing about this experiment in *Science and the Paranormal* (Scribner's, 1981), an anthology he edited with George Abell, called it "preposterous . . . not science; it's a caricature of science. Yet I imagine it is one of those that Tart would cite among the 'hundreds' that conclusively demonstrate psychic phenomena." Singer is puzzled by Tart's willingness to discontinue testing Miss Z because she "moved from the area where my laboratory was located." If astral projection is real, he declares, "it is certainly one of the scientific finds of the century. If I truly believed that I had found a subject like Miss Z who could help me demonstrate astral projection, I would follow her to the sands of Zanzibar. I'd mortgage my home to pay her to continue to work with me."

No one, least of all Tart, tried to locate Miss Z for more testing. Her name and present whereabouts are unknown. Yet this extraordinary experiment continues to be cited in psi literature in spite of no indication that anyone tried to replicate it. Here is a result so extraordinary that, if valid, it would revolutionize science. Yet the subject vanishes from the scene, and not even Tart thinks it worthwhile to try the experiment again with another subject who has frequent OBEs.

The unusual thing about PS is that replications were constantly being made with him and that he preserved his seeming psi abilities for such a long period of time. Although his testing was mainly by Milan Ryzl and Gaither Pratt, there were other psi investigators who also tested him with positive results. Our book has covered all the published reports in English. Hundreds of unreported tests, mainly by Ryzl and Pratt, were made—some successful, others total failures. As I have said before, it would be good to have details about these unpublished tests, but what data has survived I cannot say. Nor do I know why Ramakrishna Rao has never published his two carefully done experiments with PS that resulted in failures.

PS's second claim to fame is the unique specialization of his talent. Other notable psychics succeeded in a variety of test situations before their power failure, but Stepanek was successful in only one task. First it was guessing which side of a two-colored card was up when the card was hidden in an envelope. Various colors, even symbols and blank cards, were successfully used by Ryzl in early testing, but soon the use of green/white cards became standard. When such cards were replaced by ESP cards (requiring one in five choices instead of one in two), or by cards in boxes instead of envelopes, PS's clairvoyance refused to operate. Here is how JGP puts it:

> PS has always been totally *unreliable* as an ESP subject insofar as efforts
> are concerned to have him demonstrate his ability in test situations unlike

the simple test procedure with which he first started to work. Over the ten-year period of the research some modifications in testing procedure were successfully introduced, but these were changes that were introduced gradually and that came about as a result of his previous experiences with the basic test procedure. While detailed reports have not been published on all of the unsuccessful "novel" test conditions tried with PS statements made in the literature and by Ryzl in personal conversation make it clear that numerous efforts were made to get PS to demonstrate ESP ability with other procedures and that they uniformly failed.

After JGP began putting envelopes inside covers, PS's ESP began its slow migration outward. When envelopes went into covers, it focused on the envelopes and covers, with less striking focusing on colors. Soon it ceased entirely to focus on colors. When the covers (usually containing both envelopes and cards) went into manila jackets, the focusing moved to jackets and covers. And when jackets went into book bags, the focusing migrated outward again to bags and jackets.

We have explained this curious migration by conjecturing that PS had several ways of using sensory experience to score above chance. Possessing a powerful memory (you have to have one to work as an information clerk in a large library), he learned over the years to quickly memorize outside containers by what I have called their imperfections and what Pratt called their blemishes—the sort of marks that invariably can be found on any kind of container, especially cardboard ones. This was combined with a technique of placing asymmetric tactile marks on second-level containers. In earlier testing by Ryzl and others, before Pratt took precautions against glimpsing, we have suggested that PS made subtle peek moves to obtain information about targets inside containers with large flaps. We have also imagined, before Pratt adopted a policy of carefully guarding targets, that PS may have obtained access to targets, after certain tests were over, and adjusted cards to raise his score on colors after having focused on second-level containers.

After ten years of successful testing, even PS's ability to focus on second-level targets (with no reference to the colors of cards at lower levels) deserted him. His ESP became confined only to outermost containers. Because such focusing was easily explained by memorizing blemishes, JGP and other parapsychologists lost interest in continuing to test him. PS's glorious career came finally to an end. Psi researchers were no longer willing to travel to Prague or to finance trips of PS to the United States, England, and other countries. It is odd that no parapsychologist in Czechoslovakia pursued work with him, but perhaps this is explained by the small number of psi researchers in that country and by the fact that PS tried to conceal his psi fame from everyone in his native land except his parents and his lifelong friend Miss R.

The steady migration of PS's clairvoyance from color cards outward to second-level or first-level containers was naturally puzzling to JGP. In his monograph on Stepanek he has much to say about this. In the early tests, he writes, covers were not numbered. He regrets this, because had records been kept of how calls were distributed on covers, it might have been learned that focusing on them prevailed through all the early tests but went unrecognized. He reminds us that PS was trained by Ryzl to "see" through envelopes and covers as if they were transparent and to focus all his attention on the colors of cards. Pratt suggests that in trying to "see" the colors, it was impossible for PS not also to be aware of blemishes on the containers. His ESP became "trapped" by the containers on first and second levels until gradually they became more important objects for focusing than the colors he claimed he was always struggling to see.

In early work with PS, Pratt tells us, he constantly thought of his subject as responding to concealed cards. Not only was this the purpose of testing, but PS himself, whenever asked, always assured JGP he was concentrating on colors. "We were not mentally prepared to make the shift in point of view necessary to consider that the gray envelopes were being distinguished from one another by the subject's responses and that the two choices to which PS was restricted might be given without any literal reference to colors."

When a color call on an envelope coincided with the color facing that side, it was deemed psi-hitting. When the call failed to coincide with the color, it was called psi-missing. "This led us to present a picture of a complex psi process working in all possible ways or combinations on the hidden target cards: psi-hitting or psi-missing on both sides of a card; psi-hitting or psi-missing on one side with chance results on the other side; psi-hitting on one side and psi-missing on the other; and chance responses on both sides."

From our perspective, all these combinations are easily accounted for. PS was able to focus positively on both sides of cards or containers when visual and tactile information gave him cues about both sides. When he had no cues about either side, he scored chance on both. When he had cues for one side only, he focused on that side and randomly called the other. And when he took a chance on guessing a color, and was wrong, his focusing score for that side (or both sides) showed what JGP took to be psi-missing.

Both MR and JGP frequently comment on the fact that PS's tendency to repeat the same calls on certain sides of targets was usually confined to one side only. In other words, when focusing was strong on one side, calls tended toward chance on the other side. If our hypothesis of asymmetric marking is correct—and it is no more than a guess—this could be explained by the fact that in making contact by thumb or finger with the top edges of targets, it often would be difficult for PS to run his thumb or finger along the *entire* top edge. Suppose, for instance, he placed a mark near the top right corner of an edge. If he felt that mark, he would know the same side of the target was toward him, and he could repeat his previous call. Because only a small number of targets needed to be marked, it would not be possible for him to know by feeling only the right side of an edge whether the mark was on the left side or whether it was an unmarked target. This would explain why PS so seldom focused strongly on both sides of the same target.

In retrospect, JGP writes that he sees his early approach as "unnecessarily complicated." It was offered at the time "solely to satisfy the assumption that PS was responding to the concealed colors. A much simpler view of the matter is that the results show primarily a focusing effect on the *envelopes*." (By "envelopes" JGP means first- or second-level containers.) Because focusing on containers and focusing on colors are not statistically independent, it was easy to confuse the two. From the outset, JGP now thinks, PS may have been focusing mainly on containers, with only "moderately significant" hits on colors. Eventually, as we have seen, the positive deviations on colors disappeared as controls grew stronger, giving way to focusing on second-level containers and finally to focusing on just the outside containers.

JGP is also puzzled by day-to-day fluctuations in PS's performances even when he still had his powers, and which seemed to have no correlation with "observed changes in the subject's moods." He reminds us that in the tests he made with J. G. Blom (see Chapter 11), the day on which they agreed that PS was in his best form was the day on which they obtained the poorest results. When John Beloff tested PS (Chapter 13), halfway through a test Ryzl predicted a high score on the basis of PS's behavior. To his surprise, PS scored below chance. As for PS's eventual loss of ESP, which JGP calls a "slump that has extended over almost four years," he finds it impossible to explain this on the basis of any change in "sociological, psychological, or motivational factors."

Pratt discusses PS's strange confinement of clairvoyance to one basic task that could not be varied in any significant way without banishing his ESP. Even the substitution of ESP cards for bicolored cards defeated him. As we have seen, his ESP could always penetrate thick cardboard, and in the last chapter it penetrated two blankets, a book bag, and a piece of plywood. But it was unable to penetrate a shallow box. It failed to operate (except for some uncontrolled early tests) whenever PS could neither see nor touch the targets. A mitten on his right hand, in a touching test, completely blocked his ESP. A piece of cardboard taped to his palm did the same in a repetition of the test.

In seeking to minimize the strangeness of this confinement to one task, JGP reminds us that "many successful psi performers have not been able to demonstrate their ability in a wide range of test situations. . . . If a subject is accustomed, for example, to using a ouija board, an experienced investigator would be cautious about asking him to shift immediately to writing down calls for ESP test cards." However, JGP admits that PS's narrow range "is extreme in the degree of specialization he has shown."

PS was also unique, Pratt continues, in shifting his ESP from outside containers to a focusing effect on second-level containers. He discloses that Keil, working with students at the University of Tasmania, found subjects who readily learned how to make sensory responses to outside containers—something extremely easy to learn—but were unable to transfer this focusing to the same containers when they were concealed in larger ones. Pratt says he had similar failures with other subjects, and so did W. G. Roll and J. Klein.* From our point of view these failures simply reflect the inability of other subjects to think of and execute the tactile move.

JGP tries valiantly to explain in his monograph why PS's clairvoyance was never able to penetrate beyond the second level of targets.

> His approach to each target presented was from the outside inward. His job was to see through the covering layers to reach the card hidden inside. His method of trying to "see" the color on the card was not one of ignoring the cover and the enclosed envelope, but rather one of looking at them with intense concentration in the effort to see right through them. Since he was thus literally seeing the outer covers, and since he was not conscious of whether or not the ESP process was operating on each trial, he not surprisingly developed habitual ways of responding to some of the things he was seeing sensorially. Thus he consistently called some of the covers of the outside containers either "green" or "white," the only choices he was allowed to make. We know on the basis of recent studies that he might fall into such habits very quickly, and once they were formed they would have determined his responses on those objects.

"There is no clear evidence," JGP writes, "that PS has ever shown a focusing effect upon the concealed cards." No records were made of how calls were distributed on covers in early tests with cards inside covers,

---

*See "Further Forced-Choice Experiments with Lalsingh Harribance," by W. G. Roll and J. Klein, in the *Journal of the American Society for Psychical Research,* 66, 1972, pp. 103-112.

so it is possible (JGP thinks) that in these tests PS was responding only to covers, but his ESP focusing on covers was such as to increase the number of hits on the cards. In other words, from the beginning, perhaps PS's higher than chance scores on colors were no more than by-products of focusing on containers. I find this an astonishing conjecture. Surely JGP knew that in early testing PS showed significant hits on card colors that could not possibly be explained by focusing on containers.

JGP sensibly adds that if PS had become more proficient in identifying hidden colors, the focusing effect on containers would have diminished. "The focusing effect could not show up, for example, if his level of success on identifying colors were to reach the 100% level." Again, does not this statement betray a singular memory lapse? JGP seems to have totally forgotten that PS did achieve hundred-percent accuracy on fifty color cards in the test reported here in Chapter 4.

"Still thinking of the earlier experiments," Pratt continues, "we may say with confidence that PS did manage to penetrate to the hidden target, but he responded chiefly to the first concealed object he reached. For most of the experiments this was the hidden envelope, and he registered his ESP contact with it in the same way as his visual contact with some of the outer covers. . . . Where does this leave the cards? Not in as good a position insofar as direct evidence for ESP is concerned. . . ."

JGP rejects the notion that PS ignored the various containers when he made a positive score on card colors. "We are not justified in assuming that PS was penetrating through two shielding layers to reach the card by ESP if his results can be explained by penetration through only one layer to respond to the concealed envelope." Many of PS's "highly significant responses to the hidden targets were opposite to the position of the card inside the envelope."

> It is question-begging to say that PS was responding to the hidden cards with a complex intermingling of psi-hitting, psi-missing, and chance results on different sides of the cards. We can more simply say that consistent response habits were formed on some of the envelopes, with enough of them being in a direction influenced by the enclosed cards to cause a significant majority of the calls to be scored as hits when checked against the hidden cards.

PS's consistent missing on concealed cards is, of course, easily explained by our conjectures. Not knowing the orientations of cards inside sealed envelopes, he focused his attention on the envelopes. Naturally he would score above chance on some card colors and below chance on others. As for his overall positive color scores in the early tests, we have explained this by PS taking advantage of JGP's crude way of randomizing by cutting and turning the top half of a set of cards, and in some instances by obtaining access to targets and reversing a few cards. After Pratt adopted better methods of randomizing and began careful monitoring of the targets at all times, these positive deviations on card colors vanished.

There are, Pratt goes on, other subjects who have displayed unique ESP talents of a different sort. The one that comes first to his mind was an unfortunate choice—the calling displacements produced by Basil Shackleton in a famous experiment with the British parapsychologist S. G. Soal. It was in the data of this experiment that Soal was found (after his death) to have deliberately cheated. JGP notes that the "Shackleton effect" was never duplicated by other researchers. The reason, of course, was that other researchers were not willing to fudge their data to replicate it.

What about the influence of hypnosis on PS's narrow talent? Although Ryzl has made strong claims that it was his method of hypnotic training that produced PS's talent, Pratt strongly dissents. He cites failed attempts by other parapsychologists to replicate Ryzl's work and discloses that in the spring of 1967, when PS stopped off in Amsterdam on his way back to Prague, an effort was made (he does not say by whom) to revive his flagging powers by hypnotizing him. The hypnosis had no effect. Another attempt, we are told, was made in Prague in the fall of 1972 (again he does not say by whom), at a time when Stepanek's ESP had totally vanished. It too was ineffective. JGP is convinced that Ryzl's program of hypnosis had nothing to do with Stepanek's ESP talents. We of course fully agree.

As to the nature of focusing, Pratt continues to defend his early belief, which he says is shared by Keil, that it is the product of psychological conditioning, not an impregnation of a psychic "footprint" or "trace," as Ryzl contends, or the influence of a "psi field" clinging to objects, as Roll suggested. JGP reaffirms his belief that PS first learned to focus on individual targets. In later years he shifted to a more general kind of focusing in which he divided containers into two sets, based on some property such as "light" or "dark" in color, concentrating green calls on one set, white calls on the other, without reference to interior color cards. As we saw in the last chapter, by concentrating calls on the more extreme cases of the property, with random calls on fuzzy in-between instances, the result would be a focusing pattern of the sort that PS showed on later tests in which the number of targets was large. It is even possible, JGP suggests, that PS had been doing this all along. It was not recognized until late in the game because the covers had not been labeled and therefore there was no record of how calls were distributed on covers.

I have stated earlier, also in other books, my belief, that JGP, though gullible, was an honest researcher incapable of deliberately falsifying data.

On the other hand, I cannot rule out the possibility that in his strong compulsion to believe in psi he may have made unconscious errors in reporting and analyzing raw data. We have seen no less than ten instances (see Chapters 2, 6, 7, 9, 17, 18, 22, and 23) when his published data exhibited statistical anomalies hard to account for in light of standard probability laws. It seems to me entirely possible that JGP was under the impression that if a coin is tossed n times, the larger the value of n the more likely the number of heads will exactly equal the number of tails, and that this may have unconsciously biased some of his published data. If so, it casts a shadow on other data. I agree with Champe Ransom that if raw data for experiments with PS have been preserved among JGP's papers, it would be worthwhile for a skillful statistician to go over that data to determine how accurately it conforms to published data. I doubt if much of importance would come to light; nevertheless it is a task worth undertaking.

Let me now be as frank as I can about my own attitude toward Pavel Stepanek. I would be less than honest if I did not say that in my view his much-vaunted ESP talent was not genuine. I believe it was the product of subtle nonparanormal techniques that he perfected over many years, motivated by his desire for fame and money. We should remember that PS never engaged in experiments without being paid well for his time and effort. I offer this interpretation as a personal opinion—nothing more. I have tried to show that my opinion is not unreasonable. It certainly is not contradicted by any information in published papers. I am convinced that if JGP had thought of peek and tactile moves and taken simple steps to prevent them, his testing of PS would not have lasted as long as it did. One of the simplest ways to prevent both types of moves would have been to require that PS hold each target by a lower corner opposite the open end, but there is no evidence that JGP even considered such an obvious control.

If my guesses are right—and they are only guesses—I would like to add that I have no reason to look down on PS. As a lifelong enthusiast of conjuring, I admire persons who develop a skill in psi performances—in what magicians used to call "mentalism"—that can deceive intelligent investigators who are untrained in magic. I have a kind of respect for clever performers of psi magic, such as Ted Serios, Uri Geller, and Nina Kulagina, similar to my respect for skilled card mechanics and dice men who work for casinos or for themselves. If PS managed to flimflam Ryzl and Pratt, and a dozen other psi researchers, over a period of ten years, he deserves (in my book) high praise. It makes him a far more interesting and colorful personality than if he were merely someone with a mild, albeit peculiar, ESP talent that persisted for a decade before it evaporated. It is the researchers, not PS, who should be downgraded—downgraded for excessive gullibility, for failures to design experiments with adequate controls, and for persistent refusals to seek the advice of those who are the only experts on psi deception—knowledgeable magicians.

Parapsychologists with mind-sets so strong that they cannot conceive of PS as being other than an amiable man of remarkable psi talent and good will, even though he finally lost his powers, will be understandably furious with this book. All I have done, they will say over and over again, is go carefully through the published papers seeking for loopholes and inventing ingenious ways that PS might have boosted his scores by nonparanormal means, but without presenting a shred of evidence that he actually did so. I fully grant this charge. I can only claim that my conjectures are nowhere ruled out by what has been published and that they are fortified by the fact that whenever an experimental design prevented the use of the methods I have suggested, PS failed to produce results. When there were loopholes, in my opinion he moved through them. When there were no loopholes, he scored at chance.

But, critics will surely counter, is it not impossible to design *any* experiment that does not have loopholes? This is an old refrain, and it is false. Perhaps in some ultimate sense it is true, but only in the sense that nothing in science is absolutely certain. It is entirely possible that the earth is flat, but this possibility has been rendered so extremely improbable by science that no one acquainted with the evidence can reasonably deny the earth's rotundity. Who would argue that it is impossible to devise tests of the earth's roundness that will not have loopholes through which flat-earth believers can jump? In a practical sense, it is often extremely easy to devise experiments that will effectively close loopholes. If, for example, a transcendental meditator claims that while meditating he can levitate ten feet in the air and remain suspended for five minutes, would anyone argue that no definitive test of this claim can be devised? If a faith healer says he can revive a corpse, would anyone care to assert that this cannot be verified by a test without loopholes? If someone claims that he has captured a unicorn or a centaur, would every effort to refute this claim contain a loophole?

Let me give some less extreme examples. Not long ago there was a flurry of interest in psi circles over dermo-optical perception, the so-called ability of psychics to read print with their fingertips. Nina Kulagina, in Russia, was a principal claimant of this power. It is old stuff to magicians, who have been performing what they call "eyeless vision" acts for decades. Is there a simple test, without loopholes, that will prevent any psychic from demonstrating eyeless vision? There is. Just put an aluminum box over the psychic's head. Of course one can contrive extremely complicated ways a psychic might for a short time get around this—I can think of several—

but they would be much too difficult and costly for a psychic to use, and they could easily be detected. Psychics unable to read with their fingers when a box is over their head would be reduced to claiming that their finger power failed whenever controls eliminated eye power. Unfortunately, history suggests that dozens of parapsychologists would believe them.

Is there a loopholeless way to test psychic metal-bending? There is. Put a metal object on a table and do not allow a psychic near it while it is supposed to bend. Make sure the entire event is videotaped and have a magician there to observe it.

Is there a simple way to test the thoughtography of Ted Serios? Of course. Just inspect his "gismo" and his hand after the paper tube is held in front of the camera's lens, and do not allow any hand motions until the camera clicks. Jule Eisenbud, who wrote a preposterous book about Ted's powers, never took this precaution because it never entered his head that an untutored, likable chap like Ted would be capable of buying an optical device and palming it in and out of his gismo.

A few years ago a psychic claimed he used PK to turn the pages of a phone book without touching them. It was obvious at once to any magician that he was secretly blowing on the pages. James Randi, the well-known magician and debunker of psychics, faith healers, and incompetent scientists, devised a ridiculously simple and beautiful test of this claim. When time came for a demonstration on a television show, Randi sprinkled little pieces of styrofoam around the phone book. The slightest puff and the pieces would scatter over the stage. The psychic did the only thing he could do. He spent ten minutes walking around the book, sweating, scowling, at times half-smiling at the elegance of Randi's control. Finally, he announced that the strong television lights of the studio were inhibiting his PK.

Not long ago a young woman claimed that a simple card trick she had learned how to perform was actually accomplished by psychic means. She made the mistake of agreeing to demonstrate it for a group that included Randi and myself. We set up the simplest of controls (since we knew how the trick was done). After her total failure, the best she could do was weep and complain that our skepticism prevented her psi powers from operating. An official of ABC, there with a television crew to film the great event, bought the woman's excuse and was angry with us for killing the story. Naturally, the episode was never aired.

Is there a simple way to test the claims of mediums that they can float luminous trumpets in the air, or even rise bodily to the ceiling—all done, of course, in near total darkness? There is. Turn on a flashlight. It was the availability of little flashlights, more than anything else, that killed the careers of these great mountebanks. There was no way to protect themselves against some evil skeptic among the sitters who might suddenly flash a light toward them. In Stepanek's case, this was amusingly reversed. His ESP vanished when the room was dark and he was not permitted to touch targets.

Was there a simple, elegant way to eliminate all loopholes in a test of Stepanek? There was, and John Beloff actually thought of it. Just put the targets inside shallow wooden boxes with lids to prevent PS from seeing or touching the targets. Pratt was reduced to the typical lame excuse of arguing that somehow, nobody knows why, boxes upset PS. If there is any hero of this book it is Beloff, though I doubt if he will accept my accolade. For the first time in his career PS had to submit to a test that closed all loopholes. He failed, and the experiment was never tried again. Instead, JGP went back to the old "standard procedure" with all its loopholes, and Beloff went back to Scotland still firmly persuaded that PS was a powerful clairvoyant.

I believe that no one who reads this book will imagine that PS's successes can be explained by his use of unconscious sensory cues. Too many experiments will not allow such an opinion. There are, in fact, just two possible interpretations. Either PS was a remarkable psychic, with all the powers that Ryzl and Pratt and others attributed to him, or he was a clever performer who deliberately boosted his scores by nonparanormal means.

As I said in my introduction, PS replied to my first letter by saying that he could not recall details about experiments that took place so long ago and that he did not wish to answer any questions. I tried two more times, offering to send him a copy of Ryzl's *Hypnosis and ESP,* and asking if he would agree to further testing by a parapsychologist if I could arrange it. He replied to the two letters on September 18, 1988, by saying that he would indeed like to see Ryzl's monograph, but he again stated that he could not answer questions about events of many years ago, nor did he wish to reply to any questions about his personal life. The only reason he did so many experiments with Pratt, he wrote, was that Ryzl had moved to the United States. This of course is not Ryzl's view. PS added that he was pleased to learn from me that he was still in the *Guinness Book of World Records,* but he had no interest in ever being tested again.*

Pratt closes his monograph on Stepanek by quoting a remark by psychologist and psi-believer Robert H. Thouless, of Cambridge University

---

*PS's assertion that he had no interest in being tested again is hard to square with the fact that two years earlier he had participated in a test by mail conducted by J. Kappers, one of the Dutch parapsychologists involved in the experiment that was the topic of Chapter 8. As I said in an addendum to that chapter, Kappers informed me that he and two colleagues were expecting PS to visit Amsterdam in the spring of 1989 for a series of new tests.

in England: "It would probably be premature to speculate as to what such displacement [the Stepanek focusing effect] means to psi theory; we may be content to note it as part of the pattern that will be understood some time in the future."

This book is offered as a contribution toward that understanding.

Postscript, 1989

A few days before this book went to press I received a letter from Jan Kappers, of Amsterdam, reporting on the test he and two associates conducted with PS from April 9 through April 15, 1989. An earlier letter from Kappers described the protocols. I will not go into them here because Kappers will be reporting them in one or two formal papers. I will say only that the experiment involved the familiar green/white cards concealed in opaque envelopes.

The targets were prepared on the basis of random numbers generated by Dick Bierman, also of Amsterdam, who played no other role in the testing. On March 25 I wrote to Kappers to say I found his experiment soundly designed. PS was not allowed to touch the envelopes. There were eight sittings of 500 calls each, or 4,000 calls in all. PS scored 1,945 hits on the colors, or 55 below chance. The deviation was not significant enough to justify claims of negative ESP. A careful analysis showed no trace of any kind of focusing. It was, Kappers concluded in a letter, the least successful psi experiment he had ever conducted.

Accompanying Stepanek on the trip to Amsterdam was his lifelong friend, whose name, Kappers disclosed, is Dagmar Ryzlova. She is employed by a bank in Prague, where her job is the checking of accounts. I was told that the reason she and Stepanek do not live together is that their respective apartments are too small.

What should one make of this latest, perhaps final failure of PS to display clairvoyance? To skeptics, who include the overwhelming majority of working psychologists, it is another indication of how a psychic's alleged powers evaporate when test conditions are tightened to a point at which all nonparanormal causes are excluded. To true believers, such as John Beloff, Ian Stevenson, and John Palmer, it is merely one more example of the tendency of genuine psychics to lose their abilities for reasons parapsychologists are still unable to comprehend.

Name Index